SAINTS FOR NOW

SAINT FOR NOW

by Jean Charlot

SAINTS FOR NOW

EDITED BY CLARE BOOTHE LUCE

Clare Boothe Luce · Alfred Noyes · George Lamb
Kathleen Norris · Evelyn Waugh · Rebecca West
Whittaker Chambers · E. I. Watkin · Paul Gallico
Sister M. Madeleva · Robert Farren · John Farrow
Vincent Sheean · Barbara Ward · Kate O'Brien
Kurt Reinhardt · Bruce Marshall · Gerald Heard
D. B. Wyndham Lewis · Thomas Merton · Karl Stern

SHEED & WARD · NEW YORK · 1952

Library of Congress Catalog Card No. 52-10608
Designed by Stefan Salter
Manufactured in the United States of America

Contents

Saints
By Clare Boothe Luce   1

St. John
By Alfred Noyes   20

A Prayer to St. Jude, a poem
By Kathleen Norris   36

St. Helena Empress (c. 250-c. 330)
By Evelyn Waugh   38

St. Augustine (350-430)
By Rebecca West   44

St. Simeon Stylites (390-459)
By George Lamb   62

St. Benedict (480-547)
By Whittaker Chambers   75

St. Radegund (518-587)
By E. I. Watkin   86

St. Hilda of Whitby (617-680)
By Sister M. Madeleva 102

St. Francis of Assisi (1181-1225)
By Paul Gallico 117

St. Francis of Assisi
By Vincent Sheean 131

St. Thomas of Aquin (1226-1274)
By Robert Farren 146

St. Thomas More (1478-1535)
By Barbara Ward 161

St. Ignatius Loyola (1491-1556)
By John Farrow 175

St. Francis Xavier (1506-1552)
By Kate O'Brien 187

St. Pius V, Pope (1504-1572)
By D. B. Wyndham Lewis 215

St. John of the Cross (1542-1591)
By Kurt Reinhardt 231

St. John of the Cross
By Thomas Merton 250

St. Francis de Sales (1567-1622)
By Gerald Heard 261

The Curé of Ars (1786-1859)
By Bruce Marshall 272

St. Thérèse of Lisieux (1873-1897)
By Karl Stern 295

Illustrations

Sanctity
  by Jean Charlot .... Frontispiece

St. Benedict and a young monk
  by Lauren Ford 56

St. Bernard of Clairvaux
  by André Girard 88

St. Francis of Assisi
  by Jan Yoors 120

St. John of the Cross
  by Salvador Dali 152

St. John of the Cross
  by Thomas Merton 248

St. Thérèse of Lisieux
  by Thomas Merton 280

CLARE BOOTHE LUCE

*

Saints

What is a Saint? To speak in a dictionary manner, a Saint —with a capital "S"—is one of those persons recognized by the Church as having, by holiness of life and heroic virtue, attained a high place in heaven, and as being therefore entitled to the veneration of the faithful, fit to serve them as a spiritual model and able to intercede for them in the courts of God. The men and women thus recognized as Saints do not, of course, include all the holy, or exhaust all the possibilities of holiness. But of them we are certain.

The Saint's place in heaven is fixed in the mind of God. His place between heaven and earth—at God's altar, in the liturgy— is also fixed in the mind of the Church. But his place in the world is in the minds of men—always shifting ground. A Saint can go out of fashion in one century and come in again in another, as the world's understanding of his life wanes or waxes. His "popularity" depends on the seeming "timeliness" of his personal mode of holiness, or his particular spiritual message.

But how can we speak of the "timeliness" of sanctity? Is not

1

saintliness the perfecting of human nature, and therefore a thing forever pertinent to the human situation—indeed, the one thing truly pertinent? The answer is that the holiness of any Saint is partial and derivative: "I am the vine; ye are the branches." No human nature, except Christ's, has ever been wholly perfect, that is to say, perfectly holy. No single human personality can illustrate all the virtues of Christ. So none other can speak, as He spoke, to the condition of every man in every time, or provide him in all seasons and circumstances with sufficient light for his salvation. Christ's was the only pure white light of sanctity that ever showed forth in the vesture of man.

The Saints always saw their appointed task as the imitation of Christ, and the reflection of His Light. "The Lord has placed us as patterns and mirrors," writes St. Clare in her testament, "not only for all the faithful . . . (but) for those who live in the world." But the Saints were also agonizingly aware of how far short they fell of being "other Christs." Their sayings and writings abound in self-accusations that they are "unprofitable servants of Christ."

"I fear . . . the presence of the King, the sentence of the Judge" were the last words of St. Brendan. And "Priez pour moi, pauvre pécheresse," were St. Bernadette's. St. Francis, at the time when even his own brothers marvelled at his holiness, beat his heart and cried, "Oh Lord, God of heaven and earth, I have committed such wrong against Thee, and so many sins that I am worthy to be damned by Thee."

The Saints would be the first to agree with Ambrose Bierce's definition in "The Devil's Dictionary," "A saint is a dead sinner, revised and edited." Bierce, the skeptic, was referring, of course, to that cloyingly pietistic school of hagiography which depicts the Saint as a superhuman character who is indeed constantly assaulted by temptation but is constitutionally unable to yield to it. It is a sheer invention of religiosity to depict a Saint as a human

2

being who does deeds of spiritual derring-do of which no mere mortal is capable.

The very meaning of the lives of the Saints for us lies in the fact that they were sinners like ourselves trying like ourselves to combat sin. The only difference between them and us is that they kept on trying: precisely because they believed that the revision and editing of sinner-into-saint is done not by man's pen but by God's grace.

"I was like a stone lying in the deep mire," writes St. Patrick, "and He that is mighty came, and in His mercy lifted me up, and verily raised me aloft and placed me on top of the wall."

The best that any Saint has ever hoped to do, with the help of grace, is to recover for himself some fractional part of "the unfathomable riches of Christ," and, by living richly a lifetime on it, reveal to others the power of even so small a part to purchase heaven.

The portrait of a Saint is only a fragment of a great and still uncompleted mosaic—the portrait of Jesus. All the words of a Saint are no more than a faint echo of a single phrase of His— as echoed in turn by the evangelists in the Gospel. All the light of a Saint is but a moonbeam light, cast from the mirror which itself shines only in the hidden Sun of Holiness.

As the Saint's recovery of Christ's virtues is always a fractional thing, so too is his message. Not even St. John, the beloved disciple, could report all the deeds of his Master, much less embody in himself all his Lord's virtues. "There is much else besides that Jesus did; if all of it were put in writing, I do not think the world itself would contain the books which would have to be written." He might have added that there is so much else besides that Jesus *was*, that if all of it were lived out in other lives, the universe itself would not contain the Saints who would have to be born.

"Star differeth from star in its glory," says St. Paul. The lights of certain Saints shine more brightly than their neighbors', and as the world rolls along, still more brightly in some seasons than others. In this winter of our discontent, the atomic century, the authors of *Saints for Now* have gazed on a few of these stars. They were asked to choose a saint they felt they would especially like to write about, whether because the saint has a personal significance for the writer or a message for the world at this moment, or for any other reason. In what they have written we can see the appositeness to our times of these fragmented lives, these reflected lights, these echoed words of the Life and the Light and the Word of Christ.

I find here many of my own favorite Saints, and of these I shall say a brief word. There is, for example, the convert, second only to St. Paul in his greatness, Augustine of Hippo, who towered above the men of his own generation and still towers above ours. Born 1600 years ago, he is the most modern of personalities. There is hardly a movement of his heart or mind which strikes us today as alien or irrelevant to our own psychology.

Augustine came into a pagan world turning to Christianity, as we have come into a Christian world turning towards paganism. The conflicts that raged in his bosom between the tangible pleasures of paganism and the intangible joys of Christianity, between doubt and faith, self and God, also rage in ours. From birth, Augustine was a great—one would almost say greatly gifted—sinner. A precocious child, he lied, stole, cheated—as few children can do successfully. He was punished repeatedly for playing truant from the restraints of school and the necessities of education—and was nevertheless a brilliant scholar. In young manhood he recklessly pursued self-gratification, self-advancement, self-expression. He was the gayest, most sensual, most brilliant, and no doubt most egotistic student in the University of Carthage. In Carthage where, he wrote, "shameful love bubbled about me like boiling oil," he read the wrong books, expounded

4

the wrong ideas, embraced the wrong loves—and made a triumphant "success" of all of it. Lust and sophistry were his
twin idols. "For it was my sin that not in Him, but in His creatures
—myself and others—I sought for pleasures, sublimities, truths,
and so fell headlong into sorrows." But: "Thou hast commanded,
and so it is, that every inordinate affection should be its own
punishment." This furious and turbulent spirit became "entangled
in many difficulties." Financial worries, thwarted ambitions,
frustrations in friendship, and misunderstandings in love, soured
in his mind and lacerated his heart. "Soul-sick and tormented,"
he began to take stock of himself. "I was tired of devouring time,"
he wrote, "and of being devoured by it." What familiar ennui and
malaise there are in that phrase for us moderns.

He explored his interior sufferings with the same passionate
zeal with which he had explored exterior pleasures, and he quailed
to the depths of his being at the cost of reforming himself. "These
petty toys of toys, these vanities of vanities, my long-time fascina-
tions, still held me. They plucked at the garment of my flesh, and
murmured caressingly: Dost thou cast us off? From this moment
shall this delight or that be no more lawful for thee forever?"
Habit whispered insistently in his ear, "Dost thou think that thou
canst live without these things?" And Augustine, haunted by
Truth, hounded by Love, harried by Grace, "had nothing at all
to answer but those dull and dreary words: Anon, anon; or
Presently, or, leave me alone but a little while. But my 'Presently,
presently' came to no present, and my little while lasted long."

From his own *Confessions* we know the very text from Scripture
that ended his procrastination: "Not in rioting and drunkenness,
not in chambering and wantonness, not in strife and envying; but
put ye on the Lord Jesus Christ." The mighty chain of little habits
that bound his will was broken. Not Augustine, but Another would
reform him. "You shall know the Truth, and the Truth shall make
you free," is a divine command and a divine promise. St.

5

Augustine was slow to obey the command, but when he did he reaped the promise.

Thomas Aquinas' obedience, on the other hand, seems from boyhood to have been instant and persistent. His lifelong search for the Truth, the indivisible Truth that reason proves and faith reveals, was also a search for human freedom—the "liberty of the sons of God." Neither reason nor religion should fear the most scrupulous inquiry. Thomas of Aquin was the Grand Inquisitor among Saints. The best attacks ever made on religion were made by St. Thomas himself in the *Summa*. The glory of his intellect was that he never failed to adduce the best reasons that could be found *against* every position he presented. When he couldn't find them in the writings of opponents, he invented them, always stating the opposing case at its very strongest. He was a Saint in the order of reason—he showed the charity of thought: zeal to prove that a contrary proposition to one's own is right—if reason can be found to prove it. Indeed, the reasons St. Thomas gave for his own position in every question were essentially residual; they were the ones that remained after all others had been scrupulously explored and found wanting.

We live in an intellectual climate of ambiguity, of multiple and conflicting "truths," of exclusive and warring "freedoms." In a world where truth is relative, where one man's "truth" is another man's "lie," and his definition of "freedom" is his neighbor's definition of "slavery," plainly the burden of carrying the argument (if words are to be used, and not bombs) must fall on an appeal not to the mind, but to the emotions. Advertising, publicity, propaganda—the sophisticated tools of irrationalism—supersede fact, persuasion and logic, the tools of reason. We see today that our philosophers' Ivory Tower of Babel, our divided House of Truth, is about to fall around our ears in what we call "the war of ideologies." To our melancholy and perilous situation St. Thomas' sublime and heroic effort to find the Truth whose fruit is freedom speaks with awful urgency.

In passing, let us note that St. Thomas himself was quite aware that Truth in its entirety is too stupendous a castle ever to be stormed and captured by the mind of one man—or even many. The ramparts of Truth are shrouded in the mists of Eternity. And there only is where St. Thomas hoped to know Truth wholly. Of all the "immortals" in the halls of learning, none sought fame in the world less than Aquinas. How often one has heard our latter-day "intellectuals" murmur, "What happens to me when I die does not matter, so long as I live on—in my works." (Thus, denying immortality, they sigh after it.) St. Thomas, a man of encyclopaedic knowledge, of awesome literary accomplishment, at life's end thought so much of God and so little of his own works that he said, "All I have written now seems to me of little value." "Straw" he called it. Yet of this straw were made the bricks of the noble edifice of Western thought for five centuries.

St. Thomas' accomplishment was stupendous in volume. But a single unique deed has been known to earn a Saint an enduring place in history. St. Helena, for example, demonstrates the tremendous significance—in heaven and on earth—of even one holy act. Let her be invoked for aid by all those self-pitying souls who moan that their lives are "meaningless" because Providence has "cheated" them not only of opportunities, advancements, careers, but—most subtle self-deception—the chance to be "useful to others." But, you may protest, St. Helena's act was, while single, nevertheless a *great* one. She found the Cross on which Christ had died, and carried it home with her. St. Thérèse of Lisieux answers that protest: "The little way of the Cross" is her answer. Are not the lives of almost all of us made up of little things? But for most people a dozen annoyances, bothers, anxieties, frustrations, harassments a day add up to aspirins or martinis, to ulcers or neuroses or breakdowns—even to suicide. Thérèse made them add up to Sainthood.

Stooping a dozen times a day quietly—indeed furtively—she picked up and carried the splinters of the cross that strewed her path as they strew ours. And when she had gathered them all up, she had the material of a cross of no inconsiderable weight. The "little way of the Cross" is not "the way of a little cross." Try for so much as one day's dreary routine, in office or kitchen, at home or abroad, among friends or with strangers, to tread it. You will come to love St. Thérèse and to call upon her. For St. Thérèse's espousal of "pinprick martyrdom" is a long and extraordinary exegesis of Our Lord's parable of the "widow's mite." And it has swelled the treasury of heaven more than the combined gifts of many good men and women whose offerings to God could reasonably be called "substantial." "The others all gave out of what they had to spare; she with so little, put in all she had—her whole livelihood."

St. Francis, who to many is the most Christlike character in Christendom, is for that very reason plainly not a Saint whose message is to be captured in a paragraph. The barefoot little man of Assisi who married poverty for Christ's sake and whose indissoluble marriage was a long, ecstatically happy and idyllically romantic union, is a giant among spiritual giants. Volumes cannot recount the rich fruits that were borne by the vine of poverty he planted in the valley of Spoleto. I would make a trifling point: Francis is a Saint to be invoked most prayerfully when you are bedevilled by boredom.

His adorable gaiety in the dreariest hours, his brisk and bubbling gratitude to God for the mere sight of a feather wafted across the sky, or a flower blowing in a field, are all exquisite variations on "the lilies of the field," which "toil not neither do they spin," but are clad by God in far more glory than Solomon's. St. Francis' simple joy in all created matter is a reproof and a corrective for the ennui which hagrides our society!

The ragged and barefoot Francis of Assisi certainly looked very different from the purple-robed, well-slippered Francis of Sales. In the charity of Christ we find their resemblance. "Give to every

8

man who asks, and if a man takes what is thine, do not ask him to restore it." Is there anything more precious to a busy and important person, charged with weighty affairs, than his time? It is the one thing which, taken from him, cannot be restored. If you are a Very Important Personage consider, from the many points our author makes in this book, this one: the generosity of the Bishop of Annecy, who gave of his time so sweetly and courteously— even to known time-wasters. If St. Francis de Sales had shown no other virtue in his high office, this one was heroic.

Like Francis de Sales, Thomas More is a Saint who was "at home" in office, or salon, or courtroom. As Lord Chancellor to Henry VIII Thomas More gave loyal service to his King, displaying not only sagacity in the discharge of his royal duties, but such gay and charming manners, such witty urbanity in his contact with royalty, that Bluff King Hal came to dote on him. Nevertheless, Thomas More, a shrewd man, knew that to serve your King and to serve your God are not always the same thing. When he had to choose between them he made the shrewd choice—the one by which he would be judged, not in the time of men, but in the time of God, which is Eternity.

"If my head would win him a castle in France, it would not fail to go," Thomas More once said to a friend who congratulated him on having the King's favor. His head was indeed destined to go—as G. K. Chesterton put it—when Henry VIII needed it "in the storming of a larger and more ancient castle—which was also a Cathedral." Forced to choose between a King who would be "his own pope" and the Pope who sat in Rome, English Thomas More chose the Roman Pontiff. But, as his biographer in this book makes plain, he died for the principle of the Papacy, and not for the person of the Pope. He lost his whole head for a part of Christian Faith. It was not his *favorite* part, and even that part was not embodied in his favorite pontiff. He did not put a particular Pope above a particular King—or Italy above England—he put principle

9

above all. He gave to Caesar what was Caesar's and to God what was God's. Only to such men as he and such principles as his can we look for relief from the expedient corruptions and corrupt expediencies which are constantly increasing the power of the totalitarian state over our personal lives, and over our faiths and fortunes. St. Thomas More, intercede for us, in "public issues" . . . .

Obedience, before Majesty, was no less the dynamic of the life of St. John Vianney, the Curé d'Ars. One of his favorite sayings was "Do only what you can offer to God"—a homely echo of Christ's own words, ". . . What I do is always what pleases him." The harsh self-denial that he imposed upon himself when he was sent as pastor to an insignificant, fallen-away, impoverished parish was no doubt inspired by his Master's injunction, "He that would be first among you, let him be the servant of all." But it is not his asceticism which gives the Curé d'Ars his special value for our age. It is, rather, his exquisite sense of sin. His great apostolic mission was to mitigate the ravages of sin, by making people see it for what it is—opposition to God, and self-destruction.

Have you ever, by any chance, sat on a hard, straight chair in a small stuffy room for more than an hour listening to a stranger "spill his troubles"? the Curé d'Ars sat in a dark coffin-sized box— the confessional—eighteen hours a day, in the summer heat and winter cold, for twenty years, hearing the recital of the dreariest, silliest, vainest and most monotonous dialogue in the world— the intimate conversation men and women have had with the devil. He sat there in order to help them get in the end the better of the satanic argument. The Curé, an unlettered man, knew nothing about "psychology." He lived before Freud and Adler and Jung and their disciples were in due season born to provide confessional couches for a generation that had lost the sense of sin but still suffered from the devastating effects of it. But John Vianney knew what was in the hearts of men. He knew their prime need—to worship what they loved, and to love what they worshipped. And since he could tell quite easily the difference between such things as love and lust, need and greed, prudence and timidity, devotion and sentimentality, God and idol—he helped his penitents, with supernatural lucidity, to see for themselves what was godly and what was idolatrous in their conduct. "He that is not with me is against me." The little Curé did not scold or scorn the sinners who came to him. He showed them, in Christlike charity, where they were against God—in short, in what respect they were being their own worst enemies. And when they saw it, by the power of God he forgave them their sins unto seventy times seven.

It is the main point of these essays to show forth some facets of the "timeliness" of certain Saints; but whenever Saints are "collected," regardless of the editor's purpose, they have a way of making a lot of points of their own. Mysticism and miracles, penance and prayer, are phenomena common to the company of the holy. But these are mysterious matters which demand perhaps the delicate and learned commentary of the theologian. I shall make only three points, which should be as plain to sceptics as they are to the faithful: first, the astounding variety and the wonderful diversity that exist in their company; second, the paradoxes and contradictions that their lives present; and third, the way they go on working in the world, throughout the centuries.

As to their diversity, F. J. Sheed says that whenever we meet the saints in numbers, we experience a great relief from monotony. "Men are in their essential personality irreducibly diverse; but sin blots out the distinction and reduces the diversity." Sin takes all the clear, clean color out of a man and leaves him with the muddy color of sin, common and drab as earth. The word "holy" derives from the Anglo-Saxon *halig*—whole or healthy. The Saints are the health of humanity. The holy man is the only man who can be all he really is, by nature and temperament.

While God is the only Totality, He takes no totalitarian attitude

11

towards human nature or circumstance. He recruits his elect from men and women of every temperament and talent, every color, profession, class, and condition on earth. The vast calendar of the Saints includes Kings and Queens like Edward the Confessor, Louis of France, the Emperor Henry, Elizabeth of Hungary and Elizabeth of Portugal, Margaret of Scotland, and Helena; it likewise includes Saints whose background was shoddy, poor, or humble like Joseph of Cupertino, John Bosco and Mother Cabrini. There are Saints of giant intellect like Augustine, Thomas Aquinas, Bonaventure, Bellarmine, and Dominic; and there are Saints who conspicuously lacked scholarship, like Patrick, who said of himself "I have not studied as others . . . I am the most illiterate, and the least of all the faithful . . . a fool . . ." By the most charitable accounts, the Curé d'Ars and poor St. Joseph of Cupertino would have cut poor figures in one of our intelligence tests. Indeed, Joseph was so lightheaded that his miraculous flight to the church rafters seemed all but a natural manifestation of his want of mental substance.

There are gentlemen Saints like Francis de Sales and ruffian Saints like Camillus de Lellis. There are Saints who journeyed far and had high adventures in the world, like Catherine of Siena, Teresa of Avila, and Francis Xavier—and Saints who never moved more than a few miles from home or cloister, like Margaret Mary Alacoque and Bernadette, and notably (in this book) Simeon Stylites who spent most of his life on the top of a pillar. There are Saints who, before their conversion, lived riotously and fought recklessly and loved lustily in the world, like Ignatius and Augustine—and Saints who never in all their lives (it is eminently reasonable to suppose) made a single violent gesture or committed one mortal sin, like Thérèse of Lisieux. There are Saints who died in childhood like Maria Goretti, and patriarch Saints, like Anthony of Egypt, who lived hale and hearty well over a century. There are white saints and brown ones, yellow saints and black; and there

12

is no country or continent which has not bred them, or been nourished with the blood of them.

And, as though this initial variety of birth, circumstance and talent were not enough, it is enhanced by the kaleidoscopic way the Saints themselves change the patterns of their lives in obedience to God's will. They embark on terrible or glittering adventures and romantic voyages that make old fairy tales and new novels pale by comparison. The fisherman Peter drops his nets to become the head of an organization that has endured for 2000 years. The maiden Joan drops her spindle to become a great soldier and a king-maker; the soldier Ignatius drops his sword to seize a pilgrim's staff; the nobleman Francis of Assisi drops his dagger to pick up a beggar's bowl, and walks to Jerusalem unarmed through the lines of contending armies; the princess Hilda becomes a nun; the nun Catherine of Siena becomes a stateswoman. Those who have "vocations" to the priesthood, like Camillus de Lellis, Joseph of Cupertino, and Benedict Joseph Labre, have convent doors firmly closed in their faces. Those who shrink from a missioner's life wind up in far-off countries converting heathens by the thousands, like Peter Claver. Some, like Anthony of Egypt and Teresa of Avila, seek a life of eremitical solitude and contemplation, and become in the end men and women active in the world, and founders of great religious congregations. Mother Frances Xavier Cabrini, a poor and frail girl, leaves an Italian village for the great cities of America, and builds 69 convents and hospitals. The Saints, like ourselves, were born the creatures of their environment, but they demonstrate in a most astonishing way that no man need be the sport or slave of circumstance, if God go with him.

And as they differ in birth and condition and talent, so too do the Saints differ astoundingly from one another in the modes of expressing their holiness. It is perhaps the startling forms which these modes sometimes take that makes the lives of the Saints unin-

13

telligible, even repellent, to people who are sincerely eager to "understand about sanctity." Because we are prone to think of Saints as other-worldly, supernatural characters, we are likely to forget that they were conditioned as we are, by the culture of their own day, and reacted as we do to prevailing custom. Their souls made the vertical ascent to eternity, but their minds, hearts and bodies proceeded on a horizontal plane—in the context of history. The saints are, to be sure, "original and peculiar characters." But they are original chiefly because they never forget their origin which is of God, and their common peculiarity consists in remembering what is peculiar to man—his sub-angelic and super-animal nature, which permits him to stand with one foot on earth and the other on the ladder to heaven.

The individual Saint's particular way of holiness—of giving himself to God and neighbor—is as distinct from holiness itself as courtship—a mode of showing forth human love—is from love. We do not say that the Eskimo does not really desire the good of the girl in the neighboring igloo because he brings her a pail of whale blubber instead of a pearl necklace. We are wise enough to consider first the love of the giver rather than the gift of the lover. (Indeed, in this particular instance we might agree that the young man who tackled a whale to provide his lady with a love token showed more real devotion than the man who hands her a rope of pearls that *he* never dived for!)

For example, when we encounter the grim asceticism of some Saint, say of the Middle Ages, who flagellates or starves himself, clanks about in chains, or racks his body, we consider his conduct morbid, if not insane. That is because we live in an age where a scratch sends us rushing off to the medicine closet for iodine and band-aid. We would be less scandalized by his manifestation of asceticism if we were to recall that this Saint lived in an age when the most excruciating torture was publicly administered to malefactors and criminals. We might then see that his particular mode of holiness was to take upon himself a measure of the pain society was currently inflicting on its sinners, and that he was saying, in effect, "If torture is to be the lot of the sinner then torture is my lot, for all are guilty in the eyes of God." Moreover, his purgatorial asceticism may even have suggested to his neighbors that purgatory was waiting for them too, and that they might do well to show a little less harshness in their punishment of others. Saints often bear, that others may be moved to forbear.

Penance is also expiation. When the Curé d'Ars lived on slim rations of cold boiled potatoes and slept on straw bags, he took upon himself the life that many a poor farmer in France had had thrust upon him by the rich landowners who lived in the cities. In 1783, St. Benedict Joseph Labre, living out "the Son of Man has nowhere to lay his head," slept in gutters, scavenged garbage dumps for food, and emptied his ragged pockets of the smallest coin at night, so he would wake up destitute every morning. His asceticism may seem strange and unnecessarily harsh to you and me. But to many in Europe who were caught in the bloody excesses of the French Revolution that came so soon after his death or were made homeless and penniless by its terrible aftermath, the voluntary sufferings of Benedict, the Tramp of God, became familiar necessities. (It is no accident that since the advent of Hitler and Stalin, the cultus of Labre has been growing.) Saints who are the windows of God's grace are often, too, the mirror of man's inhumanity to his fellows..

Saints are paradoxical characters. They cheerfully endure themselves what they weep to see others endure. They inflict on themselves what they would rather die than inflict on their neighbors. They find riches in poverty, happiness in sorrow, and joy in pain. But the children of predilection are fathered by a Divine paradox: "He who loses his life shall save it . . ." They take the paradoxical command literally. And logically enough, with the most paradoxical consequences.

Saint Thérèse, hidden from the world in a Carmelite monastery, contemplates her hidden helpless God in the Babe in the manger. She too seeks to become little and helpless and hidden, like her infant Divinity. Later she contemplates the face of the Crucified God-Man from which all traces of human beauty and divine authority have been obliterated by tears and blood. And now she seeks this still deeper hiddenness; she tries to hide every last little trace of suffering and self, even from her hidden sisters. She cheerfully renounces even a holy desire to be a missionary sister, contenting herself with praying in the silence of her cubicle for the well-being of all missioners. And—within a decade after her death—her hidden sanctity is an open matter; she is famous to the ends of Europe. She becomes the beloved and powerful, vocation-making and money-raising and heart-lifting patron Saint of the Church's farthest-flung missions. "Pray in secret, and your father will reward you openly." The one some scornful critic called the "Saint of the Itsy Bitsy" becomes a Saint who towers over even the big Saints. Ah! The gigantic paradox of the life of the little Thérèse: microscopic acts of charity, producing macroscopic results—not only hereafter, but *here*.

Ignatius, the soldier embracing the under-fire last ditch obedience of a soldier at Armageddon, abandons all his will to the Captaincy of Christ and his intellect to His thinking. And the will and thought of Ignatius impose themselves upon thousands upon thousands of his sons in the world—shaping the minds and hearts of men for centuries.

One speaks of the "sons and daughters" of Saints—and illustrates the paradox of their chastity: they who renounced all the joys of parenthood are the world's most prolific progenitors. The filial descendants of Francis, Ignatius, Dominic, Bernard, Benedict, number in the millions: chastity proves a strangely seminal virtue.

The Saints are always working in the world. Their lives are rudimentary stuff. Their deeds are germinal. The Saints were little concerned with "social programs." Christ himself was their program. But the love of Christ inescapably includes the love of neighbor. Most of the welfare and educational reforms of the Western world spring from the words and deeds of the Saints—who sought only to reflect the words of the Master: "What you do to the least of these, you do to me."

St. Francis singing canticles to field and flower, conversing with Sister Bird, reasoning with Brother Wolf, saving from his heel the brief insignificant life of Brother Worm, is concerned only with uniting his soul in the charity of Christ with all created matter. He is listening to God. Every being to St. Francis was a word from God. He does not guess that he is becoming the original founder of the British Bird Watchers' Society, the Garden Club movement of Peoria, and the world-wide Society for the Prevention of Cruelty to Animals.

St. Camillus de Lellis haunts the hospitals to minister to the poor of his day, invades the battlefields wearing a red cross on his monk's robe to succor the wounded and carry away the dead. He knows only that he is tending the wounds of Christ in His Mystical Body. Camillus does not guess that he is fathering the modern nursing spirit and founding the institution of the Red Cross, and that thousands upon thousands of victims of bomb and fire, flood, pestilence and war rescued by that institution will owe him a prayer and a blessing.

And what the dignity and reverence in which womanhood is held (where it is so held) owe to St. Mary, our Blessed Mother, and her daughters, is beyond human estimate.

One could go on endlessly recounting the philanthropic and educational institutions that have germinated from the supernaturally inspired acts of saints like Vincent de Paul, Camillus and Francis. We owe them, and many others, an immeasurable debt for our modern orphanages, hospitals, schools, kindergartens, homes for wayward girls, the blind, the aged, the insane, the indigent and the unwanted.

The Saints have also had a shattering impact in the field of culture, economics and politics.

When, in the 8th century, St. Gregory II boldly opposed the outbreak of iconoclasm under Leo the Isaurian, and insisted that images are not the same things as idols, he was speaking as a theologian and not as a patron of the arts. He was defending the right of Christians to adorn their churches with portraits of those they venerated in heaven, on religious and rational grounds, not on artistic ones. Nevertheless, but for him, the art of sculpture, which has been one of the glories of Western culture, would have perished. No statue that stands in church or school, park or plaza stands there but by the Christian courtesy of St. Gregory.

When Joan of Arc left Domremy to put a crown on the head of the Dauphin, she was concerned only with obeying her "voices." "Thou wouldst not have any power over me at all, if it had not been given to thee from above," said Jesus to Pilate, when Pilate told Him he had the authority to crucify Him. Pilate's authority was wrongly used, but Jesus Himself did not doubt its *legality*. The Dauphin was an impotent, treacherous, cowardly prince— but he was the *lawful* ruler of the French people, and not to be overthrown by an unlawful pretender, however superior he might be in his person. This principle of legality in government, through which God's will works in the world of politics, is the very one we invoke today against revolution by force, foreign aggression, and even "benign" dictatorship. It is a pity that Joan herself did not make more explicit that that was what she was defending; her mission might then not have been so easily misunderstood by later generations who have tended to make her a sort of patron saint of chauvinism and a narrow nationalism.

The early Christian martyrs like Felicity and Perpetua who gave themselves gladly to the beasts of Caesar in the Colosseum sought only one thing there: to die in Christ so that they might live the resurrected life He promised them. They would have been astounded, and incredulous, if they had been told that their small band was engaged in overthrowing the ancient and mighty Empire of Rome, with most of its laws, customs and institutions.

The fact is, the Saints give little thought to changing the world around them. They are too busy changing the world within them. They are not out to reform Caesar, but to conform themselves to Christ. If there is one text in Scripture that exemplifies the Spirit of Christianity towards the world it is St. Paul's "God was in Christ in order to reconcile the world to himself."

The Saints were reconcilers, not revolutionists. And yet—their efforts to reconcile the world to Christ, through themselves, effected the greatest political, economic, cultural revolution on earth. It is a revolution still in process, against which tyranny, dictatorship, mob rule, Communism, are always to be seen as counter-revolutions.

Ideas have consequences. The Divine Ideas that filled the hearts and minds of the Saints have had—and continue to have—sublime consequences in history.

ALFRED NOYES

*

St. John

In the history of Christendom St. John has a central position of his own. The disciple whom Jesus loved has been beloved by mankind for two thousand years. His mind caught glimpses of the universal plan as few other minds have caught them, while his tenderness goes down to the deep fount of human tears.

St. Augustine reminds us that the son of the fisherman Zebedee had rested his head upon the breast of his Master and had "heard the beating of his heart." He goes on to say: "In this same Gospel we find what sort and how great a man was John, that from the dignity of the dispenser it may be understood of how great a price is the Word which could be announced by such a man."

Apart from the writings that bear his name (the Apocalypse, the Gospel and the three Epistles) there are few references to St. John in the New Testament, but, if we had to depend on these references alone, there is enough to give him one of the chief places in the history of Christendom. Those few references, although they are quite incidental, do at once suggest the complete portrait

20

as soon as the light of the fourth Gospel is allowed to play on them. It is rather like catching a momentary glimpse of a face in the twilight and having your first impression not only confirmed but explained by a sudden illumination.

We have first the bond of natural affection between Our Lord and the young nephew of his own mother (Westcott gives very good reasons for supposing that the mother of Our Lord and the mother of John were sisters). Then there is the affectionate smile as of a divine humour in the name Son of Thunder, which Our Lord gave to the young man who wanted him to call down fire from heaven upon that inhospitable village of Samaria. Could any title be more appropriate to the future author of the Apocalypse?

St. Matthew tells us (Chapter xx) of a time when some of the disciples were contending for pre-eminence in the favour of their Master. This happened before they had grasped the full meaning of his "kingdom." The mother of John and James may have expressed herself in terms that sounded like earthly ambition, but it seems at least probable that the natural bonds of relationship might have induced something of that forgivable rivalry of affection. Their eager affirmation that they were prepared to die for him whose favour they were soliciting, and to drink of his own cup of agony, indicates the kind of pre-eminence that John and his brother were seeking. The rivalry of affection apparently lingered on, and is certainly illuminated in the last chapter of the fourth Gospel by Peter's question about the beloved disciple, "Lord, and what shall this man do?" It is illuminated still more by John's anxiety to correct the further misunderstanding about the rebuke administered, in turn, to Peter: "If I will that he tarry till I come, what is that to thee?" The rumour spread that Christ meant by this that John would not die. Perhaps, after all, this arose from the misinterpretation of some wish expressed by the beloved disciple, that his nearness to the Master on earth might be renewed beyond death. The misunderstanding might be natural enough, if the wish was ex-

21

pressed in the somewhat apocalyptic terms of the story in Matthew.

St. John makes no direct reference to the incident recorded by Matthew, but I cannot help thinking that there is a real connection between the rebuke, "it is not mine to give, but it shall be given to them for whom it is prepared of my Father," and the later promise: "In my Father's house are many mansions. If it were not so, I would have told you. I go to prepare a place for you." This is recorded only by St. John, and, with infinite tenderness, clarifies what had hitherto been seen only dimly.

St. Luke tells us that it was St. John who was sent, with St. Peter, to make ready the guest chamber for the Last Supper.

Matthew, Mark and Luke all associate James and John with St. Peter in the story of the Transfiguration, which John omits altogether—probably for the reason that the others have told it so fully, his desire being to write what the others had omitted, or give precision to what they had sometimes told with the natural discrepancies of minds confronted with a light from beyond the world.

St. John gives that vital personal memory of the moment when Our Lord spoke of his approaching betrayal by one among them. Simon Peter beckoned to the disciple whom Jesus loved, "that he should ask him of whom he spake. He then lying on Jesus' breast saith, Lord, who is it?"

On the occasions when John speaks of "the disciple whom Jesus loved," he clearly does it to confirm and deepen the authority of the personal testimony. He is simply saying, this is the witness of one who rested his head on the breast of Christ, and his use of the third person is evidence, not of his vanity, but exactly the opposite. He avoids the use of the capital I, except in passages of the Apocalypse where it is used with a kind of astonishment: "I John saw the Holy City." But elsewhere he avoids egotism by the use of the first person plural, associating himself with the other eyewitnesses: "That which we have seen. . . ."

After the Resurrection this close association with St. Peter is confirmed by an incident related only in the fourth Gospel. In the dim light of the early morning the disciples, who had been fishing on the lake, hear someone calling to them from the shore. They are a little too far away (St. John gives the exact distance) for their eyes to recognize the solitary Figure standing at the water's edge. A question, whether they had caught anything, is enough, and the quick intuition of St. John breathes at once the heart-shaking words, "It is the Lord." Peter immediately plunges into the sea in his eagerness to fall at the feet of the risen Christ.

There is something quite beyond the power of art in what I can only call the supernatural reality of that scene, the breathless quiet in which it all takes place. It was no pious theologian of the second century, but the son of the fisherman Zebedee who had heard the waves breaking on that lonely shore, and now almost enables our own eyes to see that strangest detail of all, the little fire that had been lighted on the beach by that lonely Figure, as if he wanted to make them feel at home with him in the very moment when his appearance might have overwhelmed them with awe.

St. Luke again associates St. John with St. Peter in the Acts of the Apostles, when, after the Resurrection, that strange boldness had come upon the disciples. St. Peter himself, in the incident at the Gate called Beautiful, emphasizes this association in his reply to the lame man who asked an alms: "Peter, fastening his eyes upon him with John, said, Look on us . . . Silver and gold have I none; but such as I have give I thee: in the name of Jesus Christ of Nazareth rise up and walk. And he took him by the right hand and lifted him up; and immediately his feet and ankle bones received strength . . . And as the lame man which was healed held Peter and John all the people ran together unto them . . . And when Peter saw it he answered unto them . . . Why look ye so earnestly on us, as though by our own power or holiness we had made this man to walk . . . But ye denied the Holy One and the

23

Just, and desired a murderer to be granted unto you, and killed the Prince of life, whom God hath raised from the dead; whereof we are witnesses."

Almost immediately they were seized and imprisoned by the priests and the captain of the temple. The next day they were brought before Annas and Caiaphas, those formidable and exalted personages who had contrived the death of Jesus.

This moment was one of the great turning points in human history. With no worldly resources whatsoever, those two men—Peter who only a short while ago had denied his Master and had sworn "I know not the man," and John the beloved disciple, standing at Peter's side as only a short while ago he had stood beside the Cross—were asked that menacing question: "By what power, or by what name, have ye done this?"

From Annas and Caiaphas, the murderers of Christ, it was a menacing question indeed, but there was fear in their hearts as they asked it, for they saw before them two poor unlearned men transfigured by the power of the spirit; the one silent, but with a light shining upon his face like that which so blinded Dante when he saw him in his vision of Paradise, and the other moved to speak as they had never heard man speak before, except that greater man whom they had murdered:

"Be it known unto you all . . . that by the name of Jesus Christ of Nazareth, whom ye crucified, whom God raised from the dead, even by him doth this man stand before you whole. This is the stone which was set at nought of you builders, which is become the head of the corner. Neither is there salvation in any other: for there is none other name under heaven given among men, whereby we must be saved."

The Court then threatened and commanded them that they should use that name no more; and the association of the two Apostles became even closer; for we are told that, now, both of them answered:

"But Peter and John answered and said unto them, Whether it be right in the sight of God to hearken unto you more than unto God, judge ye. *For we cannot but speak the things which we have seen and heard.*"

In this last sentence we hear the voice of John, the eye-witness, introducing that cry which rings and re-echoes, or pulses like a deep undertone of music, through all his writings from the first to the last:

"That which was from the beginning, which we have heard, which we have seen with our eyes, which we have looked upon, and our hands have handled, of the word of life . . . That which we have seen and heard, declare we unto you."

The most poignant and profound sayings of Christ are those recorded by St. John; their implications are of a kind that only the intuition of St. John could immediately recognize. They are not the words of one who is merely man, but it is the same voice that we hear in Matthew xi, 29, and the words carry the evidence of the speaker's infinity within themselves.

> *Visus, tactus, gustus*
> *In te fallitur,*
> *Sed auditu solo*
> *Tuto creditur.*

If we had only the phrase in Matthew "Take my yoke upon you and learn of me," it might have seemed the utterance of a tyrant or a dictator; but when it is followed by the words "for I am meek and lowly in heart," we feel instinctively that here God is gently stooping to men, that men may rise to God.

Of the sayings of Christ in the Synoptic Gospels that can be compared to those in the fourth Gospel, there are one or two which I venture to think can only have been recorded on the authority of St. John. At the crucifixion the others were standing "afar off." Who but St. John could have told them the words to the penitent thief: "This day shalt thou be with me in Paradise," and "Father, forgive them, for they know not what they do"? St. Matthew puts into Our Lord's mouth a quotation from the Old Testament, but it is St. John, the eye-witness, who hears his very voice saying "I thirst." It is surely no idle fancy to suppose that St. Luke, not being one of the twelve, must have derived his insight into the mind and heart of Our Lord's mother from the disciple who knew her best. "Behold thy son; behold thy mother." It is only St. John who records those words. No other disciple was there to hear them. No other could have opened to St. Luke that heart in which the memories of the divine Child were so divinely laid up. St. John had heard them in the house to which he took her. It may have been from her lips that he learned something about that first ecstasy of the Magnificat, so that he was able later to tell St. Luke, in whose Gospel, though in different terms, it breathes the same profound message as the prologue to the fourth Gospel, of the Word made flesh that came to dwell among us.

Unless we are to make a rule of doubting everything of which we have direct testimony, there seems to be no reason whatsoever to doubt that under the Roman persecution of the Christians St. John was exiled to Patmos, and that there, remembering the destruction that had come upon Jerusalem in A.D. 70, and foreseeing the destruction that would yet come upon the world, he wrote the Apocalypse.

It was natural enough in the circumstances that the latent fire in his character should flame into that tremendous imagery drawn from the Hebrew prophets and amplified by his own prophetic vision of the Dies Irae. Behind it, around it and above it all there is the sense of that eternal Being, the Logos, who becomes articulate for man: "In the beginning was the Word, and the Word was with God, and the Word was God."

In the fourth Gospel St. John illustrates his meaning for his Hellenistic hearers by his use of the Greek philosophical term. In

26

the Apocalypse he illustrates his meaning by the use of two letters of the Greek alphabet, and hears the voice of the Eternal saying: "I am Alpha and Omega, the first and the last." This eternally existent Reality is the ground, not only of the whole created universe, but of those words, "I am the Resurrection and the Life."

It is not from Philo or any Greek philosopher that St. John draws his inspiration in the prologue. But just as a student of Plato, coming upon the great passage in which he says that there can be no communication between God and man except through a mediator, might feel that this helped him to understand the place of Christ in the universe, so John, feeling as strongly as St. Augustine that the Platonists could never give him the Voice that said "Come unto Me," nevertheless used one of their phrases to illustrate his own infinitely deeper meaning.

In both the Apocalypse and the fourth Gospel the Word becomes flesh and is "tabernacled among us." The prologue to the latter, despite its illustrative use of a philosophical term, moves like a great piece of music to a Hebrew measure: "He came unto his own, and his own received him not." The words are none other than those of John, the Palestinian Jew.

The co-existence of fiery passion and exquisite tenderness in a single character is a fact of human nature which did not escape the observation of Shakespeare, its profoundest secular student. We find it in the terrible passion of Lear, and the heart-rending gentleness of his last words to Cordelia. And so, suddenly, in the midst of the thunders of the Apocalypse, we hear the voice of St. John, melting into the tones that he had caught from the Master of Compassion:

"And I John saw the holy city, new Jerusalem, coming down from God out of heaven, prepared as a bride adorned for her husband.

"And I heard a great voice out of heaven saying, Behold, the tabernacle of God is with men, and he will dwell with them, and

27

they shall be his people, and God himself shall be with them, and be their God.

"And God shall wipe away all tears from their eyes; and there shall be no more death, neither sorrow, nor crying, neither shall there be any more pain: for the former things are passed away.

"And he that sat upon the throne said, Behold, I make all things new. And he said unto me, Write: for these words are true and faithful."

At the end of the Apocalypse there is again that solemn insistence on the personal testimony, and even more solemn warning to those who would impugn it. The "eye of the heart" can hardly fail to recognize in the close of the Apocalypse a reminiscence of those words which were later recorded in the fourth Gospel: "If I will that he tarry till I come, what is that to thee?" The disciple whom Jesus loved knew well the true meaning of that question.

It is the voice of St. John and no other, that we hear from Patmos, echoing the very words of Jesus, and replying to them in words that burn with the disciple's passionate longing for the end of his earthly exile and the fulfillment of his Lord's promise in the life to come:

"Surely I come quickly, Amen. Even so, come, Lord Jesus."

Brief as the record may be, it is momentous, and the man depicted in it stands out as one of the central figures of history. His portrait may be amplified by the traditional stories, some of them legendary while others are impressed with the character of the man and have all the marks of truth.

The most notable of these is the story of his last days at Ephesus: We see the aged Apostle borne in the arms of his disciples into the Ephesian assembly, and there repeating over and over again the same saying, "Little children, love one another."

There seems no reason whatever to doubt the manifold allusions to his residence in Ephesus, the centre of the region in which he had founded so many churches, nor is there the slightest reason to doubt the statement of Polycrates (Bishop of Ephesus) within a short lifetime of St. John's death, that St. John was buried in that city. It is easy to cast doubt upon a thousand things the most probable and natural, if each is taken in isolation. It is not so easy when they consistently interlock and interweave in harmony not only with each other but with the known facts of history. Still less easy could it have been for some obscure and unidentifiable man in the second century not only to pass off his writings as the work of St. John, but also to speak with such overwhelming authority that his Gospel was accepted and read in the Churches as that of St. John at a date when disciples of the Apostle, men of authority and learning, were still living.

If the destructive critics were able to take away the fourth Gospel from St. John there would be a curious result, which not one of them seems to have envisaged: In place of the Apostle who could naturally speak to the Churches of Asia with authority, and could give the most solemn attestations of what he had seen and heard, recording and recalling as no other had recorded the most clearly divine of all Our Lord's utterances—instead of the beloved disciple, whose personal relationship had naturally given him the knowledge and power to do all this, we should have an unknown Elder of the same name. This Elder of the second century (quite immune from canonization) not only left us a book that, by the universal consent of Christendom through seventeen centuries, surpasses the Synoptic Gospels in its spiritual sublimity, but also records the most poignant and piercing utterances of Christ himself, and records them in such a way that they have moved the hearts of men and established their belief in his divinity as no other words have ever done. The words

I am the Resurrection and the Life

belong to something higher than the natural order. With their personal claim they are words quite impossible to be spoken to a mourner at the graveside by any merely human being. For centuries they have run through the hearts of millions, not only of Christians, but of those who may have come simply to stand by the grave of a friend. Sceptics and men without hope, forlornly brave, have heard them in the distance and wondered, as if in their exile a voice had reached them from their native country. These words, and others like them in the fourth Gospel, are not the record of a pious meditation, but of a memory so vital that, even in a strange land, they cleave to the mind and heart of the hearer.

It may be recalled that in what Chesterton described as "the noblest use of a quotation in the English language," they rise as a memory in the mind of a man who had hitherto wasted great gifts, but was about to find redemption by laying down his life for a friend. He was only a character in a tale, but the tale was a parable and it embodied a vital truth. As he walked through the blood-stained streets of revolutionary Paris, apparently without hope in this world or any other, those words rose like a great ship's anchor from the depths. He walked "with the settled manner of a tired man, who had wandered and struggled and got lost, but who at length struck into his road and saw its end.

"Long ago, when he had been famous among his earliest competitors as a youth of great promise, he had followed his father to the grave . . . These solemn words, which had been read at his father's grave, arose in his mind as he went down the dark streets, among the heavy shadows, with the moon and the clouds sailing on high above him. 'I am the Resurrection and the Life, saith the Lord; he that believeth in me, though he were dead, yet shall he live; and whosoever liveth and believeth in me shall never die.' "*

In the mind of the man who first recorded them, they echoed and re-echoed with a far greater memory:

"That which was from the beginning, which we have heard,

* Dickens, *A Tale of Two Cities.*

30

which we have seen with our eyes, which we have looked upon, and our hands have handled, of the Word of life."

They were recorded and recalled, and solemnly attested, by an old man, remembering the greatest thing, the central fact, in the history of mankind.

He remembers, with an exactness possible only to an eye-witness, the scenes in which he had taken part. He remembers places he had visited with the Master in his youth, before the destruction of Jerusalem, as only a Palestinian Jew and an eye-witness could remember them. Of Jerusalem as it was before the destruction he remembers minute details, of which only memory could supply the record. And these details of places and buildings are introduced so naturally and easily that they seem to flow like music from the recollection of his own youth.

He remembers the Brook Kidron, that "winter torrent," the Pool of Bethesda with its five porches, "by the Sheep Gate." He speaks of the details of the Temple as one familiar with them, and perhaps what he does not directly mention is even more significant in an indirect allusion. If Westcott is right in one magnificent flash of intuition, it seems indeed more than probable that it was the symbolic tracery of the great golden vine over the Gate of the Temple, as Our Lord passed it under the Paschal moon, that suggested to him that other imagery, recorded only by St. John:

"I am the vine, ye are the branches: he that abideth in me, and I in him, the same bringeth forth much fruit."

The manner in which these memories were recorded is not in question here. Whether they were written by his own hand or dictated to another who wrote them down, they are attested in words that ring with the conviction that their truth is a matter of life or death. He remembers vivid little details of action that no other could have remembered. Not only does he remember that in his youthful eagerness, after the first strange rumour had been brought to them that the stone had been rolled away, he outran Peter on

31

their way to the tomb, but also how he hesitated before entering, until the other disciple caught up with him. Though he does not say so, we recognize in it the natural shrinking of his supremely sensitive nature from plunging directly into that tremendous, heart-shaking mystery.

Most vivid and most moving of all is the reality which St. John alone gives to the strange moment in which Mary Magdalene caught her first glimpse of One whom she believed to be dead, and, in the early morning mist, or through the mist of her own tears, failed to recognize him. It was only from her own lips that St. John could have learned what the other disciples at first regarded as a wild tale. It was only the beloved disciple who could so instantly and so sensitively have recognized the loving kindness that must have broken her heart with joy if it had not already been broken with sorrow.

"She turned herself back, and saw Jesus standing, and knew not that it was Jesus. Jesus saith unto her, Woman, why weepest thou? whom seekest thou? She, supposing him to be the gardener, saith unto him, Sir, if thou hast borne him hence, tell me where thou hast laid him, and I will take him away. Jesus saith unto her, Mary. She turned herself, and saith unto him, Rabboni; which is to say, Master."

These are not words to be picked up and turned over and dissected by the little doctors who have lost their souls between the pages of a lexicon. They are the words not of meditation, but of a vital experience. The life-blood beats in them, and they are pregnant with the most profound emotions of the human soul.

There is the same tenderness in the great discourse with which a little earlier Our Lord seems to be preparing his disciples for his departure, yet draws them still nearer to his living presence, the eternal presence of Christ in God: "Let not your heart be troubled; ye believe in God; believe also in me." There, and there alone, is the complete answer and consolation to those who, although they believe in God, find it impossible to love him if they know him only in his transcendence of space and time and of all the conditions of human thought.

To St. John the Word of God is not the Logos of the Greeks nor the Memra of the Hebrews, but true man, in whom God had become articulate. This is what he means by calling Christ the Word. This, as St. John saw it and expressed it for the universal Church, is the meaning of the Incarnation.

At a certain stage in his evolution, man himself had been able to lay hold upon a higher order of things, which raised him above the level of the beasts that perish, and enabled him to see, at least in the distance, the shining towers of the City of God. At this point he was met half-way:

> "So, through the thunder comes a human voice
> Saying, 'O heart I made, a heart beats here!
> 'Face, my hands fashioned, see it in myself!
> 'Thou hast no power nor mayst conceive of mine,
> 'But love I gave thee, with myself to love,
> 'And thou must love me who have died for thee!'"

This is the perfect interpretation of that passage in John where Philip says, "Lord, shew us the Father and it sufficeth us," and is met with the question, so quiet, so gently touched with loving reproach, so profound in its implications, yet filled with infinite compassion for our human weakness: "Have I been so long time with you, and yet hast thou not known me, Philip?" St. John alone recorded it, perhaps because no other instrument was sensitive enough to catch those divine undertones.

The human mind has its own focus, and, crude as the phrase may seem, it is in Christ that the transcendent Godhead is focussed into definition for the human mind. Here again St. John gives the complete answer to those who look upon Christianity as a merely anthropomorphic religion.

One of the most moving instances of this is a single brief sentence, as subtle in its apparent simplicity as nature itself. It occurs in that wonderful discourse of farewell, where the Master of all Compassion tells his disciples that they will meet again in a life beyond death: "If it were not so, I would have told you." Who but St. John could have caught the quiet implication of perfect knowledge in those words which lifts them into the Eternal Realm; and once more there is infinite tenderness in them, the compassion of a father for his children, or of a celestial surgeon who would not be afraid to tell the worst to those who could bear it and who trusted him:

"If it were not so I would have told you."

In reading that discourse, we feel a fuller realization of that other assurance in the Old Testament:

"Yea, though I walk through the valley of the shadow of death, I will fear no evil, for thou art with me."

The first Epistle of St. John is a letter from an old man, solemnly attesting that which he had seen and touched and handled. There is a recollection in these words of that other scene in the room with the locked door, when the sceptical Thomas fell at the feet of the risen Christ with the cry, "My Lord and my God." If the story of the Resurrection were indeed a myth, this incident, again recorded only by St. John, gives it a unique character. It would be the only myth in which so fierce a doubt of its truth ("except I shall . . . put my finger into the print of the nails . . . I will not believe") formed a part of the story, and the overwhelming sincerity of that brief conclusion is only dramatic because it is so intensely true a picture of a living man, torn with an agony of doubt, and suddenly receiving that answer which seemed beyond all hope: "Reach hither thy hand."

"That which we have seen and touched and handled," reports St. John in his old age, and in some of the words that follow we

34

seem to hear the very tones that he had caught from his Master: "Little children, it is the last time." Is it too much to imagine that these words, murmured perhaps as the old Apostle lay in a trance of memory, were an echo of words that came from Our Lord himself on the evening before he went to his betrayal, there is so much sorrow in them and so much tenderness to souls that are to him like little children.

But in conclusion I must go back to those words which, to me as to many and many another, in times of doubt have remained as a great anchor. Those who have never known the darkness of doubt are fortunate, perhaps; but they can never have known the re-assurance that breathes through those words of Christ, recorded by St. John:

"If it were not so I would have told you."

*

Prayer to St. Jude

Oh, great Saint Jude
Whose traitor-sounding name
By man's perceptions crude
Confused is with the obloquy and blame
Of him who to our gain and his disaster
Betrayed so kind a Master;
We, seeing more clear, concede thee what was thine;
The glory of a place beside that board
Whereon, awaiting their predestined hour
Of bowing to all-Good, all-Love, all-Power,
Lay bread and wine
Before that Host adored
Through whom our hope and our salvation came;
Thy kinsman, and our Lord.

Oh, thou, the sad day done,
Taking the homeward road
To thine obscure abode

36

In the long shadows of the setting sun,
To meet the frightened crowd
Sobbing aloud,
With thine Aunt Mary silent in their midst,
Leaning upon
The faithful arm of John;
Saint Jude, who didst
Join them in unbelief
And utter agony of grief,
And in a voice of pain and terror cried:
"Saw'st thou—and thou—
Saws't thou indeed my Cousin crucified?"
Oh, by the memory of that hour of birth
Wherein Heaven's door opened to us of earth,
Befriend—befriend us now!

St. Helena Empress

We are advised to meditate on the lives of the saints, but
this precept originated in the ages when meditation was a more
precise and arduous activity than we are tempted to think it today.
Heavy apparatus has been at work in the last hundred years to
enervate and stultify the imaginative faculties. First, realistic
novels and plays, then the cinema have made the urban mentality
increasingly subject to suggestion, so that now it lapses effortlessly
into a trance-like escape from its condition. It is said that great
popularity in fiction and film is only attained by works into which
readers and audience can transport themselves and be vicariously
endangered, loved and applauded. This kind of reverie is not
meditation, even when its objects are worthy of high devotion. It
may do little harm, perhaps even some little good, to fall day-
dreaming and play the parts of Sir Thomas More, King Lewis IX
or Father Damien. There are evident dangers in identifying ourselves with St. Francis or St. John of the Cross. We can invoke
the help of the saints and study the workings of God in them, but
if we delude ourselves that we are walking in their shoes, seeing

38

through their eyes and thinking with their minds, we lose sight of the one certain course of our salvation. There is only one saint that Bridget Hogan can actually become, St. Bridget Hogan, and that saint she *must* become, either here or in the fires of purgatory, if she is to enter heaven. She cannot slip through in fancy-dress, made up as Joan of Arc.

For this reason it is well to pay particular attention to the saints about whom our information is incomplete. There are names in the calendar about which we know nothing at all except those names, and them sometimes in a form that would puzzle their contemporaries. There are others about whom, humanly speaking, we know almost everything, who have left us a conspectus of their minds in their own writings, who were accompanied through life by pious biographers recording every movement and saying, who were conspicuous in the history of their times, so that we can see them from all sides as they impressed friends and opponents. And mid-way between these two groups are the saints who are remembered for a single act. To this class Helena eminently belongs. In extreme old age, as Empress Dowager, she made a journey into one part of her son's immense dominions, to Jerusalem. From that journey spring the relics of the True Cross that are venerated everywhere in Christendom. That is what we know; most else is surmise.

Helena was at a time, literally, the most important woman in the world, yet we know next to nothing about her. Two places claim to be her birthplace: Colchester in England and Drepanum, a seaside resort, now quite vanished, in Turkey. The evidence for neither is so strong that Englishman or Turk need abandon his pretension. She was probably of modest rank, not servile, not illustrious. Constantius married her early in his rise to power and abandoned her later for a royal match. She may have been brought up at one of the post-stables on an Imperial trunk road and have there attracted Constantius's attention on one of his official journeys. Or she may, conceivably, have been what legend makes her,

39

the daughter of a British chief. She bore one son, Constantine the Great, probably at Nish in Serbia. After her divorce she settled at Trier (Trèves) where the Cathedral probably stands on the foundations of her palace. Almost certainly it was there that she became Christian. Lactantius, who was tutor to her grandson Crispus, may have helped instruct her. At the very end of her life she suddenly emerged for her great adventure. She died at Constantinople and her body was thereupon or later moved to Rome. Her tomb never became a great centre of pilgrimage. She, herself, never seems to have attracted great personal devotion; but she was a popular saint. Numberless churches are dedicated to her; numberless girls baptized with her name; she appears everywhere in painting, sculpture and mosaic. She has fitted, in a homely and substantial way, into the family life of Christendom.

There is little of heroism or genius in any of this. We can assume that she was devout, chaste, munificent; a thoroughly good woman in an age when palaces were mostly occupied by the wicked; but she lived grandly and comfortably, whereas most of the saints in every age have accepted poverty as the condition of their calling. We know of no suffering of hers, physical, spiritual or mental, beyond the normal bereavements, disappointments and infirmities which we all expect to bear. Yet she lived in an age when Christians had often to choose between flight, apostasy or brutal punishment. Where, one may ask, lies her sanctity? Where the particular lesson for us who live in such very different circumstances?

For the world of Constantine, as we catch glimpses of it, is utterly remote from ours. There are certain superficial similarities. Poetry was dead and prose dying. Architecture had lapsed into the horny hands of engineers. Sculpture had fallen so low that in all his empire Constantine could not find a mason capable of decorating his triumphal arch and preferred instead to rob the two-hundred-year-old arch of Trajan. An enormous bureaucracy was virtually sovereign, controlling taxation on the sources of wealth, for the pleasure of city mobs and for the defense of frontiers more and more dangerously pressed by barbarians from the East. The civilized world was obliged to find a new capital. All this seems familiar, but for the event of supreme importance, the victory of Christianity, we can find no counterpart in contemporary history. We cannot by any effort of the imagination share the emotions of Lactantius or Macarius. Helena, more than anyone, stands in the heart of that mystery.

She might claim, like that other, less prudent queen: "In my end is my beginning." But for her final, triumphant journey she would have had no fame. We should think of her, if at all, as we think of Constantine: someone who neatly made the best of both worlds. The strong purpose of her pilgrimage shed a new and happier light on the long years of uneventful retirement, showing us that it was by an act of will, grounded in patience and humility, that she accepted her position. Or rather, her positions. We do not know in what state Constantius found her. She certainly did not choose him for his hopes of power. Those hopes, indeed, proved her undoing and dismissed her, divorced, into exile. In a court full of intrigue and murder she formed no party, took no steps against her rival, but quietly accepted her disgrace. Constantine rose to power, proclaimed her empress, struck coins in her honour, opened the whole imperial treasury for her use. And she accepted that too. Only in her religious practices did she maintain her private station, slipping in to mass at Rome among the crowd, helping with the housework at the convent on Mount Sion. She accepted the fact that God had his own use for her. Others faced the lions in the circus; others lived in caves in the desert. She was to be St. Helena Empress, not St. Helena Martyr or St. Helena Anchorite. She accepted a state of life full of dangers to the soul in which many foundered, and she remained fixed in her purpose until at last it seemed God had no other need of her except to continue to the end, a kind old lady. Then came her call to a single peculiar act of service, something unattempted before and unrepeatable—the finding of the True Cross.

We have no absolute certainty that she found it. The old sneer, that there was enough "wood of the cross" to build a ship, though still repeated, has long been nullified. All the splinters and shavings venerated everywhere have been patiently measured and found to comprise a volume far short of a cross. We know that most of these fragments have a plain pedigree back to the early fourth century. But there is no guarantee which would satisfy an antiquary of the authenticity of Helena's discovery. If she found the True Cross, it was by direct supernatural aid, not by archaeological reasoning. That, from the first, was its patent of title. There are certain elements about the surviving relics which are so odd that they seem to preclude the possibility of imposture. The "Label," for example—the inscription *Jesus of Nazareth, King of the Jews*—now preserved in Santa Croce, seems the most unlikely product of a forger's art. And who would have tried to cheat her? Not St. Macarius certainly. But it *is* nevertheless possible that Helena was tricked, or that she and her companions mistook casual baulks of timber, builders' waste long-buried, for the wood they sought; that the Label, somehow, got added to her treasure later. Even so her enterprise was something life-bringing.

It is not fantastic to claim that her discovery entitles her to a place in the Doctorate of the Church, for she was not merely adding one more stupendous trophy to the hoard of relics which were everywhere being unearthed and enshrined. She was asserting in sensational form a dogma that was in danger of neglect. Power was shifting. In the academies of the Eastern and South-Eastern Mediterranean sharp, sly minds were everywhere looking for phrases and analogies to reconcile the new, blunt creed for which men had died, with the ancient speculations which had beguiled their minds, and with the occult rites which had for generations spiced their logic.

Another phase of existence which select souls enjoyed when the body was shed; a priesthood; a sacramental system, even in certain details of eating, anointing and washing—all these had already a place in fashionable thought. Everything about the new religion was capable of interpretation, could be refined and diminished; everything except the unreasonable assertion that God became man and died on the Cross; not a myth nor an allegory; true God, truly incarnate, tortured to death at a particular moment in time, at a particular geographical place, as a matter of plain historical fact. This was the stumbling-block in Carthage, Alexandria, Ephesus and Athens, and at this all the talents of the time went to work, to reduce, hide and eliminate.

Constantine was no match for them. Schooled on battle-fields and in diplomatic conferences, where retreat was often the highest strategy, where truth was a compromise between irreconcilable opposites; busy with all the affairs of state; unused to the technical terms of philosophy; Constantine not yet baptized, still fuddled perhaps by dreams of Alexander, not quite sure he was not himself divine; not himself the incarnation of the Supreme Being of whom Jove and Jehovah were alike imperfect emanations; Constantine was quite out of his depth. The situation of the Church was more perilous, though few saw it, than in the days of persecution. And at that crisis suddenly emerged, God-sent from luxurious retirement in the far north, a lonely, resolute old woman with a single concrete, practical task clear before her; to turn the eyes of the world back to the planks of wood on which their salvation hung.

That was Helena's achievement, and for us who, whatever our difficulties, are no longer troubled by those particular philosophic confusions that clouded the fourth century, it has the refreshing quality that we cannot hope to imitate it. The Cross is very plain today; plainer perhaps than for many centuries. What we can learn from Helena is something about the workings of God; that He wants a different thing from each of us, laborious or easy, conspicuous or quite private, but something which only we can do and for which we were created.

St. Augustine

The Mediterranean was a magic pool in the heart of the ancient world. The peoples who dwelt on its shores swam in it and sailed on it and breathed its salt, and were given the powers of magicians. They practised the arts and sciences and crafts with an aptitude not to have been anticipated in the kindred of apes. On its northern shores Greece and Rome drew an especially powerful magic from the waters, so powerful that the enchantment radiated all over Europe, all through time down to the present age. On its southern shores was Carthage, where the enchantment was of a different sort, more suited to a soil which engendered lions and elephants and snakes and jungle vegetation almost as fierce. That city also should have radiated power, that should have run down the continent to its southward tip, and Africa should have worked out its destiny in the light. But Cato and his sour like held the mean man's myth that the prosperous man can only prosper at the expense of another man, and saw Carthage as the competitor of Rome, and provoked the Punic Wars. The victory of the Romans in those wars left Carthage rubble and turned North Africa into a

44

mere colony, where African men of genius were still born, but had to work without the support of their own national tradition. The sacrifice was in vain. For as the Roman Empire fell apart, North Africa experienced economic and administrative decay which produced poverty and anarchy, and it was harried on its seaboard by pirates and on its southern frontiers by tribesmen. It got no help from tottering Rome, and it was forced to succumb before the barbarian invasions. It appeared that all civilisation was being totally and finally destroyed. It was during this period, in A.D. 354, that there was born in North Africa a man named Augustine who was fatuous enough to ignore the catastrophe which was about to overcome him, engaged in an exhaustive enquiry into the nature of things which were about to lose their human audience, and set down his findings in manuscripts which seemed destined to be lost almost as soon as they were completed under the sands drifting from the spreading desert across burned and looted cities. It was an insane enterprise: and the most canny of writers composing in the illusion of perpetual peace cannot have hoped for such immortality as he attained. His works are the foundation of modern Western thought.

This was a stupendous act of faith. Every expert on international affairs would have told Augustine that he and his work were doomed. Had he not disregarded them, Christendom might have had as insubstantial an intellectual system as Islam, and there is not the slightest indication that anybody could have performed the task in his stead. With magnificent audacity he took as his subject matter a certain complex of ideas which intrude into every developed religion and are present in Christianity also: the idea that matter, and especially matter related to sex, is evil; that man, wearing a body made of matter, living in a material world, and delighting in the manifestations of sex, is tainted with evil, and must cleanse himself before God; and that this atonement must take the form of suffering. He examined these ideas from a philosophical point of view and discussed how they looked in the new light cast on the world by the life of Christ, and checked his conclusions by his own personal experience, which he used with a candour new in literature. The construction thus built stood up so well that the Western mind made it its home, and its finest achievements since then have consisted largely of modifying and extending the original structure. The teachings of Augustine are, of course, directly transmitted by the Roman Catholic Church to its members, and with various modifications by the Protestant churches to theirs; and they pervade Catholic and Protestant literature. Shakespeare was born about twelve hundred years later than Augustine, but if his work is examined for evidence of his general conceptions he proves to accept the same assumptions that Augustine makes when, in his *Confessions*, he deliberates on the religious and philosophical significance of the events of his life. But it is easier to prove his domination of the modern world negatively. Our recognition of Goethe as a unique figure can be accounted for by his freedom from Augustinian conceptions; and in our own day the influence of André Gide, not sufficiently explained by either his creative or critical works in themselves, is derived from his organisation of an anti-Augustinian revolt.

But it would be a mistake to think of Augustine as having thrust on us an intellectual schedule so competently prepared that we adhere to it because there is no better. Rather is it that Augustine, being an exceptionally vital human being, in whom all human characteristics appeared in an intense form, and being given to self-examination, which he conducted with all this idiosyncratic intensity, predigested our experiences for us. He worked out the sum for us to the last stage, which each of us must work out in the light of the unique knowledge we derive from our unique circumstances. He was able to do us this service because he was one of the greatest of all writers. There is a peculiar vitality about his writing, which came to him, perhaps, as the favoured heir of a rich racial heritage.

46

For tradition says that he was a Numidian, one of a people akin to the Berbers and Tuaregs, who were non-Semitic and sometimes fair-haired and blue-eyed, but dark of skin and with features cast in a non-European mould. There is very little doubt that he came of native African stock, whether of this branch or another. A pagan grammarian named Maximus once wrote to him a hostile letter in which he mocked at the Punic names of some Christian martyrs, and in his reply Augustine rebukes him for having, in a letter written "by an African to Africans," thrown ridicule at the Punic language which he describes as "our own tongue." He also, in a poem addressed to a friend who had followed him to Italy, speaks of the ancient race to which they both belonged, as if this marked them off from the Italians who surrounded them. This race had its strong vein of literary genius. Many Latin writers, whom we assume to have been Europeans, such as Terence and Apuleius, were, in fact, native Africans.

In the works of Augustine there is a dark abundance, a deeply coloured fecundity, which is beyond the range of nearly all Europeans. He lacked the delicacy which makes a writer happy in responding to the disciplinary demands of poetry, but that was all he lacked. He had to contend with the difficulty that he had always something to say, that the ideas flowed as fast as the ink from his pen, that his pages are crowded with arguments and illustrations, with hasty accounts of truths he has discovered on the planes of the flesh and the mind and the soul. This is a real handicap. Many a writer has earned a reputation for deliberation and restraint for no other reason than that he cannot muster more than one idea to a page, which suits readers who have not the capacity to deal with a more copious flow. To connoisseurs of impoverishment Augustine appears gross and unclassical, but it is not grossness but power which makes him, in his *Confessions* and in his correspondence, able to pick up a character and transfer it in its totality from life to literature. In this field he recalls the greatest of Russian writers,

47

Aksakov; and this is a significant parallel. Aksakov was brought up on the eastern steppes of Russia, at the end of the eighteenth century, facing the cultured West, but with a primitive world, unblurred by self-consciousness, behind his back. Augustine looked North to Rome but he had wild Africa behind him, and he too possessed a frontier freshness, seeing civilisation with eyes that were not too tired.

Again and again he draws characters so fully, so intensely, that it seems to us we know them in life, in our lives, that we have to strip them of the modern clothes in which we have re-dressed them and put them back into toga and tunic. There is our familiar friend, Alypius, whom we like. Who would not? When he sat on the Assessor's bench in Rome he found it easy to refuse large bribes, even when powerful and dangerous men tried to force him to take them with menaces, but found it very hard indeed not to take advantage of the customs by which the praetors were able to buy books at cut prices on the side. He was a very simple soul, and unlucky such often are. When he was a student in Carthage, he was going through the market-place at noon (when most of the shops would be closed) repeating to himself a lesson he had to learn by heart, when he saw a man drop an axe and run away very fast. He thought that very odd. The man was running at a speed which was really quite remarkable. Alypius picked up the axe, and examined it, and wondered what it was all about. As the man was a burglar, who had been disturbed while robbing a silversmith, and the axe was the old Roman equivalent for a jemmy, the police fell into a natural misapprehension about Alypius' part in the incident, and his friends had a great deal of trouble to get him released. He carried his artlessness into fields where it normally knows no survival. When Augustine was greatly concerned about his need for the love of women, and meditated marriage, Alypius could not at first understand what Augustine was making all this fuss about. "For he had made a trial of that act in the beginning of his youth; but not

48

having engaged himself by it, he was sorry for it, rather, and de-spised it; living from that time until this present most continently." But he was always open to argument, and as Augustine would go on and on about it, and he had a great respect for Augustine, he admitted that perhaps he had formed his adverse opinion of sexual intercourse too hastily, and decided that there would be no harm in looking into the matter again. But he never set his heart on it, and was not greatly disappointed when Augustine decided that celibacy was better after all.

But Augustine did not fall into the error of bolstering up that delusion, "the little man," innocent and harmless, as the children of men are not. Mildness was Alypius' salient and, it might have been thought, his essential and unalterable characteristic; but at Car-thage, which was a place of heated and uncensored inclinations, he became an addict of the gladiatorial shows. This meant quite sim-ply that he was given up to blood-lust, for these shows involved the brutalisation and slaughter of helpless men and beasts. He was shocked out of his vice by a public denunciation of the shows delivered by Augustine when he was a teacher at Carthage Uni-versity, and the cream of his mildness rose to the surface again. But later, in Rome, when he was a mature man, his friends one day haled him to the Coliseum by sheer force, and though he covered his eyes again "a mighty cry of the people, beating strongly upon him he (being overcome by curiosity, and as it were prepared, whatsoever it were, to condemn it even when seen, and to overcome it) opened his eyes," and the love of cruelty flamed up in him again. "So soon as he saw the blood, he at the very instant drunk down a kind of savageness," and for a long space of time, until another spiritual upheaval cured him, he was what he had been before, a connoisseur of murder. It is as disconcerting to read this of Alypius as it is to visit an American town and learn that the quiet little house-agent led the mob in a recent race-riot; as it was to meet the Nazi who was also a good and kind family man and rate-

49

payer; as it is to contemplate the atrocity of history and consider that statistically it is certain that this must be the work of the average man. But it is the special usefulness of Augustine that he was never alarmed by the disconcerting, it had to be set down on paper as justly as everything else.

This was true even when he himself was the disconcerting object. His *Confessions* tell a story which we may judge to have been embarrassing even by the standards of his time, for there is no autobiography like it. Penitent Christians, cleansing their bosoms by avowing all, have found it not impossible to own that they have in their day come near committing the sin against the Holy Ghost; but nobody has ever recounted in such detail the story of a purposeless, ungracious youth, dipping, as the thirties came along and there was nothing done, to the sordid. He was born in an untranquil home. He was the son of one Patricius, the owner of a small estate near Tagaste (now Souk Ahras, in the Algerian hinterland, near Constantine), and his wife Monica. Augustine always speaks of his father in tones of moral reprobation, but he seems on Augustine's own showing to have been simply a typical country gentleman of the age, needy because the economic system was falling to pieces round him, harassed because he was one of the select but unlucky class of *curiales*, who were responsible for the taxes of their district, and, not unnaturally in these circumstances, hot-tempered. Like most of his class in that transition era, he was a pagan, but was to be baptised before the end of his life. His mother Monica was a Christian, born of a family firm for at least two generations in the faith, and she was ardent in her devotion and active in church work. Of Monica Augustine gives a fuller picture than he gives of his father, indeed in all literature no son has ever painted a more detailed and a more intimate picture of his mother. But by a curious chance this has been obscured from us. When she had been dead for a thousand years or so her story appealed to some Italians, who started a cult in her honour, and they made a soft-eyed Italian lady of her, passive in all but prayer; and this image has replaced the picture Augustine drew from life, and which is in fact all we know of her, and which represents an entirely different type of woman. According to him she was passionate, in spite of a remarkable power of self-control, vigorous, competent, full of good sense and worldly wisdom, dominating, and able to hold her own in argument. She is much more lovable than the popular legend, though the disparity is at first shocking to people who come on the *Confessions* late in life.

There was the making of much trouble here. Patricius' fortunes went from bad to worse; in spite of great efforts he had for a time to withdraw Augustine from school, and the lad idled at home, getting into mischief. There was the not quite eradicated difficulty of belonging to the conquered race. There was the religious difference between husband and wife; when Augustine was a child he accepted his mother's Christianity, but as an adolescent stood with his father in his paganism. There was also the imminence of war and the threat of dissolution which overhung civilisation, and the imperfect quality which that civilisation had attained in this particular spot. For all these people (again like the Russian landowners in Aksakov's pages) were thorough toughs. Augustine and his friends were studying philosophy at the highest level it has yet reached, and the North African mind was in touch with all that had been achieved in art and science; but when his mother entertained her friends it was as likely as not that they would fall to comparing the disfigurements that had been left by their husbands' blows, and Monica's only comment was that they deserved what they got for having answered back their husbands. In this violent and vexed world Augustine developed into an unsettled adolescent, and then into a clever wastrel.

He was, of course, recognised as brilliant. He won a high place in the Rhetoric Schools of Carthage, we hear of him being crowned in a poetical competition, he became a professor of Rhetoric. But he was consumed by sensuality, of a quite heartless kind, until he fell in love with a woman with whom he lived in a union as close and stable as marriage, though they were not married. There was probably some legal impediment: she may have been a manumitted slave, and therefore forbidden by law to marry a man of superior legal status. He was faithful to her and they had a son, whom he called Adeodatus, Given-by-God, and marvelled over, not having expected that "though children be against our wills begotten, yet being born they even compel us to love them." But he was not easy in the relationship, which was displeasing to him by reason of its irregularity, and to his father, who had wanted him to make a good marriage within the Imperial caste system. He made similar arrangements that pleased nobody over his religious life. His mother was firm in her Christianity, his father was still a pagan, but he himself became a Manichaean.

The heresy of Manichaeanism, then about a hundred and fifty years old, has since played an important part in history, and is always starting up again in our own time. If a playwright or a novelist feels the need for religion, and is unwilling to take the trouble to find out what the orthodox faith accepts as proven truth, but feels the need to formulate a theory of the purpose of life, he is practically certain to achieve a restatement of the Manichaean heresy. It posits an extremely crude dichotomy between matter and spirit, invents a God Who is in active conflict with Satan and might yet be beaten, and takes only a shadowy interest in any of the personages of the Gospel story. It has been highly intellectualised and ethicised in subsequent centuries, but in those days it was very much as its inventor Mani had left it, a Persian fairytale about the two powers, the kingdom of good and the kingdom of evil, which went to war and got smashed up and confused, so that now it is the business of the virtuous to recover the scattered particles of light which got thrown into the darkness and are still embedded in it. The universe was conceived as a sort of decontamination centre, where this salvage work is being done. There are all sorts of picturesque oddities in the story: in the sun dwelt Primal Man, and in the moon Primal Woman, and the Signs of the Zodiac, like dredger buckets, lifted up such particles of light as were rescued from the darkness by the virtuous, to be stored by these two celestial custodians. This sort of legend was well below Augustine's intellectual level, but he remained a Manichaean for nine years. During this time Augustine's father died, and Monica, who had been left in straitened circumstances, had to find money for the assistance of her heretical son and his concubine and child. Her material situation must have been harassing, and she was so deeply distressed by his spiritual state that, in spite of their deep attachment, she would not see him.

Time was going by. He was at the end of his twenties, with nothing achieved. The dreariness of the situation can be realised if a modern parallel is imagined: the case of a pious Roman Catholic widow, left with only a small amount of insurance, who has several children, one of whom is a young man of brilliant intellectual gifts, who fails to make a living, has a mistress and an illegitimate child, and practises one of the queerer Californian religions. But, of course, there was something more here than mere misfortune befalling a blameless woman. There was a conflict in Monica as well as in Augustine. By that time infant baptism was favoured by many strictly orthodox Catholics; but Monica had never had Augustine baptised. In his childhood, before he had renounced his mother's Christianity and adopted his father's paganism, he had been gravely ill and had begged to be baptised, but she had refused, on some trivial ground. Moreover, though she had early recognised and deplored his strong sexual nature, she had done nothing to help him by arranging an early marriage for him. It is typical of Augustine's honesty that, in spite of his adoration of his mother, he sets down these two instances in which she failed him, without malice, but without any attempt to mitigate them.

That honesty continues to operate when he goes on to the next and most lamentable phase of his story. This began by what might have been supposed to have been a step in the right direction. He left the Manichaeans. He had a speculative mind, but a great deal of horse sense, and the astronomical fantasies were more than he could stand in the long run. Also he spent some time with a famous Manichaean bishop named Faustus, and found him a silly fellow. Augustine never despised reason, and was later to bid his followers put "far from us the thought that God detests that whereby he has made us superior to other animals, far from us an assent of pure faith which should dispense us from accepting or demanding proof." But this rejection of heresy did not take him very far. He did not become a Christian, and he could not get on with his work. It seemed to him that he might do better away from Carthage, which had many painful associations for him, and he took his mistress and his child to Rome to start afresh. This step was passionately opposed by Monica, who travelled from Tagaste to Carthage to beg him not to go, and he only managed to get on board his ship by telling her that he must leave her for a while to say goodbye to a friend who was sailing from the harbour. Her excessive emotion over what was a reasonable course of action is an indication of the extent to which things were wrong in this troubled family. In Rome good Alypius was already installed as a civil servant, and he beat the drum for his brilliant friend and got him some pupils. But though students in Rome were more orderly than they were in Carthage they were apt to bilk their teachers. Augustine fell into financial difficulties, and was ill. Moreover he could not win peace of mind, not only in the commonplace sense, but in the literal sense of peace of the intellect. He tried to find contentment in the doctrines of the Sceptics, who held that the human mind is incapable of enquiring into the nature of things, and that all one can do is to fold one's philosophical hands and cultivate blandness, but the attempt was vain.

54

At last he had a stroke of good fortune. He was made Professor of Rhetoric at Milan, which was the seat of the Imperial Court. But there was something dubious about this appointment, for it was obtained on the strength of recommendations from Manichaean friends, who might have been less active in the matter had they known of Augustine's alienation from their faith. But this dubiety brought him under the influence of a figure who was shining with candour and rectitude, the Bishop of Milan, St. Ambrose. This was a superb human being, an aristocrat not cast down by the plight of aristocracy in the foundering Empire, who had been the governor of a province before he was, by the curious custom of the time, conscripted a bishop, and who was an inspired preacher and interpreter of Scripture. Ambrose was too much wrapped in the preoccupations of his exacting office to pay much attention to Augustine, as is recorded wistfully but without malice in the *Confessions*. But Augustine was profoundly impressed by Ambrose, and when Monica came to Milan, about a year after he settled there, he was able to tell her that he had become a catechumen and was only waiting for some sign of the Divine Will to be baptised.

But he was still in a state of miserable futility and discontent. Alypius and eight or nine of his African admirers had thrown up all other ties to follow him and be his pupils, and they were living in a common household, reading the Neo-Platonists and worrying about the future in a way that was quite contrary to Neo-Platonic doctrine. They had no money. Augustine was in bad health, and could not undertake much beyond his official duties, and found those distasteful, because of the lip-service he had to render to Imperial majesty. They thought of becoming a closed community devoted to scholarship, persuading some rich man who loved learning to support them; but Augustine was firm that he could not live without a woman, and this hardly fitted in with the idea of a secular monastery. Then it occurred to them that Augustine might save the situation by marrying a rich wife. He expressly says in his *Confessions* that there was no question of marrying in order to have children and build up a family; he was simply moved by the expectation that he would find a sexual mate and that "by means of ample patrimony, it were possible that all those whom you wish to have living with you in one place could be comfortably supported, and that by this reason of her noble birth she could bring within your easy reach the honours necessary for a man to lead a cultured existence."

To this end Monica went into the marriage market and found a bride for him. This meant that he had to part with the woman who had been virtually his wife for fourteen years. "When that mistress of mine which was wont to be my bedfellow, the hinderer as it were of my marriage, was plucked away from my side," he wrote, "my heart cleaving unto her was broken by this means, and wounded, yea, and blood drawn from it." She was sent home to North Africa, and proved what her relationship with Augustine had meant to her by taking a vow of celibacy. What is quite horrible is that when Augustine and Monica sent her home, they kept her son, who was a clever and lovable boy. This was to be a worse crime than then appeared, for he was to die in a year or two; but it was immediately exposed as unpardonable by Augustine's behaviour. For the bride his mother had chosen for him was so young that there could be no question of her marriage for at least two years, and to fill in this time he took another concubine, so that nothing was gained by this separation of the mother from her son, it was gratuitous cruelty. How twisted and confused were all the people in this group at the time can be judged from an examination of Monica's motives. She must, of course, have been under grave material compulsion. Her means were small, and for some reason none of her children, neither Augustine nor his brother nor his sister, were self-supporting. She also professed to be moved by the desire that her son should repudiate his mistress and marry, so that

ST. BENEDICT AND A YOUNG MONK

by Lauren Ford

his sexual life could conform to the Church's requirements, and he could be baptised. But that makes it very strange that she should have chosen a bride so young that Augustine would be obliged to wait for her, for with her knowledge of his nature she must have known that he would not wait in a state of celibacy. If these had been a group of White Russians in Munich, of Middle Western expatriates in Paris, one would certainly know what to think of them all: the needy widow who forces her clever unsuccessful son to send away his aging mistress so that he can marry a rich young girl, but insists that the poor woman should leave her child behind, because he is an attractive and promising boy. But what is significant is that it is through Augustine's own candour that we know what to think of them.

This deed could not be undone; but the hideous phase of which it was a part suddenly passed. The darkness in Augustine's mind grew blacker, and there came an afternoon when an agony fell upon him. He wandered about in his garden, horribly aware of his own baseness and its contrast with virtue, and of the paralysis afflicting his will which prevented him from choosing to be other than base. He had been talking to Alypius, but in his distraction left him, letting a book of the scriptures fall as he rose. Then he heard the voice of a child from a neighbouring house, chanting in a singsong, "Take . . . up . . . and . . . read. Take . . . up . . . and . . . read." But the chant went on. He began to suspect that this was a sign; and he remembered how St. Anthony of Egypt had taken up a hermit's life because he had opened a copy of the Gospel and read a text that seemed to be spoken directly to him. So he assumed that it was the book he had cast down that he was being ordered to pick up and read. The text that met his eyes was a verse from the Epistle to the Romans which read: "Not in rioting and drunkenness, not in chambering and impurities, not in contention and envy, but put ye on the Lord Jesus Christ and make not provision for the flesh in its concupiscence." The trouble was over. He felt

57

easy and confident. He had no need to worry about a rich wife or place-hunting or budgeting for the costs of a community or satisfaction of his emotional appetites. He had simply to become a Christian and give himself wholly to the service of the Church. Putting his finger in the book to keep the place, he went to Alypius and told him what had been happening during the last few minutes, and found that Alypius also had been passing through a crisis of torment, of which he had said nothing. Alypius took the book from him and read the next verse, which ran, "Now him that is weak in faith, take unto you," and he applied it to himself and announced that he would follow Augustine into the Church. They went into the house and told Monica, who had never anticipated such a transformation of Augustine's earthy character. She had prayed that he might marry, and keep to a Christian rule of life, it had never occurred to her that he might renounce the world for the sake of the Church, and she was full of amazement and rejoicing.

Thereafter everything went well with them, there was an end to this phase of ambiguity and squalid striving and cruelty. Augustine and Monica and Adeodatus and Alypius went to a friend's villa on the hills above Lake Varese, and there he spent the winter teaching some African pupils, and writing some treatises, which delight by their pictures of the Italian scene and by his character-sketches of his pupils, and by their crystalline serenity. At Easter he and Adeodatus and Alypius were baptised at Milan by Ambrose. Then they set their faces towards their home, and in June they were at the port of Ostia, waiting for a ship to take them to Africa. Actually Italy was in a state of grave disorder, for the usurper Maximus was about to cross the Alps and sweep down on Milan, and the Emperor Valentinian had before him the long flight which was to end in his captivity and death. But these people were tranquil, and one day, when Augustine and Monica were sitting by a window that looked down on a garden in a courtyard, they talked of the love of God and were raised to a moment's understanding of Him. "And while we were thus talking of His wisdom and panting for it, with all the effort of our hearts we did for one instant attain to touch it," wrote Augustine, "then sighing, and leaving the first fruits of our spirit bound to it, we returned to the sound of our own tongue . . ." The account of this moment records the most intense experience ever commemorated. The passage has the massiveness of Milton; but Milton, perhaps for the very reason that he was master of our human tongue, never soared to a region where he heard another, and it is that which Augustine persuades us he has done.

Monica felt that she had no need for further life, and indeed it was only a few days before she died; and in Augustine's account of his bereavement men and women who have not yet lost a beloved parent can learn beforehand what sorrow they will feel. He did not shrink from reliving any moment of suffering, since his truthful spirit insisted that he must write down what had really happened. In that year Augustine was thirty-two; and he was seventy-six when he died. All the remaining years were spent in the service of the Church. He missed the summer sailings to Africa that year and went to Rome, where he wrote some treatises against Manichaeanism, probably at the behest of the new Pope, Siricius, who was a great foe of these heretics. In the following August he went back to North Africa, and used his share of his father's estate which was waiting for him there to found a small religious house. There he lived very happily for three years, writing busily. But after that he fell a victim to the prevalent danger of those days, involuntary episcopacy. As the Roman Empire fell apart, Christianity was taking over its territory. It gave the populations a sense of security, and therefore they needed priests who could preach them the doctrine of salvation; and they needed priests too to warn them of what was stable orthodoxy, which would give them shelter, and what was heresy, which would lead them into profitless warrings;

and they needed priests to distribute charity, to settle disputes, to replace function after function that fell from the hands of the dwindling bureaucracy. So a congregation which lacked a priest (and priests were scarce) were apt to seize any able person of character who incautiously came within their orbit, drag him to the altar, and forcibly consecrate him. This often happened to Government officials who had no inclination towards the priesthood, but it could also happen to the religious man who had found his proper vocation in the monastic life and had no taste for pastoral duties. Thus it was with Augustine, who, when visiting the town of Hippo (now Bona in Algeria) in order to convert a pagan, was kidnapped and made a presbyter, and later a bishop.

For the rest of Augustine's life he conducted with astonishing success two parallel careers. He was a prolific author, pouring out definitions of the faith, reconsiderations of political and philosophical problems in the light of Christianity, blue-prints for contemporary social action, explosive contributions to controversy on matters of theology and scholarship, and immensely long letters of advice to persons troubled by spiritual perplexity. He also was an administrator with duties that perpetually extended as civil disorder increased in pace with poverty, as the forces of heresy multiplied and grew madder, and the threats of invasion from the southern tribesmen and the northern barbarians came nearer and nearer to realisation. It can be said with certainty that no man ever worked so hard for so long. He was still in harness when the vandals sailed from Spain on Africa and swept the Roman and Visigoth defenders out of their way. He was still in Hippo when it was besieged, and died in the hours of defeat, praying stoically, "I ask God to deliver this city from its enemies, or if that may not be, that He give us strength to bear His Will, or at least that He take me from this world and receive me in His bosom." To the end he was under the government of truthfulness, and did not pretend he found a pleasure in the chastening hand of God. But it never failed him during these years of double service. Not unnaturally he had made many mistakes during the forty years when he was both writer and man of action, he had often been tactless and obtuse and disrespectful to the merits of others; but he had always written down what he was in his own correspondence. He would not bury the truth.

Augustine made many gifts to humanity, including a great deal of entertainment. There is very little of his writing, on whatever subject, which does not warm the interest in a few sentences, and he had an immense range. His description of the ecstasy that uplifted his mother and himself as they stood at the window reveals the substance of mysticism to the least mystical of readers, and proves its right to primacy over all other experience; and his letter to a certain pious Lady Ecdicia, telling her not to be an ass and to stop annoying her husband, is a masterpiece of humour, and not unconscious humour either. But the quality by which he has rendered most service to humanity is probably his truthfulness. He demonstrated it beyond all doubt when he described without mitigation how deep he had been at Milan in a web of futility and nastiness. Let it be remarked that he did not wallow in his state, he was not smacking his lips over his abjection in order to make an effective contrast with his later uprightness. He was simply describing that phase as it had been. Bearing that in mind, it is significant that this same man asserted in all his writings that he was in constant relations with a living God. Many other people who have written of such relations have been weaklings who could not bear to look facts in the face and might be suspected of inventing a God to obviate the necessity of considering the universe a systemless chaos. But Augustine is not subject to such suspicion. When he said that he knew God it must be accepted that something really happened which his perceptions and his intellect interpreted as the knowledge of God; and none of us can claim perceptions as delicate or intellect as strong.

61

St. Simeon was a Peculiar Person; of that there can be no doubt. To live on top of a pillar for thirty-odd years marks a man out in history whether he has the incidental value of being a saint or not. And so St. Simeon was a favourite of mine long before I was a Catholic, long even before I knew he was a saint. Somebody produced a one-act play at school, I remember, in which this weird creature appeared as hero; whether the play was funny or not I can't remember, though being a school play it probably was. Anyway, this was my first introduction to St. Simeon, and to the fact that in the past some people had stood on pillars and done nothing else for years on end. But this had all happened long ago: I was hazy about dates, and Simeon became simply one more figure of the dim and distant past, along with Alcestis, Orestes, Hector, the Trojan War, Venus, Helen of Troy, Brutus and Cassius; and such for a long time he remained. But from the beginning there was a slight difference between this Peculiar Person and the real or mythical heroes of the classical past who appeared wrapped in shawls or imitation togas, standing before pseudo tent-flaps or rickety walls, on the bare boards of the school platform every Tuesday at four o'clock during the winter term. For whereas nearly all these famous figures were men of action, who did great things and suffered for them, Simeon seemed to have become famous— if he was famous, and I had never heard of him before—by doing absolutely nothing. He had done nothing and yet got paid for it, so to speak. This struck me as pretty shrewd. I was lazy by nature in those days—or rather, I was a boy—and my idea of the good life was a perpetual holiday, with a game of cricket occasionally to relieve the monotony, and I thought that old Simeon had hit on an easy thing which in later life, if possible, I would do my best to emulate.

He was a romantic figure, too, because the details of his life were wrapped in mystery. There was the one bald fact of the pillar; but all sorts of intriguing questions arose as to how he lived there. How did he get his food, for instance? Was it sent up to him in a basket at regular intervals, or did he rely on the good nature of any casual passer-by? One thing seemed certain—he would not go down for it. There was a saying about Mahomet and a mountain, and it seemed that in this case the mountain would most definitely have to go to Mahomet; and then there was that other mysterious saying about faith moving mountains, and it did not seem beyond the bounds of possibility that this miraculous old man—I imagined him as very old indeed, and of course bearded—had been miraculously fed by birds or angels, as the tribes had been fed by manna in the wilderness. Of course, there was always the simple possibility that he had lived on his pillar without food, but this seemed far too prosaic a solution to be true.

Then there was the further question of sleeping. Was Simeon in danger of falling off in more senses than one every night? For some reason, arising, I believe now, from the similarity in sound between Stylites and stilts, and also stiles, I was inclined to think of the old gentleman as performing some kind of balancing act on the top of a very flimsy wooden structure, rather like a music-hall comedian; and when I did get it into my head that the pillar was made of stone it still appeared to me as very tall and very slender, with Simeon not so much seated as perched there, and I could not imagine how he ever managed to get a good night's rest. Of course, not doing any work all day he would hardly get tired, but still he would need a few hours' sleep every night presumably, and how did he manage to get it?

There was the final and fundamental question, the most intriguing of all, as to what he did with his time. What could he do all day? He had solved the problem of living without working, and for that I admired him tremendously; but it did seem to me, even at that early age, that there was something rather too negative about an existence which involved simply not doing anything at all. My idea of the good life was certainly one from which work was entirely absent, but this was only a clearing of the ground, so to speak, to make way for endless games and amusements, and the number of possible games that could be played on top of a pillar seemed to me to be limited, even when, as seemed likely from the play, there was a neighbour perched on his own pillar, not too far away for neighbourly intercourse. The problem remained: what did Simeon do all day?

This question, childish as it was and childish as it sounds, was nevertheless the fundamental question raised by the figure of this old man perched up there aloft. "Why should the aged eagle spread his wings?" is a later question, the question of the disillusioned, the "disenchanted," the question of those who have reached a certain age, and who can see no reason for going forward any further. It was not a question that presented itself to me then. I thought of life, lazy as I was, as activity, pleasant activity. Simeon remained with me as a personification of glorious futility.

And yet it was obvious to me that he was, though futile, by no means a failure. Apparently, judging by the one-act play, people often went to see him—even crowds of people. This seemed to me perfectly understandable. I was going to school in the 'thirties, the sporting decade in which records were being broken daily. There was Malcolm Campbell in his "Bluebird," record-breaking along some stretch of sand in far-away—California, was it? Daytona, perhaps? There were non-stop dancing and piano-playing, couples going round and round some dance-hall in Blackpool until they either stopped or dropped. And also at Blackpool was some modern fakir, a one-time minister of religion, I think, who lived in a barrel or did something or other in a barrel, and in whom the police force seemed to be taking an interest. Then in the 'thirties came Gandhi's visit—Gandhi in his sheet and spectacles, the man who fasted for phenomenal lengths of time, and always seemed to get his way in the end. Gandhi the religious Indian, the Christian clergyman fakir, the sporting and dancing record-breakers, all seemed to have something in common with the mythical figure of old Simeon on his perch, something essential to the type of person who wants to go one better than everybody else in some mad direction or other, someone who wants to shine and get into the newspapers. Simeon had succeeded, as Gandhi had succeeded; but was such success really worth it?

I never really bothered my head very much with the effort to answer this question. It was sufficient that I had managed to place old Simeon in his correct category. I had heard of Diogenes too: it seemed that at all times, and in all kinds of places, peculiar people had managed to do peculiar things, and get applauded for them.

Then for a long time I forgot about Simeon. I passed into a civilized world from which genuine cranks were ostracized, and into which only the sham oddities, those who know the rules, and if they break them know how to break them *comme il faut*, are received with open arms. Simeon grew very remote indeed. After all, he had lived so long ago, and in Cilicia. Times had changed.

65

We were not so rough now. Those hairy men of the past, always bearded, always either grotesque in their voluminous clothing—there was a pre-Raphaelite picture of Moses being held up to see the Promised Land from afar in the Manchester Art Gallery—or else disgustingly under-clad in their loin-cloths and little else—they were all so remote. Unlike them we dressed sensibly; we used our Gillette blade daily; we bathed; we lived in civilized houses, not tents; we went to the pictures. Simeon became almost pre-historic; it would have been no surprise to learn that he had ridden to his pillar on a dinosaur or a pterodactyl.

But then times changed again. The civilized world prepared for war; went to war. The velvet glove was whisked away; the iron hand appeared. When you are encompassed by a world at war, Simeon's glorious futility begins to seem less futile and more glorious. I discovered with delight that some sections of the civilized world took old bearded madmen like Simeon seriously. There was Helen Waddell's *Desert Fathers*, for instance. Then, in a beautiful picture of the desert fathers, each in his separate little orbit of ground, encircled with flowers and being visited by tamed animals, I found a flowering wilderness, and this seemed to me a blessed counterpoise to the wildernesses that were being made of the modern cities as the bombs fell thicker and thicker. I began to wonder whether those old madmen had been so mad after all, and whether maybe Simeon was not such a fool as he looked.

Since then I have learned a little more about St. Simeon; only a little, but enough to increase rather than diminish my youthful astonishment at this astonishing man. Apparently he was not always old and bearded after all, in fact as a boy he seems to have been quite a normal son of a shepherd—that is to say, a young shepherd himself—until one day, after going to church, he became suddenly convinced that he must go into a monastery. Of the mystery, the providentiality of that impulse, what is there to be said?

His mode of entry into the monastery was unusual but characteristic: he lay on the ground outside the gates of the building for five days and nights, until finally they let him in. He seems rather to have enjoyed the experience, for once in the monastery he started doing more outrageous things of a similar kind. When the others objected, he ran off to a deserted tank, hid himself there, was discovered and dragged back by main force. He did not see why they should object to his eating only one day a week when he was giving the rest of his food to the poor; nor why he should not bind his body with a tight cord so that the flesh grew over it, if he felt it necessary thus to chastise the rebellious flesh. His fifth-century monastery was not given to what we should describe as self-indulgence, but evidently it was too soft for Simeon, for after a year he was off again, and this time for good.

He went to a nearby mountain, the Telanassus; and it was here that he eventually became famous, ensconced on his pillar. He did not immediately go to the top of the mountain but lived in the comparative luxury—after an introductory fast lasting forty days— of a little house under the peak. He spent three years here; then he went up higher—to the top. At once, lest he might in a moment of weakness wish to escape, he walled himself in. But he was taking no chances; remembering that stone walls do not a prison make, he obtained a large iron ball, and chained himself to it. One day Meletius, the Bishop of Antioch's vicar, visited him. If the will was truly there, he remarked, the chain would be unnecessary. For all his austerities, Simeon was not above taking a hint from a prelate, and obediently he unhooked himself. The will did in fact prove to be there, for the saint remained on his mountain-top until he died.

According to his two friends, disciples and biographers, Anthony and Theodoret, the result of all this splendid isolation was an immense number of conversions amongst the wild Arabian tribes who had ignored Christianity's milder missionaries. God, says Theodoret, is pleased to raise up saints distinguished by different marks of sanctity appropriate to different times; and the wild Iberi, Persians, Ishmaelites and Armenians evidently needed a man as wild in his sanctity as they were savage in their lives before they could be brought to the waters of baptism. Anyway, they were so impressed by the ferocity which this old man of the mountains vented upon himself that they flocked to him in droves to be converted. I have wondered whether a sense of humour of a rather shrewd and countrified kind was tucked away somewhere behind the austerities; for Simeon, in an effort apparently to flee from his increasing popularity, did not move horizontally but vertically. The will was still there; not even notoriety could break it; and Simeon's pillar, which had begun by being six cubits high, rose to twelve. In the end it reached a height of thirty-six cubits, and still the shaggy converts came. Simeon seems to have taken little pride in his elevation, for at a word from his superiors, the bishops and abbots of the surrounding regions (was Meletius one of them, one wonders?), he showed himself perfectly willing to come down to earth; but the authorities, having tested his obedience and humility, decided not to clip the old eagle's wings after all, and Simeon remained on his high pillar, up on the mountain peak.

From this vantage point he preached, it is said, twice daily, sometimes for hours on end. Of course he fasted and prayed. He healed the sick. He even became a sort of judge. It was here that his uncomprehending mother came to visit him and die, wailing that flesh of her flesh should so cruelly have mortified itself; and her son wept with her. Here too came a thief, Jonathan by name, to be protected, converted and dead, all within a week. And here at last the old man himself died, after being clasped to his pillar in prayer for three days. The body was taken down by the faithful Anthony, carried to Antioch, and buried with great pomp and reverence.

I have a feeling that this saint is still looked a bit askance at, by the "average" Catholic, as he is certainly a figure of fun to the average non-Catholic. And for a time, when my one wish was to be utterly orthodox in all things, both great and small, I tried to feel the same way about him and to convince myself that sanctity was more appropriately achieved in drawing-rooms with St. François de Sales than on the top of a pillar with St. Simeon. But as the times change again, becoming ever again the same, and the world prepares for another world war, waged with atomic weapons this time, I begin to return to my old favourite, and with increased fervour. Extraordinary ages call for extraordinary characters; extraordinary diseases for extraordinary cures. St. Simeon is for me the perfect figure of the extraordinary saint. I think we need more of him.

For what, after all, do we—do I—admire St. Simeon so enthusiastically for? It is for that terrific talent of his for doing nothing. There is no finer slap in the eye to the modern world than that. It is a phenomenon that the modern world finds not only incomprehensible but reprehensible and even criminal, and there are strong reasons for thinking that the modern world needs a good slap in the eye. St. Simeon stands—or sits, or perches—as the pure contemplative, the eagle up aloft in his eyrie gazing at the sun, the look-out man in the crow's nest. I know that the text-books will tell you—and the lives of most saints truly witness—that the life of contemplation does not mean a life that is physically inactive; that the great contemplatives have been great men of action. But it is the other kind of contemplative life, the other kind of sanctity, that I think the modern world needs.

> "Teach us to care and not to care
> Teach us to sit still."

St. Simeon had certainly learned to sit still, and he if anyone amongst the saints of Christendom can teach us how to do the same.

For why can't we sit still? Why must we be always doing? It is because the active life of the West does not feed the soul, because it so destroys our spiritual resources that even the briefest respite from it brings a sense of boredom. I am sure that most of the restlessness of the West arises from this fear of boredom, and boredom means being brought face to face with our own emptiness. Therefore that childish question: what did old Simeon do all day?—is highly relevant. If we could say no more about him than that he faced boredom, wrestled with it, did not succumb to it—did not descend from his pillar—but conquered it and remained up there, *doing nothing*, then I think that would be sufficient to make him a worthwhile study and counterblast to the present day.

But Simeon didn't go right away from the towns, from civilization; he went so far and no further; far enough to be away, to be out of it all, not far enough to be ignored and forgotten. Perched up there on his pillar, he was and is a living reproach to the active city-dwellers, the everlasting compromisers who aim to make the best of both worlds—and certainly manage to make the best of this one. He was a thorn in the flesh of the civilized hide of mankind, that hardened hide which is so firm against the supernatural. Simeon did nothing—except live for God: hence he became St. Simeon. But even if we forget about the achieved sanctity, the supernatural fruit of what in fact he did "up there," while seeming to do nothing—if we forget all that and concentrate merely on the human gesture, then there is still plenty for us to admire. I take St. Simeon as my favourite saint because he dwells, so to speak, at the easternmost end of western Christendom, because he embodies all that otherworldliness of the East which has managed to get christianized. He has, most of the West may say, only just managed to get in: we need to be warned, they will add, against all that is extreme in his example, particularly the spiritual pride that may so easily lie behind such an extraordinary mode of life. Precisely the opposite seems to me to be the truth. For the Christian religion, like the rest of the world, is suffering from an overdose of Westernism: we need a potent injection from the East, the more violent and the more remarkable the better. The prime characteristic of Westernism is that it puts this world first—puts it first not only unreflectingly, but as its first principle of action. Simeon did the opposite. He may not, like Léon Bloy, have spat on the world, but he turned his back on it, and he turned his face to the sun. Simeon represents a type that has always fascinated me, that of the outcast, the Ishmael, the scapegoat. But he is an outcast of a peculiarly intransigent kind: he does not go and hide himself away in a hole in the desert, he goes a certain distance (not too far) from the town and there "sets up shop." He is, if you like, an exhibitionist, in the most literal meaning of the word; he is determined to make an exhibition of himself. Presumably he had a reason for doing so; and presumably, since he is Saint Simeon, his reason was a valid one. I take it that his reason was to cock a snook at the world, to behave as impertinently towards civilization as civilization behaves towards God. It is a transvaluation of all values to go and live up in the air, feet off the ground, permanently. It is to behave as daringly as Icarus, except for the solid rock of sanctity underneath. There is a cheekiness about it that offends more modest, more self-effacing types of saintliness; an oriental extravagance, divested of all oriental splendour, that strikes me as particularly appropriate and relevant today.

Our time has seen, thanks chiefly to Graham Greene, a revival of interest in the theme of the hunted man. It is a theme dear after all in its sentimental guise to the English heart; hence the popularity of Galsworthy's *Escape*. Presented less sentimentally by Greene, it reveals a deeper religious fact, of a kind traditional in our literature and finding one of its most compelling expressions in Francis Thompson's *Hound of Heaven*: "I fled him down the arches of the years." I think the time has come when the religious undertones of another familiar figure should be sounded—the figure of the Guy. Not the American guy, the good guy, but the English guy, the guy shortly to be burned in effigy by the boys I

71

have been helping to cart autumn prunings away from my garden. They will have a big stuffed guy up above their fire, and fortunately they will be quite indifferent as to whether it is a Catholic or a Protestant or a Hottentot they are burning in effigy. But it has occurred to me that if St. Simeon appears at first sight as a similar sort of guy, someone if not to be burned by the mob at least to be taken pot-shots at, a most helpless "sitting target" for all the pagan scorn of mankind—then at second sight he may teach us to have pity on all poor guys, and realize that in a surprising number of cases the English guy may turn out to be the American guy—the regular *guy* becomes the *regular* guy. Guy Fawkes and St. Simeon, raised up above the jeering populace, have after all a heavenly prototype, and every guy deserves our pennyworth of thanks, if only in memory (if one may speak so without blasphemy) of that Greatest of all the Guys who have ever been raised up above the self-righteous heads.

I mentioned Léon Bloy, the great modern outcast, another guy or curio. No one, perhaps, has fulminated more violently against the modern world than he; no one has revealed so frankly the great amount of pure hatred of mankind that may be mixed up in a fervent and in fact quite overpowering love of God and the poor. If we were warned against the dangers in such a spirit (which nevertheless helped to produce a Maritain), there would no doubt be reason in the warning. But in St. Simeon we see all that is positive in Bloy's reaction against the civilized world extracted from the merely human husk that is harmful: the great assertion of No Compromise.

I do not know—I do not even know if anyone knows—the contents of any of St. Simeon's lengthy sermons. What I do know is that the people went to him—he did not go to the people; and that they went in droves. Imagine this figure perched up on the top of a high stone a few miles outside London, say, or New York. What would our modern reactions be? Would St. Simeon have any news value now? Suppose he was visited by flocking sightseers, out of a sense of fun, and suppose he made this simple announcement, that the world being as it is, he had been obliged to adopt his peculiar way of life because it was the only way he could follow in his pursuit of holiness. What could we reply? That our virtue is such that we feel safer in the cities? Or that our faith is so luke-warm that we prefer to remain as we are?

I do not think that I am in any danger now of confusing St. Simeon with the mere record-breakers. I do not imagine now that he wanted to outshine anyone else. But I am still firmly convinced that he wanted to shine—with holiness. "Let your light so shine before men. . . ." "A city that is set on a hill cannot be hid. . . ." "Neither do men light a candle and put it under a bushel. . . ." And though holiness may shine in drawing-rooms, and saints may brave the rigours of afternoon tea and scandal for our enlightenment and encouragement, nevertheless our world seems to demand a differ-ent kind of sanctity, a sanctity whose impulse from the human side is as extraordinary and as radical as the world we live in.

But after all, I do more than admire this saint, I really love him. And why? Because I am a timid modern, a vitiated city-dweller; also (I must confess in a whisper) a bit of a guy myself, a bit of an English guy, a Peculiar Person. St. Simeon is myself as I would like to be, if I had the heroism of the saint instead of the cowardice of the sinner. I should like to have the courage to face mockery from those who mock what I love; I should like to welcome the brickbat. I should like to be up there on a pillar, instead of down on the ground with the crowd, hiding my sympathy with the man up aloft. There is safety in numbers, and so Simeon went up alone; there is dizziness for the timid at the prospect of great heights, and Simeon faced it. The modern world has developed its own methods of conquering space. Perhaps Simeon's way of conquering it was better: he reduced his contact with earth to a minimum, but he remained earth-bound. He is an excellent symbol of our faith, which is sanctified commonsense. The funny thing is that sanctified commonsense takes such uncommon forms.

I think of that man of rock, a sage, a man of God. "Come in under the shadow of this red rock." It is because he lives in my mind with all the strength of the rock he lived on that I long to creep in under the shadow of that pillar and that sanctity of his; because he rises there like a beacon out of a better land and a better time, when sanctity was more gaunt, more simple, more heroic; when the eternal choices were clearer under the everlasting stars, Heaven and Hell closer, the sword of the spirit more ruthless. Mankind has always hankered after a Golden Age, set either backwards or forwards in time; if in the past, with great men ten feet high, if in the future, winged. Simeon was not winged, but he had done his best to get away from earth; he was not ten feet high, but he had managed to get higher still. My picture of him is largely imaginative, you see: he is my perfect spiritual father.

St. Benedict

Queen Victoria left this world almost at the moment that I chanced to enter it. Her memory, when I was old enough to identify it, fell thinly across my earliest childhood. People still spoke of "the Queen," as if in all history there had been only one and everybody must know at once that Queen Victoria was meant. Somewhat later, I sensed that her going had stirred a deep-set uneasiness, as if with her a part of the mainland of human experience had sunk into the sea and no one quite knew what further subsidences and commotions to expect. Yet, in those far-off days, no one ever chanted to me that grim line of the Queen's favorite poet:

And the great aeon sinks in blood:

though I was not very old when I had the "Death of Arthur" read to me in full, and, after the depressingly long glories of the winter moon, I noted with relief that

The new sun rose, bringing the new year.

With the rest of my generation, I grew in that sun's illusory light. For the historical skies of my boyhood were only infrequently troubled, chiefly by a triad of figures powerful and unpredictable enough to thrill from time to time the nerve of reality. They were, of course, in America, Theodore Roosevelt: in England, King Edward VII: and, on the continent of Europe, bestriding it like a self-inflated colossus, the German Kaiser. Each had a characteristic motif, too, like a Wagnerian hero: a little repetitive phrase that set the historic mood or forecast that each, for good or ill, was about to vault again upon the world stage, to give some new tingling turn to the plot. Thus, from the heart of Europe, would come characteristic variations on the Bismarckian theme of *Blut und Eisen*. In America, rose blithe shouts of "Bully! It's bully!" While Edwardian England had reversed the plea in which Swinburne exhorted Walt Whitman to "send but a song oversea to us," and both shores of the Atlantic rocked to the surge and thunder of Tarara-boom-de-ay.

Long before I had the slightest notion what the barbaric sounds might mean, as language or destiny, I listened fascinated to people chanting:

> A Brussels carpet on the floor:
> An elevator at the door:
> Tarara-boom-de-ay; Tarara-boom-de-ay!

It was not only because of its gayness that it embedded itself in my memory. For what others found gay, I found indefinably ominous, as fixing a tone, a touch of dissolution that, even as a sensitive child, I could not possibly have explained to myself or anybody else. But one day, much later, the echo of Tararaboom-de-ay fused itself unexpectedly with something that would seem to have nothing to do with it—a more or less random remark by one of my college instructors in Contemporary Civilization. Contemporary Civilization, a course required for all freshmen at Columbia College, was taught by several young men whom I remember chiefly as rather lugubrious—disillusioned veterans of the First World War, and a conscientious objector who had refused to take part in it. One day, the objector, staring at some point far beyond the backs of our heads, observed that "the world is entering upon a new Dark Ages."

It was one of the few things that I carried away from Contemporary Civilization, required for all freshmen. And it was not so much the meaning of the words, which I was far too unfledged to understand, as the toneless despondency with which they were uttered that struck me. That, and their acceptance of the Dark Ages as something relevant, and possibly recurrent in history.

For under the sunlit skies of my boyhood, the Dark Ages were seldom mentioned: if at all, chiefly by way of contrast to the light of our progress. For the voice of that time was, at least as it reached me, wholly incapable of the irony with which, little more than a decade later, Jean de Bosschère would ask: *"Qui se leva pour dire que nous ne sommes pas en plein jour?"*

The Dark Ages were inexcusable and rather disreputable—a bad time when the machine of civilization in its matchless climb to the twentieth century had sheared a whole rank of king-pins and landed mankind in a centuries-long ditch. At best, it was a time when monks sat in unsanitary cells with a human skull before them, and copied and re-copied, for lack of more fruitful employment, the tattered records of a dead antiquity. That was the Dark Ages at best, which, as anybody could see, was not far from the worst.

If a bright boy, leafing through history, asked: "How did the Dark Ages come about?," he might be told that "Rome fell!"—as if a curtain simply dropped. Boys of ten or twelve, even if bright, are seldom bright enough to say to themselves: "Surely, Rome did not fall in a day." If a boy had asked: "But were there no great figures in the Dark Ages, like Teddy Roosevelt, King Edward and the Kaiser?", he might well have been suspected of something like an unhealthy interest in the habits and habitats of spiders. If he had persisted and asked: "But isn't it clear that the Dark Ages are of a piece with our age of light, that our civilization is by origin Catholic, that, in fact, we cannot understand what we have become without understanding what we came from?", he would have been suspected of something much worse than priggery—a distressing turn to Popery.

I was no such bright boy (or youth). I reached young manhood serene in the knowledge that, between the failed light of antiquity and the buzzing incandescence of our own time, there had intervened a thousand years of darkness from which the spirit of man had begun to liberate itself (intellectually) first in the riotous luminosity of the Renaissance, in Humanism, in the eighteenth century, and at last (politically) in the French Revolution. For the dividing line between the Dark Ages and the Middle Ages is not fast, and they were easily lumped together.

To be sure, even before Queen Victoria died, the pre-Raphaelites had popularized certain stage properties of the Middle Ages. And on the Continent there had been Novalis, to mention only one name (but no one in my boyhood mentioned Novalis). There had been Huysmans (we knew Huysmans, but his name was touched with decadence). There was a fad of the Gothic and figures like Viollet-le-Duc: while an obscure American, Henry Adams, was even then composing *Mont St. Michel and Chartres*, and inditing certain thoughts on the Virgin and the Dynamo that would echo briefly above the clink of their swizzle sticks in the patter of my generation.

I was in my twenties, a young intellectual savage in college with thousands of others, before the fact slowly dawned upon me that, for a youth always under the spell of history, the history I knew was practically no history at all. It consisted of two disjointed parts—the history of Greece and Rome, with side-trips to Egypt and the Fertile Crescent: and a history of the last four hundred years of Europe and America. Of what lay in between, what joined the parts and gave them continuity, and the pulse of life and breath of spirit, my ignorance was darker than any Dark Age. Less by intelligence than by the kind of sixth sense which makes us aware of objects ahead in the dark, I divined that a main land-mass of the history of Western civilization loomed hidden beyond my sight.

I turned briefly to medieval history. But the distinguished teachers who first guided me into the Dark Ages seemed, even to my blindness, not too sure of their own way. They knew facts, more facts than I would ever know. Yet in their understanding of the facts something was missing, something that would enable them to feel that the life of the times they were exploring was of one tissue with the life of ours, that neither could be divided from the other, without an arterial tearing, that neither could be understood without the other. Their exposition, even of so obvious a problem as the causes for the fall of the Roman West left me with a sense of climbing railless stairs above a chasm at night. Rome fell, I learned, because of the barbarian hordes and a series of great barbarian leaders. H. G. Wells would presently startle me with the information that the hordes had been comparative handfuls among the populations they conquered, while, somewhat later, I would come to believe that the barbarian leaders were scarcely more barbarian than the Romans, that many of them were disaffected officials of the Roman state and their conduct was not so much that of invaders as what we should now call Fifth Columnists.

Or I was taught that Rome's collapse was due in part to the disrepair of the Roman roads and the breakdown of communications. Or the resurgence of the Pontine marshes and the high incidence of malaria at Rome. Or that the conquest of the East had introduced alien and indigestible masses into the Empire, and corrupted Rome, and so it fell. But even a collegiate savage

79

could scarcely fail to note that it was precisely the corrupt Eastern half of the Empire that survived as a political unit, and, for another 800 years, stood against the vigorous East, and was the bulwark of the fallen West.

There were other facts and factors. My ignorance could question them only so far, and then not their reality for the most part, but their power to explain by themselves an event so complex and so thunderous as the crash of a civilization. Some more subtle dissolvent, I sensed, must also have been, undivined, at work. I thought I had caught a hint of it in Salvianus' *moritur et ridet*: "The Roman Empire is luxurious, but it is filled with misery. It is dying but it laughs—*moritur et ridet.*" But Salvian, we learned with a deflecting smile, was an extremist, though, in the hindsight of disaster, his foresight would scarcely seem overstated. What interested me was that men had smiled complacently at Salvian's words when he spoke them, and men still smiled at them complacently a thousand years later—the same kind of men, I was beginning to suspect, upon, I also suspected, a similar turning point of history.

In any case, for me it was too late. What the missing something was in the crisis of Rome I was not to learn in classrooms. The crisis of civilization in my own time had caught me in its undertow and soon swept me far beyond that earlier Dark Ages. Not until it had cast me back upon its rocks, by grace a defeated fugitive from its forces, would I again find peace or pause to seek to determine what, if anything, that mortal experience had taught me about the history of our own time, or any other.

This century was half gone, and with it more than half my life, that at that moment seemed all but to have ended in an ordeal with which my name is linked, when someone, seeking only to comfort me, once more directed my eyes to that point in the past from which, some thirty years before, I had abruptly taken them. Anne Ford, my friend of many years standing, sent me from the Monastery of Gethsemani a little silver medal, blessed in my family's name and mine, by Father Louis—Thomas Merton of *The Seven-Storey Mountain*, who, as a later student, had sat in the same college classrooms, listening to some of the same instructors I had known. On the medal was an image of St. Benedict.

I found myself asking who St. Benedict had been. I knew that he had founded a monastic order, which bore his name, and that for it he had written a famous Rule. I knew that he had uttered a precept that I had taken for my own: *Laborare est orare*—to labor is to pray. I had once written a little news story about plans for the restoration of his monastery of Monte Cassino after its destruction in the World War of 1939. What I had written had presumably been read at least by one hundred thousand people (so much for journalism in our time). But a seeker after knowledge at any age, certainly one fifty years old, must begin by confessing that he probably knew less about St. Benedict than many a pupil in parochial school. Nor, had I asked a dozen friends, regarded as highly intelligent by themselves and the world, could one of them have told me much more about St. Benedict than I knew myself. The fact that such ignorance could exist, could be taken as a matter of course, was more stunning than the abyss of ignorance itself.

For the briefest prying must reveal that, simply in terms of history, leaving aside for a moment his sanctity, St. Benedict was a colossal figure on a scale of importance in shaping the civilization of the West against which few subsequent figures could measure. And of those who might measure in terms of historic force, almost none could measure in terms of good achieved.

Nor was St. Benedict an isolated peak. He was only one among ranges of human height that reached away from him in time in both directions, past and future, but of which, with one or two obvious exceptions, one was as ignorant as of Benedict: St.

81

Jerome, St. Ambrose, St. Augustine, Pope St. Leo the Great, Pope St. Gregory the Great, St. Francis of Assisi, Hildebrand (Pope Gregory VII).

Clearly, a cleft cut across the body of Christendom itself, and raised an overwhelming question: What, in fact, was the civilization of the West? If it was Christendom, why had it turned its back on half its roots and meanings and become cheerfully ignorant of those who had embodied them? If it was not Christendom, what was it? And what were those values that it claimed to assert against the forces of active evil that beset it in the greatest crisis of history since the fall of Rome? Did the failure of the Western World to know what it was lie at the root of its spiritual despondency, its intellectual confusion, its moral chaos, the dissolving bonds of faith and loyalty within itself, its swift political decline in barely four decades from hegemony of the world to a demoralized rump of Europe little larger that it had been in the crash of the Roman West, and an America still disputing the nature of the crisis, its gravity, whether it existed at all, or what to do about it?

Answers to such questions could not be extemporized. At the moment, a baffled seeker could do little more than grope for St. Benedict's hand and pray in all humbleness to be led over the traces of the saint's progress to the end that he might be, if not 'more knowledgeable, at least less nakedly ignorant. The biographical facts were synoptic enough and chiefly to be found in the *Dialogues* of Pope St. Gregory the Great or inferred between the lines of St. Benedict's Rule.

Benedict had been born, toward the end of the fifth century, of good family in the sturdy countryside of Nursia, which lay close enough to Rome to catch the tremors of its sack, in 410, by Alaric's West Goths (the first time in 800 years that the City had fallen), and the shock of its sack by the Vandals, who, in 455 completed the material and human havoc that the West Goths had begun. To a Rome darkened by such disasters, Benedict had been sent to school as a boy of fourteen or fifteen. There he was shaken by the corrupt customs of his schoolmates, it is said. But we may surely conjecture that he was touched, too, like sensitive minds in our own day, by a sense of brooding, indefinable disaster, of doom still incomplete, for the Dark Ages were scarcely more than begun.

The boy fled from Rome, or, as we might say, ran away from school, and settled with a loose-knit congregation about thirty miles from the City. There he performed his first miracle. When, as a result, men called him good, he fled again. For, though he was a boy, he was clearly old enough to fear the world, especially when it praises. This time he fled into the desert wilderness near Subiaco, where for three years he lived alone in a cave. To those who presently found him, he seemed more like a wild creature than a man. Those were the years of the saint's conquest of his flesh, his purgation, illumination and perhaps his prayerful union with God. They must also have been the years when he plumbed all the perils of solitary austerities and the hermit life, by suffering them.

At any rate, the saint left Subiaco to enter on his first experience in governing a community of monks. He returned to Subiaco, and, in twelve years, organized twelve Benedictine communities. His days were filled with devotion and with labor and touched with miracles. But again human factors threatened failure. St. Benedict with a few companions withdrew to Monte Cassino, some eighty miles southeast of Rome. There he overthrew an ancient altar of Apollo (for paganism was still rooted in the countryside), and there he raised his own altar. On those heights, he organized his community, ruled his monks, performed new miracles, distilled his holy experience in his Holy Rule. There he died at a date which is in dispute, but was probably about 547, when the campaigns of the Eastern Roman Empire to recover Italy from the East Goths had so permanently devastated the Peninsula that the irruption of the Lombards into the ruins brought a new horror rather than any novelty in havoc.

Against that night and that ruin, like a man patiently lighting a wick in a tempest, St. Benedict set his Rule. There had been other monastic Rules before—St. Pachomius' and St. Basil's, for example. St. Benedict called his the *Holy Rule*, setting it down and setting it apart from all others, with a consciousness of its singular authority that has led some biographers to speculate whether he had not been prompted by the Holy See to write it. Perhaps it is permissible to hazard that his authority need have proceeded from nothing more than that unwavering confidence which commonly sustains genius.

What was there in this little book that changed the world? To us, at first glance, it seems prosaic enough, even fairly obvious. That, indeed, is the heart of its inspiration. In an age of pillar saints and furiously competing athletes of the spirit, when men plunged by thousands into the desert, in a lunge towards God, and in revulsion from man, St. Benedict's Rule brought a saving and creative sanity. Its temper was that of moderation as against excesses of zeal, of fruitful labor as against austerities pushed to the point of fruitlessness, of discipline as against enthusiasm, of continence of spirit and conduct as against incontinence.

It has been said (by T. F. Lindsay in his sensitive and searching *St. Benedict*) that, in a shattered society, the Holy Rule, to those who submitted to its mild but strict sway, restored the discipline and power of Roman family life.

I venture that it did something else as well. For those who obeyed it, it ended three great alienations of the spirit whose action, I suspect, touched on that missing something which my instructors failed to find among the causes of the fall of Rome. The same alienations, I further suspect, can be seen at their work of dissolution among ourselves, and are perhaps among the little-noticed reasons why men turn to Communism. They are: the alienation of the spirit of man from traditional authority; his alienation from the idea of traditional order: and a crippling alienation that he feels at the point where civilization has deprived him of the joy of simple productive labor.

These alienations St. Benedict fused into a new surge of the human spirit by directing the frustrations that informed them into the disciplined service of God. At the touch of his mild inspiration, the bones of a new order stirred and clothed themselves with life, drawing to itself much of what was best and most vigorous among the ruins of man and his work in the Dark Ages, and conserving and shaping its energy for that unparalleled outburst of mind and spirit in the Middle Ages. For about the Benedictine monasteries what we, having casually lost the Christian East, now casually call the West, once before regrouped and saved itself.

So bald a summary can do little more than indicate the dimensions of the Benedictine achievement and plead for its constant re-examination. Seldom has the need been greater. For we sense, in the year 1952, that we may stand closer to the year 410 than at any other time in the centuries since. If that statement seems as extreme as any of Salvian's, three hundred million Russians, Poles, Czechs, Slovaks, East Germans, Austrians, Hungarians, and all the Christian Balkans, would tell you that it is not—would tell you if they could lift their voices through the night of the new Dark Ages that have fallen on them. For them the year 410 has already come.

E. I. WATKIN

*

St. Radegund

The period when the Western Empire fell to the barbarians and the succeeding Dark Ages are often regarded as similar to our own. In some respects the resemblance is undeniable. In both cases security and prosperity are followed by disorder and insecurity. Both witness widespread and appalling suffering and the destruction of priceless remains of past culture. Both are tormented by wars and the fear of war, "men's hearts failing for fear of what may come on earth." In other respects, however, the periods are the antithesis each of the other. Ours is a period of a triumphant and seemingly still advancing secularism, whose strength lies in the physical sciences and their technical achievement. And never before has the State been so powerful, ruling vast masses despotically, sacrificing them lavishly for its economic and military purposes, and well-nigh irresistible. In a mechanised mass civilization in which economic values are supreme, the individual is dwarfed to impotence and spiritual values fade out of sight.

In the post-Roman period on the other hand, power and achievement lay with religion and its representatives. The wisest and morally best, whatever of culture survived in the progressive decay and persistent anarchy, served the Church. Like the ark riding the deluge the Church preserved with her religious treasure, not only culture and the graces of cultured living, but even the elementary decencies of civilised behaviour, and did so in face of violence from without and in spite of unworthy servants within.

In this time, so like yet so totally unlike our own, lived the great woman venerated as St. Radegund. Born about 518 (some two years before the Romano-British general incorrectly known to posterity as King Arthur won the last of many victories in which the cavalry he had trained defeated the Saxon invader) she died ten years before St. Augustine landed at Ebbsfleet to convert Kent.

Yet St. Radegund is no shadowy figure more legendary than historical. Nor, like so many contemporary saints, is she the subject of some wholly unreliable life concocted by a hagiographer of later centuries in accordance with a conventional recipe, and often with unashamed plagiarism from the lives of other saints. Her life is known from contemporary sources, related by those who knew her intimately. Her friend of years, the poet Venantius Fortunatus, wrote her life. And a little later a nun of the convent she founded, brought up by the saint, Baudonivia by name, wrote a supplementary life. Neither, it must be admitted, rose to the height of the opportunity. Neither has given us the full-length portrait for which they possessed such ample material. Each felt it his or her duty, not to depict the woman known so long and so well, but to make a stained-glass window in her honour and for their readers' edification. Consequently the bulk of these lives consists of the two ingredients of hagiography as then practised: an account of austerities and an account of miracles. Fortunatus does not even mention, though Baudonivia does, Radegund's foundation of the convent at Poitiers or the event which gave it its name—the arrival of a relic of the True Cross which the Byzantine Emperor Justin sent at her request. Nevertheless, here and there the saint's personality pierces through in a word or action.

87

And in his poems Fortunatus has revealed another aspect of her character, a more humanly attractive woman in lighter moments of cultivated relaxation and warm friendship, indulgent, too indulgent perhaps, to the weakness of souls of stuff less stern than her own.

Finally, to place her life and work in its historical setting and in wider connections, we have the information of St. Gregory, the saintly Bishop of Tours who played such a prominent part in the public life of his time, and the historian whose writings illuminate so vividly the historical scene of sixth-century Gaul. And Gregory knew the saint well and laid her body in its tomb.

Radegund was a German princess, the daughter of Berthaire, a Thuringian king. At that time Thuringia was ruled by three brothers. One of the three, Radegund's uncle Hermenefred, murdered her father, and with the aid of the Frankish King, Clovis' son Theuderic, defeated the third and became sole ruler. Thus Radegund's infancy was darkened by a crime of savage violence such as was almost common form in the annals of these barbarian kingdoms. But although he killed her father, her uncle Hermenefred showed no ill will to his little niece. Perhaps he intended her to be the future bride of his son Hamalafred. Radegund had a brother who was probably younger than herself, and Hamalafred was the big brother of her first childish days. Her affection for him is evident from a poem written in her name by Fortunatus and embalming her memories of him. He was father and mother, sister and brother to her. She cherishes memories of her cousin taking her in his arms and kissing her.

But these days of home life did not last long. Her uncle Hermenefred broke faith with his Frankish allies. Theuderic, assisted by his brother Clothaire, attacked and crushed the Thuringian chief. Hamalafred fled to the East to enter, it would seem likely, the service of the Eastern Emperor. Radegund was ten or twelve years old. Clothaire carried her off—one of the many

ST. BERNARD OF CLAIRVAUX

by André Girard

The two themes St. Bernard best loved were mother love, treated in the *Sermons on the Blessed Virgin*, and spiritual love, treated in the *Sermons on the Canticle of Canticles*.

These latter boldly take the text of the Old Testament poem, regarded by so many as a pagan love song, and show that the woman of the poem is the Church, that the man, the beloved, is God, and that the Church's love for its creator is most naturally expressed in terms of passionate human love.

St. Bernard chose so difficult a theme in reaction against the frivolousness of the day. In his great mass of letters, also, we find his spiritual counsels couched in terms of passionate love, thus giving this emotion its place in the highest spirituality.

No less moving are his commentaries on mother love: to all who hear him he offers the blessings of the maternal love of Our Lady. As he teaches, no one is excluded from it, every man can count at every moment upon the aid of the Mother of God. In all he says upon this, we can catch echoes of what his mother Aleth was to him. Reserved, tender, constant in prayer, ever attentive to the Spirit, she prepared him to be the saint he was.

displaced persons, as common then as today—and brought her up at Athies with a view to possible future marriage. With her he took her brother, who was probably brought up with her. Whether she was now baptised or already a Christian I do not know. Since the conversion of the Franks was so recent, it seems unlikely that Thuringia was Christian.

She received as good an education as time and place could afford, and acquired the appreciation of letters she would show later; but above all the profound religious devotion which issued in sanctity. Certainly at the time of her marriage she was already in spirit a religious, a woman of cultured tastes, regal bearing and personal beauty. As soon as he judged her age sufficient, Clothaire decided to marry her. She made a somewhat futile gesture of flight, but bowed to the inevitable, and they were married at Soissons. A girl much less sensitive, refined, holy and modest than Radegund might well have shrunk from such a husband. For, like most of his race, Clothaire was a savage of uncontrolled passions. Though even as pagans the Franks were monogamous, the chiefs had always been permitted a harem, and conversion had not disposed them to renounce their privileged polygamy. It is often quite impossible to tell which of a king's wives was his wife as the Church understands the term. Nor did the Gallic bishops, and though many are reckoned among the saints, take any action against their polygamous rulers. Clothaire certainly was no monogamist. We hear of six consorts of whom Radegund was the second.

With his own hand he had murdered two of the children, sons of his brother Clodomer. And shortly before his death he set fire to a hut containing his rebel son—he had, it is true, pardoned an earlier rebellion—and burned him alive with his wife and daughters. Such was the man to whom this sensitive, cultured and devout girl was bound in matrimony.

As queen, we are told, she lived a life more suited to a nun in her cloister. She lavished money and food on the poor and on

89

religious. She gave away a tithe of her revenues. At Athies she built a hospice for the sick poor, where she bathed the women herself and washed the men's heads, and finally gave her patients a hot drink. At the royal table she refused the banquet spread before her and contrived to eat unobserved a meagre vegetable meal. And she would rise from table to attend, or sing herself, the Divine Office. At night she would leave her husband's bed to pray in her oratory, outstretched on sackcloth, returning numb with cold. Throughout Lent she wore a hair shirt under her royal robes, and when Clothaire was absent redoubled the length and fervour of her devotions. Whole nights she would spend at prayer in chapels lit by tapers her own hands had made. Sometimes Clothaire would notice her absence from his table, to be informed that she was engaged in her devotions. A husband of far milder temper might well have resented her austerities and protracted absence from her place beside him. But surprisingly his violence, it would seem, was never more than verbal, and even so he would apologise and offer presents in atonement. No doubt he found consolation in women of earthier mould. But the fact remains that this uncontrolled savage was evidently in awe of Radegund. He was conscious of a supernatural power in her which he shrank from offending, and when he did so he was afraid. For the Catholic religion, however superstitiously and crudely understood, was a reality to these Merovingian chiefs. Nor is human conduct of a piece. The vivid writings of St. Gregory of Tours read like a combination of the *Acta Sanctorum* and *The Daily News*.

Clothaire entertained for Radegund not only awe but reverence. She was even able to obtain from him the lives of many condemned criminals. And she caused a surviving pagan sanctuary to be destroyed. The ill-assorted union continued about six years and might have dragged on indefinitely if her husband had not, for some unknown motive, had her brother murdered. This was too much. Radegund, not held back by children, decided to leave Clothaire and embrace her religious vocation. She made her way to Noyon where St. Medard was Bishop, and asked him to give her the veil. Understandably, he hesitated to separate the Queen from her royal husband, the more so when a band of Frankish nobles threatened him in his cathedral. Radegund retired to the sacristy, put on the religious habit, and returning to the altar, told Medard that if from human respect he refused her request, God would require her soul at his hands. Since he did fear God, he consented and consecrated her a deaconess.

At this time of anxiety and dedication, Radegund was comforted by a vision promising her a place in Our Lord's breast—as we would put it today, in His Heart. Her first step was to lavish in alms or the adornment of churches her royal wardrobe of rich garments and jewels. After a visit to St. Martin's shrine at Tours—the holiest sanctuary in Gaul—she retired to Saix, an estate given to her by Clothaire. She redoubled her austerities. Fortunatus tells us that from the time of her consecration she ate nothing but vegetables—not even fish, eggs or fruit—and drank only honey water or pear juice. Yet Fortunatus addressed a poem to her with a present of fruit. She must therefore have relaxed her rule on occasion. She continued and increased her charities. Every Thursday and Saturday she washed the heads of a crowd of filthy paupers, ridding them of their scurf, cleansing their sores, even removing vermin and pouring oil into wounds. Women she washed from head to foot with soap, gave them clean clothes and a meal at which she waited upon them herself, wiping the hands and mouths of those too weak to do it for themselves. The sick and blind she fed with a spoon. Every Sunday she provided a meal for the poor at which she handed round the first cup of wine herself.

But her special delight was to serve lepers. She laid their table, washed their faces, hands, nails and sores with warm water, waited on each of her guests and sent them away with a present of money or clothing. The leprous women she embraced, and kissed their

91

faces. A maid ventured to remonstrate: "Most reverend lady, who will kiss you if you embrace lepers in this way?" "If *you* don't kiss me," was her reply, "I couldn't care less."

Radegund now moved on to Poitiers, which would be her home for the remainder of her life. Here she erected her convent, first called St. Mary's and later dedicated to the Holy Cross. She gathered there some two hundred nuns, many from noble Frankish or Gallo-Roman families and some of royal blood. She adopted the rule of St. Caesarius, of which she obtained a copy from the younger St. Caesaria. The convent was strictly enclosed against its inmates leaving their enclosure. The nuns could not even follow their foundress to her grave, but watched the funeral from the walls. But it was by no means so strictly kept against visitors from outside. Fortunatus, as we shall see, could dine in the parlour in the company of Radegund and the Abbess Agnes. The convent was equipped with well-appointed baths. They must have been of the normal Roman type, in which hot air played a considerable part— much like a modern Turkish bath. These baths cannot have been strictly or permanently in the enclosure, for the men serving the convent, workmen and agricultural labourers, were allowed to use them from the beginning of Lent to Pentecost. Austere as she was, Radegund was not, like so many saints, tolerant of dirt. Many recorded incidents prove her love of bathing and cleanliness. Altogether the Abbey was an imposing edifice and spacious, "occupying more ground than villas or townships."

Radegund appointed as Abbess, Agnes, a young woman whom she had brought up and who was, as Fortunatus is never tired of insisting, her spiritual daughter, a woman of charm and culture and of a gentle and gracious disposition. The humility of her intention is unquestionable, but it is quite clear that Radegund was the Superior in fact though not in name. Agnes was not the woman to assert her will against that of her spiritual mother, and Radegund was nothing if not strong-minded. She knew what she thought right and did it.

She stoutly refused to allow the daughter of King Chilperic to leave the convent at her father's command and make a marriage politically desirable. Many of her two hundred nuns were holy women. Many, however, were far from holy. Many were women of noble or royal birth who did not regard Merovingian wedlock as an attractive prospect but preferred the life of maiden ladies in an aristocratic community. Radegund, we can hardly doubt, made concessions to their human weakness.

All this while, Clothaire had taken no steps to reclaim his wife or punish her desertion. As we have seen, he entertained for Radegund an awe born of a genuine if superstitious faith.

There came, however, a moment when the resentment of injured pride, combined perhaps with a genuine affection for his lost queen, moved him to take action. He came to Tours with the intention of proceeding to Poitiers to take her back. Radegund wrote to St. Germanus, Bishop of Paris, who had accompanied the King, begging his intervention, and betook herself to prayer. Germanus implored the King to abandon his purpose. He was successful. Not only did Clothaire leave Radegund in peace, he wrote to her begging her to forgive his abandoned design. After Clothaire's death Radegund secured a solemn pledge of protection for her Abbey from his four sons, bearing their signatures or marks, and at the same time placed it under the special care of the Gallic episcopate.

Her personal austerities were now carried even further. She kept every week-day as a fast. All the year round, except in Easter time and on great feasts, her bed was sackcloth and ashes. She took more than her share of the most menial tasks. She swept the floors, even the dirtiest. She drew water, cooked and cleaned vegetables and washed the kitchen utensils. She brought in wood and lit the fire. She tended the sick. She even cleaned the latrines. This was too much for one historian, who writes, "The meanest, most disgust-

93

ing offices, such as no modern pen would venture to describe, were performed by a Queen of France." But she was no longer a queen, not even officially an abbess. This dirty work—a thousand years before Queen Elizabeth's godson invented the water-closet—had to be performed by someone. We should rather admire the humility which did not shrink from performing the most unpleasant service.

Nor did Radegund forget the welfare of the country. She would write to the kings, constantly at war, entreating them, unfortunately without much effect, to make and keep peace.

The Caesarian rule encouraged, indeed demanded, education. Every nun must be able to read—she must also know the Psalter by heart. And two hours every day were to be spent in reading. This was congenial to Radegund, who loved books. She read Gregory either of Nyssa or Nazianzen, Basil, Athanasius, Hilary, Ambrose, Jerome, Augustine, Sedulius and Orosius. Whether she read the Greek Fathers in the original or in a Latin translation we are not told. Whatever time was left over from Psalmody or domestic chores she devoted to reading or hearing others read. And she would often comment to her nuns on what was being read. Sleep she cut down to a minimum. Even when she lay down for a brief rest, a nun was deputed to read until she fell asleep—another form of the habit of reading in bed. "When the reader thought she had fallen off and stopped reading . . . she would say: Why are you silent? Go on reading and don't leave off." Baudonivia, who tells us this, may well have been the reader in question. A little inconsiderate you may think. Possibly. As I remarked earlier, human conduct is not of a piece and even saints are not exceptions.

In the main, however, Radegund, so severe upon herself, was indulgent to the human weakness of others. "Stern and unbending towards herself," Baudonivia observes, "she was full of compassion for others." We can translate this general statement into concrete details through the poems addressed to Radegund and Agnes by Fortunatus. Here we see her as the Christian humanist, indulging particular friendships, enjoying cultured conversation and permitting—even encouraging—in a friend an enjoyment of the good food and wine she denied to herself. The friendship between Radegund, Agnes and Fortunatus made the parlour of Holy Cross an oasis of learning and peace and civilised living in a desert of war and savagery. This aspect, however, of Radegund's life cannot be studied without knowledge of the friend on whom it centered, the poet Venantius Fortunatus or, to give him his full name, Venantius Honorius Clementianus Fortunatus.

Fortunatus was an Italian, born near Treviso and educated at Ravenna. He came to France about 565 to return thanks to St. Martin for the cure of a diseased eye. He made himself popular with bishops, noblemen and princes by addressing to them complimentary poems. St. Gregory of Tours in particular befriended him. Finally he settled at Poitiers and his friendship with Radegund and Agnes began. Though he is not enrolled in the Martyrology, his feast is kept in several dioceses. He is therefore entitled to the name of saint—though the honours of sanctity were easily won in the sixth century. Indeed, if a Merovingian bishop does not figure among the saints, he was not, one suspects, a very satisfactory bishop. And when he died Fortunatus was Bishop of Poitiers. In his earlier days he certainly tried to make the best of both worlds. His first principle of conduct was to avoid being mixed up in any unpleasantness. Since being involved in unpleasantness might mean torture and death, I am not disposed to blame him for this.

Characteristic of Fortunatus is his picture of himself given at the beginning of a letter to St. Felix, Bishop of Nantes; lying on the beach yawning and dozing with a volume of his friend's composition in his hand and dipping lazily into it until, so he says, Felix's eloquence roused him from his torpor.

Fortunatus' best-known compositions are the Passiontide hymns, *Vexilla Regis* and *Pange Lingua gloriosi lauream certaminis*. He also wrote the *Salve festa dies*, the poem which celebrates so jubi-

lantly nature's resurrection from the grave of winter to greet her
risen Lord, in better days sung in part as a processional before the
Masses of Easter and Ascension.

His numerous poems to Radegund and Agnes are in quite another vein: occasional verses and tokens of friendship. Radegund
he regarded as his spiritual mother; Agnes, about the same age as
himself, as his spiritual sister. And his friendship for his "mother"
and "sister," though pure as light, was warm. When Radegund
enters her Lenten retreat the sky clouds over for him until the
sunshine—Radegund, "my light"—returns at Easter. Her return
indeed brings harvest and vintage in April. And Agnes is his heart's
delight, *"deliciae animae meae,"* his "honey." He wishes he could
help Radegund in the kitchen and scullery, in the garden, or fetch-
ing water from the well. He expresses his pleasure in his friends'
singing on St. Martin's feast. Away from home and oppressed by
anxiety, he wishes he could put on Daedalus' wings and fly back
to them. He joins Agnes in urging Radegund to drink some wine
for the sake of her health.

Presents pass between them to the accompaniment of verses by
Fortunatus. Did the season permit, he would send lilies or roses.
But he can send nothing more than vetches—some species or other
of brightly coloured wild pea—and violets. And a poem equally
charming apologises for a bunch of violets and crocuses. He sends
chestnuts in a basket woven by himself, plums from his orchard, or
his life of St. Marcellus. Trifles, but "between friends," he observes,
"trifling gifts are gracious beyond their worth." And he apologises
for the poor container in which he sends a present of fruit.

He often thanks for presents of food, food parcels or meals served
to him in the parlour. He thanks his friends for vegetables steeped
in honey, followed by a mountain of meat surrounded by delicacies
from sea and land. All, he says, is now in his stomach. He thanks
for meat served on a silver plate with vegetables swimming in
gravy, for vegetables on a marble dish tasting sweet as the honey

which flavoured them, fowls on a glass dish, apples deliciously scented and a jug of milk. There is a cream mould bearing the marks of Agnes' fingers. He thanks Agnes for eggs and plums. Radegund and Agnes had told him to eat two eggs, but, he must confess, he has drunk four in an eggflip. He writes of a dinner at the convent when table and sideboard were smothered with roses; and of another dinner when he hopes that by her conversation Radegund will redouble the satisfaction he receives from the feast of milk, vegetables, eggs and butter with which, as he rather crudely says, he has distended his stomach. But his critics will take most scandal at a poem in which he confesses to having drunk not wisely but too well, so that the wine went to his head. He became muddle-headed, could hardly keep his eyes open. He was in no condition to compose or write verses. The dinner table, in fact, seemed to be swimming in wine. However, on his return home, before he goes to bed, he sends these verses of excuse. Certainly a strange scene when a saint dines with a saint in the convent of Holy Cross. I hope none of my readers when next they hear *Vexilla Regis* sung on Good Friday will be distracted by the thought of its author in so different an aspect as man and poet. In this instance, at any rate, Radegund seems to have pushed indulgence too far, though we do not know what she said or wrote to Fortunatus when he returned to sobriety. But we must remember that drunkenness, within limits at least, was regarded at that time as a venial offence. The biographer of St. Sampson, the contemporary Celtic saint, relates to his credit that no one ever saw him the worse for drink.

But, as he insists himself, Fortunatus appreciated his friends' conversation more than the menu. He found it more satisfying. Nor was it always serious. He speaks of Radegund's "delicious and versatile humour." It is in keeping with this lighter vein that she played a game of chance, in the nature, it would seem, of draughts.

Fortunatus was undeniably an epicure and a *bon vivant*, though he could appreciate Radegund's abstinence. But his hymns prove him a man of strong Christian faith and personal devotion. We cannot in fact better sum up his character than in the words of an eighteenth-century epitaph: "He united the natural enjoyment of the pleasures of this world with a 'prayerful hope' of those of the world to come."

Radegund shared to the full the contemporary devotion to relics. Her most famous relic was that of the True Cross. She sent to Constantinople to ask for it from the Emperor Justin II. It was probably on this occasion that the metrical letter composed by Fortunatus in her name was sent to her cousin Hamalafred begging him, wherever he might be, to reply. He must surely have been known or believed to be in the Imperial service. Despite some absurd rhetorical touches, it is a moving document. The affection of a child for the older cousin is recalled and revived.

Justin was gracious. He sent a relic of the Cross in a reliquary adorned with gold and jewels, other relics, and a copy of the Gospels bound in gold and studded with gems. But it would seem that news was returned of Hamalafred's death. For another metrical letter was written in Radegund's name to a relative named Artachis, which informs us of his death and of her grief.

These precious relics were at hand, when a hitch arose. The Bishop of Poitiers, Maroveus, refused to perform the ceremony of their solemn reception. The motive of his hostility to Radegund, shown on other occasions, is obscure. Possibly he disapproved of her government of her convent. Possibly he was jealous of a royal foundation placed under the official protection of the Frankish kings and the Gallic episcopate and regarded it as an unwelcome *imperium in imperio*. Nothing could be done but to invite a bishop from outside to preside over the function. This, however, would be the intrusion of one bishop into the diocese of another. Today a matter of this kind would be referred to the Holy See. But Rome was far off and the Church of Gaul, though in communion with

Rome and acknowledging in principle Papal supremacy, was an Erastian institution. Radegund, therefore, turned to her stepson, King Sigebert, and he deputed Bishop Euphronius of Tours to act.

So the Cross made its triumphant entry into the convent, henceforth to bear its name, and was solemnly enshrined. Now it was that Fortunatus rose to his opportunity and composed for the occasion the two hymns which ever since have celebrated throughout the western Church the victory won on Calvary—the *Vexilla Regis* and the *Pange Lingua gloriosi proelium*. The *Pange Lingua* indeed was and is set to the marching tune of the Roman legionaries, sung at least since the days when they followed Julius Caesar to his conquests.

It is quite usual today—perhaps in reaction from past excesses— for the biographer of a saint to pass over without mention the miracles which bulk so largely in the original sources. They seem to be a nettle which even Catholics shrink from touching. No faithful historian, however, can reject unexamined or ignore miracles related by such contemporaries as Fortunatus and Baudonivia in detail, and often with the names of their subjects. In the limited space of this short study it is impossible to evaluate the many cures attributed to Radegund. Some were, perhaps, the result of her medical treatments reinforced by suggestion, but to others recorded by eye-witnesses no natural cause appears assignable.

A year before her death, Baudonivia tells us, Radegund dreamed she saw a handsome young man richly clad. When he drew close and addressed her in affectionate terms, she took alarm and repulsed his attentions. He told her He was the heavenly Bridegroom she had loved so well and that she would be a priceless jewel in His crown.

The material, and to a large extent the form even, of visions authentically divine in origin are drawn from the subject's subconscious. A genuine intuition, therefore, of heavenly reward may well have taken a form determined by the saint's lifelong desire for the pure affection of a man genuinely loved, a desire shown by her love for her murdered brother and her cousin and her friendship for Fortunatus, a desire frustrated and polluted by her union with Clothaire. It was, however, as the dream also shows, mixed with the knowledge that it had been and must be sacrificed for the love of Christ. The dream, perhaps told to Baudonivia, at the time reveals the woman in the saint, and her womanhood as the material of her sanctity.

As she lay ill on what proved to be her deathbed, she was insistent that Psalms should be sung. Or she would speak of the judgment and heaven, even at times when she seemed to be talking in her sleep.

On August 13, 587, the end came. Bishop Maroveus was conveniently away on a visitation and in no hurry to return. The funeral could not wait for him nor for an appeal to the civil power. Once more the Bishop of Tours was called in. He was now the historian St. Gregory; and he and Baudonivia have both left us accounts of the funeral. Both speak of the beauty of the dead woman's face. "It was as lovely as a lily or rose," says Baudonivia. "It surpassed the beauty of lilies or roses," says St. Gregory. And Baudonivia remarks that the sight filled St. Gregory with awe "as if he saw the most holy Mother of the Lord Jesus herself."

Around the bier the nuns stood lamenting. But the language of their rhetorical panegyric owes much to convention and something probably to Gregory. Weeping, they crowded on to the wall as the funeral cortège passed beneath, and sobs interrupted the Psalms and antiphons of the clerics. The body was laid, packed with spices, in the wooden coffin Radegund had prepared. But the lid was left open, to be closed by the diocesan when he celebrated the funeral Mass.

Fortunatus wrote no elegy. His grief lay too deep for verse. We hear nothing of Agnes. Presumably she followed her spiritual

100

mother shortly to the grave. Two years later there was another abbess at Holy Cross.

When St. Catherine of Siena was reproached for the indulgence she showed to Francesco Malavolti, a disciple who in her absence had returned to his unconverted life, "Never mind," she replied, "one day I shall cast such a noose around his neck that he shall never escape from me any more." She did. After her death Malavolti became an Olivetan monk. So, I conjecture, *mutatis mutandis*, Radegund might have replied, if blamed for her indulgence to Fortunatus' addiction to the pleasures of the table and occasional excesses in drinking. After her death she held him fast and brought him closer to herself as he drew closer to God.

Certainly he was judged worthy to be chosen shortly before his death Bishop of Poitiers, and in that office he died in the odour of sanctity.

O fortunatus nimium Venantius.

101

*

St. Hilda of Whitby

Regularly organized, credit-crammed summer sessions were fairly young on this morning of which I speak. We were young, too, a half dozen round-cheeked, eager-eyed novices. A professor from a midwest state university had come to teach us Old English. I have never forgotten this sentence with which he began: "It is hardly necessary to tell a group like you that English literature was mothered by a Benedictine nun." We filled in his pause with confused conjectures to be happily resolved as he added "Saint Hilda of Whitby."

For a number of years and in various high school and college English courses Hilda of Whitby had flitted in and out of my classes, never with any emphasis or apparent importance. Here this June morning she suddenly became a reality, a person who through the long, crowded years since has dominated my thinking, my acting, with quiet, positive persistence. Without surrounding her with the aureoles of the old-fashioned heroine I found in her the qualities of common sense, good judgment, courage of which I have had such sore and constant need. I found in her a love of words, of poetry, of the Sacred Scriptures, of study and of students. As a woman, a teacher, a student, a nun she filled my young world with a companionship which has still the bloom and the joy of that summer morning on it.

Hilda dawned on me, not in a single apocalyptic flash but progressively and through the years. My first experience in her recorded life came during our reading in class the twenty-fourth chapter of the fourth book of Bede's *Ecclesiastical History*. Here was Hilda the teacher, the administrator. Through the Old English text I watched her organize a course and a workshop in creative writing, in the writing of poetry, in teacher training. I watched her deal with the gifted student, the inspired student, the genius. She did not exploit him on the radio or the television of her day. She set him to studying and to paraphrasing the Scriptures. What she did and how she did it I have set down in my own English from the text of St. Bede. Deliberately, I have preserved a literal rather than a free translation in order the better to taste the flavor of the text. It is one of the pivotal passages in our literature:

"In the monastery of this abbess (Hilda) was a brother singularly distinguished and honored with a divine gift by which he was accustomed to make songs that belonged properly to piety and to virtue; so that whatever he learned of spiritual writing from scribes, after a little while he translated into poetry with the greatest sweetness and inspiration and brought forth into well wrought English (language). And because of his songs the minds of many men were inflamed with contempt of the world and were associated with a heavenly life. And although many others among the English people after him wrote pious songs there was none that could equal him; because he had not learned his song craft from men nor through men, but he was divinely helped, and received his gift of song craft from God; and for this reason he could never make any falsehood or any useless song, but always that which belonged to piety and such as befitted a pious tongue to sing.

103

"He was a man established in secular life until the time that he was infirm with age and had never learned anything of singing. And for that reason often at banquet, when there was deemed an occasion for rejoicing that all in turn should sing with the harp, when he saw the harp coming near to him, then he arose for shame from the group and went home to his house. Once when he did this, he left the banquet hall and went to the cattle shed because the keeping of the cattle was entrusted to him; when he had in due time laid his body down to rest and was sleeping a man stood before him in a dream and addressed him and greeted him and called him by his name: 'Caedmon, sing me something.' Then he answered and said: 'I cannot sing; and for that reason I left the banquet hall and came here because I did not know how to sing.' Then he who was speaking with him said: 'Nevertheless you can sing for me.' Then he said: 'What shall I sing?' He said: 'Sing for me of creation.'

"When he had received this answer he began at once to sing in praise of God, the Creator, the verse and the words that he had never heard. . . . Then he arose from sleep and all that he had sung in sleep he kept fast in mind; and to the words he soon added many words in the same meter of worthy songs to God. Then he came in the morning to the town reeve who was his alderman: he told him what gift he had received; and he took him at once to the abbess and informed and told her this. Then she called together all the most learned men and the teachers and commanded him to tell the dream and to sing the song to those present, that the judgment of all of them might decide what and from whence it had come.

"Then it was evident to all of them, just as it was, that this heavenly gift was bestowed on him by God Himself. Then they told him and discussed some heavenly text and word of heavenly wisdom: they directed him then, if he could, that he would turn it into the harmony of a poem. When he had received this matter, then he went home to his house, and came back in the morning, and sang to them the best wrought song and fulfilled what was committed to him.

"Then the abbess began to accept and to love the gift of God to this man, and she exhorted and advised him that he leave the world and receive monkhood; and he consented to that gladly. And she received him into the monastery with his goods and associated him to the community of God's servants and commanded him to study the making of holy stories and narratives. And all that he could learn by hearing he kept in mind and ruminating like clean kine he turned it into the sweetest song. And his song and his poetry were so winsome to hear that his teachers themselves wrought and learned at his mouth."

The story never grows old nor the woman who with Caedmon dominates it.

Through the years I find myself returning to the firelight and the recreations in the community rooms of that great double monastery of Whitby.* I watch her, the abbess, presiding over and sustaining the high and holy spirit of the group. But with Caedmon I slip out to the barn to live again that unique hour when English poetry like Christianity was born in a stable.

Then, on the great morning after, I accompany him and the town reeve to the Abbess Hilda with the first of all official reports on poetry in England. The conference which she called is easily the most important single meeting ever held on the subject. I like to set up the program as it might appear today, the Abbess Hilda presiding. Brother Caedmon makes the key speech in his report on his dream and his song of creation. There follows the panel discussion on the sources of the song in which the teachers and students together with the town officials participate. They come to a unanimous decision, that the song craft of Caedmon is a heavenly

---

* This Benedictine foundation which Hilda made included an abbey for the monks and a convent for her nuns.

gift from God himself. Hilda, acting on their resolution, receives Caedmon into the monastery and sets up her school of creative writing with him as the unique poet-student and teacher.

The whole story becomes completely contemporary, with Hilda in the place of pre-eminence which thirteen centuries have not changed.

Through the years, too, the question not infrequently arose, "What places would you want most to visit if you went to Europe?" My answer was always quick, positive, unvarying; "To Assisi for Saint Francis, to Norwich for Dame Juliana, to Whitby for Saint Hilda." Eventually, my wish was realized in precisely this order.

On a faultless July afternoon I found myself climbing the winding streets of the old fishing village of Whitby, past the traditional grave of Caedmon and its fine Celtic cross, up to the majestic site of the monastery itself. The bay below is circled by cliffs, somber and all but perpendicular.

Inside, the harbor walls cut out by the beating of the waves are white and shining. These bright cliffs against their black enclosure properly explain the name *Whitby*, given to the place by the Danes after their invasion and their destruction of the abbey built by St. Hilda and called Streaneshalch. Really, she is not Hilda of Whitby at all but Hild of Streaneshalch, the light of the beacon. There on the rock-bound promontory I looked out over the same North Sea that she knew. The bleak Northumbrian winds still discipline this austere land. Majestic ruins of her great monastic foundation still keep guard with them.

That day at Whitby sent me back to the old histories for the very meager facts of the life of my saint. Under the date A.D. 680 I found in the *Anglo-Saxon Chronicle* this brief entry: "the same year died Hilda, Abbess of Whitby." The statement could scarcely be more simple. The life at the end of which it puts a period was simple, too, I thought, in its directness, its clarity, its achievements, and in the means to these ends. Death in 680 terminated for this

106

Northumbrian woman, Hilda of Whitby, an experience rich in human being, a career wise in administration, in ecclesiastical foundations, in education, in public relations; a life wise in its own day, and more significantly wise seen in the perspective of thirteen hundred years.

Moving backward sixty-six years I came to the story at its beginning. The seventh century was an age of beginnings: the first perturbed and perverse gravitations of hostile tribal kingdoms towards a united nation; the first pentecostal rebirth of individuals and families and peoples from paganism to Christianity. Hilda was a child of both.

She was born, according to St. Bede, in 614, of noble parents. Her father, Hereric, was the nephew of King Edwin; her mother Bregusuit. Tragedy and predilection marked her infancy. Under decree of banishment by Cerdic, king of the hostile Britons, her father lived a fugitive from home. He never returned to his wife and little daughter. Ultimately, in the fierce and fearful rights of way of the time, Cerdic poisoned him. His stricken wife Bregusuit, mourning his loss, was visited by the comfort of a dream. This is the dream as I read it in Bede's *Ecclesiastical History*:

"She fancied in a dream, that she was seeking for him most carefully, and could find no sign of him anywhere; but, after having used all her industry to seek him, she found a most precious jewel under her garment, which, whilst she was looking on it very attentively, cast such a light as spread itself throughout all Britain; which dream was brought to pass in her daughter that we speak of, whose life was a bright example, not only to herself, but to all who desired to live well."

The remote preparation for her great mission began with Hilda's baptism. Under the year 627 the *Anglo-Saxon Chronicle* has the entry: "This year was King Edwin baptized at Easter, with all his people, by Paulinus." Bede says, in the *Ecclesiastical History*: "In the year 627, King Edwin was baptized, with his nation, at Easter."

107

And of Hilda, the king's niece, he writes: "She also embraced the faith and mysteries of Christ, at the preaching of Paulinus, the first bishop of the Northumbrians, of blessed memory, and preserved the same undefiled till she attained to the sight of Him in heaven."

For this gently born girl of thirteen the experience must have been literally skyscraping. The exchange of the loveless gloom of ironic pagan myth for the solicitous, merciful love of God meant deliverance and hope and joy. The sacramental meeting with Christ marked a new life. The Our Father, the Gloria, the Creed of the Apostles were texts upon which to build a new earth and a new heaven. Hilda must have accepted them all with the rich spontaneity of her youth and the sturdy stability that was her birthright. Over and over I picture her, with Bishop Paulinus and King Edwin; the bishop, "tall of stature, a little stooping, his hair black, his visage meagre, his aspect both venerable and majestic"; the king of such great majesty that banners were carried before him even "when he rode about his cities, towns, or provinces with his officers."

I follow her to the thresholds of many martyrdoms. The faith that had come to Northumbria was purchased not only by the baptism of water but of blood. In 633 Cadwalla, the king of the Britons, with Penda of Mercia, rose in joint rebellion. Great numbers of Northumbrian Christians were killed in the slaughter. King Edwin was killed in this fight for his faith on the plain of Heathfield the twelfth of October 633.

Hilda was nineteen. Six years of ardent Christianity had given to her youth the strength and nobility of apostolic zeal. The martyrdom of her uncle brought her face-to-face not only with life but with death for Christ. The alternatives were everywhere about her. All Northumbria was a prey to savage persecution that "spared neither the female, nor the innocent age of children." There was no safety except in flight. When the bishop Paulinus sailed from Whitby to Kent with her aunt, Queen Ethelberga, and her royal cousins, she was left perilously alone and lonely.

108

The picture of this young girl looking out from the great headland to the sea that was putting itself between her kinsfolk and probable martyrdom is singularly moving. That hour held in itself her own gift of possible martyrdom for her people and the Church in Northumbria. God asked life rather than death from her in His infinite pattern of providence.

Ten years passed in the turbulence of persecutions and the tragedies of apostasies. One does not live among martyrs without achieving something of vicarious martyrdom. One does not share the wisdom of holiness without becoming in some measure wise, in some degree holy. Hilda's young womanhood had surrounded her with such companionships. She was now thirty-three years old. Neither the eminently obvious nor the practically inevitable had happened to her. A Northumbrian gentlewoman, she had not been given in marriage to a kindred prince, nor carried off as spoils or hostage by a hostile one. Considering the temper of the times and the lot of hundreds of girls as gently born and reared as she, one can fairly infer that she was rather well able to take care of herself in the recurrent ravages of war and worse.

Hilda hoped that she might enter the monastery at Cale (Chelles), France, where she might "live a stranger for our Lord" in her quest for the kingdom of heaven. Histories of the time record that her sister, Heresuid, the mother of Aldwulf, king of the East Angles, entered this monastery after the death of her husband, King Anna. As yet there were no monasteries for women in Northumbria.

Hilda left Whitby for East Anglia where she waited an entire year under the protection of her nephew, the king. The delay was providential. Bishop Aidan of Lindisfarne gave her first a small tract of land on the north bank of the river Wear where, with a few companions and for a single year, she led the monastic life for which she had hoped.

Monasticism had come to England from Iona, which Columba had founded, as early as 563; through the Benedictine monks from

109

the Continent, Augustine and his four companions in 596. The pattern, whether Latin or Celtic, was one of holiness, wisdom, culture. Hilda's life and thought had been fashioned by these.

Meanwhile, a devout woman named Heiu had founded a convent called Heruteu, or "the Island of the Hart," in Northumbria under the spiritual direction of Bishop Aidan. She is said to have been the first woman in Hilda's country to be clothed in the holy habit and to become a nun.

The little community across the river Wear was hardly more than a year old when Bishop Aidan named Hilda abbess of the monastery of Heruteu. She was then about thirty-five. Her years of study and training under the learned men who had been her teachers prepared her for this new responsibility. St. Bede says: "Bishop Aidan and other religious men that knew her and loved her, frequently visited and diligently instructed her, because of her innate wisdom and inclination to the service of God."

With her disciplined mind and her aptitude for organization she "began immediately to reduce all things to a regular system." How contemporary, even how efficient and American it all sounds! Her vocation, her desire to go abroad for its fulfillment, her finding her mission and her work at home in the first Northumbrian convent have nothing of the remote or the primitive about them. They are a story of here and now.

We must not miss this very dear and human detail. King Oswy in gratitude for his victory over Penda and the pagan Mercians dedicated his little daughter Elfleda to God. He gave the child, with her dower of land, into the care of Hilda, at Heruteu (Hartlepool). Few girls have been more fortunate in their home, their school, their teachers.

About two years after Elfleda had been entrusted to her cloister, the Abbess came into possession of a considerable tract of land a little south of Hartlepool. The precedent for land-grant schools was centuries old even then. The place was called Streaneshalch,

110

for a holy light that had marked it as blessed. Here on the high headland, three hundred feet above the sea, she built her great double monastery, Whitby. Here her life came to flower and fruit. Here Elfleda, the king's daughter, grew up, first as a student in this convent school and then as "a teacher of monastic life." The pattern is repeated the Christian world over today, on lower spiritual and cultural levels, it may be. How often, when putting brick on mortar against the mountain-side of Utah or the levels of Indiana have I looked back to it and to the intrepid woman directing it.

The scope and quality of that seventh-century life and culture are written large in the story of the monk Theodore and the subdeacon Hadrian. About the year 655 or 660 the sees of Canterbury and Northumbria were deprived by death of their bishops. Kings Egbert and Oswy sent to Pope Vitalian petitioning the consecration of an archbishop for the Churches of England.

In the *Ecclesiastical History* the story runs thus. There was at the time in a monastery near Naples a certain Hadrian, African-born, "well versed in Holy Writ, experienced in monastical and ecclesiastical discipline, and excellently skilled both in the Greek and Latin tongues. The pope, sending for him, commanded him to accept of the bishopric, and repair into Britain. He answered, that he was unworthy of so great a dignity, but said he could name another whose learning and age were fitter for the episcopal office." After repeated protests he presented to the pope Theodore, a monk born in Cilicia who happened at that time to be in Rome. He was "well known to Hadrian, born at Tarsus in Cilicia, a man well instructed in worldly and divine literature, as also in Greek and Latin; of known probity of life, and venerable of age, being sixty-five years old." Hadrian offered him to the pope to be ordained bishop, and prevailed; but upon these conditions, that he should conduct him into Britain, because he had already travelled through France twice upon several occasions, and was, therefore, better acquainted with the way." The episcopal transaction could

111

scarcely be more succinct, more informed with practical humility and prudence. It is not without its amusing human side. "Hadrian, being ordained sub-deacon, waiting four months for his hair to grow, that it might be shorn into the shape of a crown; for he had before the tonsure of Saint Paul, the apostle, after the manner of the eastern people."

Theodore arrived at Canterbury on Sunday, the twenty-seventh of May 668. Immediately he visited the whole of Christian England, accompanied by Hadrian. They were everywhere entertained, everywhere available to their people. English Catholics were for the first time united under and obedient to one archbishop. Neither Church history nor the history of education presents a finer picture than this of the sixty-eight-year-old archbishop and his devoted and indefatigable priest Hadrian as they both, well read in sacred and secular literature, "gathered a crowd of disciples and there daily flowed from them rivers of knowledge to water the hearts of hearers; and, together with the books of holy writ, they also taught them the arts of ecclesiastical poetry, astronomy, and arithmetic." And this, in the name of *Motu Proprio* and all our modern schools of chant: "From that time also they began in all the Churches of the English to learn sacred music."

This was the pattern and the environment of the monastery at Whitby, one of the happy places of this happy time, where "all who desired to be instructed in sacred reading had masters at hand to teach them." Here under the holiness of her wisdom and the wisdom of her holiness, Hilda reclaimed for her spiritual family the great virtues of the early Church. Problems of personal inequality, of poverty and wealth were solved by the virtues of common life and community of goods. Holiness and happiness were the effect of the virtues on which the Abbess most insisted: justice, charity, peace. Kings and princes knew the qualities of her prudence and came to her for advice. What is better, they accepted it. This is the more significant since she obliged those who came to her for direction to devote themselves to the study of Holy Scripture and to be the very patterns of justice. The modern study club and seminar and great books group do not sound so erudite and impressive in the presence of these seventh-century intellectuals.

Indeed, Hilda can well serve as a model for our contemporary schools of sacred theology for the laity. Her students were so well instructed that among the men numbers were "found fit for ecclesiastical duties and to serve at the altar." As a matter of fact, five bishops were consecrated from the monastery of Whitby; a sixth would have been but for his untimely death. Two of these came in succession to the Church of York, one to Dorchester. Oftfor was the eminent scholar of the group. He had studied both "the reading and the observation of the Scriptures"—a nice combination—under Hilda's direction at both her monasteries. A true student, he went on for further study to Archbishop Theodore in Kent. The continuity of the intellectual and spiritual life here is as thrilling as the chronicle is ingenuous. For, says that beautiful scholar and saint, Bede: "having spent some time in sacred studies he also resolved to go to Rome, which, in those days, was reckoned of great moment," as when would it not be! But this was the seventh century.

The very greatness of Hilda as a scholar in sacred theology and Scripture emerges in the lives and works of her disciples. What work of translating, transcribing, copying, illuminating must have glorified their days!

While literature was building in the minds and cloisters of her monks, Hilda had been busy with the erection of the monastery of Hackness, thirteen miles from Whitby. Here Frigyth acted as superior. She had been busy with problems of Church discipline. The controversy over the time of keeping Easter is probably the only one which has significance for us today. A synod was called to meet at Whitby in 664 to represent the respective claims and to establish the practice "celebrated by all at Rome." Hilda quite

113

logically supported the practice of her own country. Though she took no part in the discussions, she shared the sharp rebuke that came from Rome. The choice of Whitby as the proper place for the synod indicates the importance that it had achieved in the life of the Church within the first ten years of its founding.

With all her major activities as religious superior and administrator, student, scholar, Hilda found time for great and gracious friendships. There were the kings under whose protection she had grown up, the great ecclesiastics who directed her spiritual life. There were scholars from Tarsus and Carthage and Rome. There was Caedmon. The baby daughter of King Oswy, Elfleda, grew up in her convents and for a lifetime enjoyed the heritage of her love. Begu, a nun at Hackness, and the acting superior of that monastery, Frigyth, shared so closely in her life and work as to know her death by special revelation. An anonymous nun at Whitby, and a devoted friend of Hilda, had this same experience. The great abbess transacted the whole business of life with a very certain splendor of being.

Her long years of intense activity had been years of illness as well. For six years before her death she suffered constantly from a violent fever. This became the occasion for increased zeal in her work. Publicly and privately she exhorted her people to use their health and strength in perfect service to God. Her own example taught them as effectively as her words. After seven years of illness her condition became acute. At cock crow one morning she received Holy Communion for the last time. Gathering her community she counseled them to preserve their blessed "evangelical peace among themselves and with all others." Death came as she was speaking. This was November 17, 680.

These were the days when the preternatural and the supernatural shared actively in the natural order and lives of men. Chronicles recorded comets and eclipses with significant fidelity and details. Portents and omens brought their forewarnings of life and of death. Dreams and visions not uncommonly carried tidings of good or ill days in anticipation of the events themselves. This had happened to Caedmon and to Bregusuit, the mother of Hilda. Now came a manifest vision to the convent of Hackness. On a night Begu heard the familiar sound of the convent bell that was ordinarily rung to wake the sisters and to call them to prayers at the death of any of their number. She was a sister well past middle age and had been a religious more than thirty years. She was well past the age of emotional pseudo-ecstasies, but as she opened her eyes it seemed to her that the roof of the convent opened and a great light shone down from the skies. In this light she saw the soul of Hilda carried by angels to heaven.

She looked about the dormitory and found that all the other sisters were sleeping undisturbed. She got up quickly and hurried to her superior Frigyth to tell her that the Abbess Hilda had just died. Frigyth called the sisters to the Church, where they spent the remainder of the night in prayer and the singing of psalms for the soul of their beloved abbess. At daybreak the brothers came from Whitby with word of her death, but they already had the news from heaven.

The chronicle has nothing more to say. But what need? For here she is under my roof, at the very heart of my living and being, this wise, versatile woman, this very Benedictine nun. If there is a problem of building under adverse circumstances, I look at the floor plan of her double monastery at Whitby. If there is a question of educating teachers, she is before me with her best students studying in Rome. If the matter is one of recruiting faculty, I find her drawing on episcopal scholarship from Tarsus to Carthage. As for going to conventions, she was hostess for a synod. Mothering Caedmon, she pioneered in workshops of creative writing. She became the mother of English literature. Her universality encompasses me. I find myself leaning hard upon her human sturdiness, leaning with even greater dependence upon her recorded prudence. The decades since the June morning of our first meeting, the centuries since her actual life, shrink into the measure of inconsequence.

Just here I am interrupted. An interminable questionnaire arrives, asking how many complete or partial scholarships we will grant to students, to displaced persons, to graduate students. How many? To whom? I'll ask the abbess. I'll ask St. Hilda.

Of all the men who have made an impact upon the world and the human heart, next to Jesus, time has least diminished Francis of Assisi.

If one thinks of oneself standing for a moment poised between two worlds, his and ours, and looks back upon him with modern eyes, his life becomes even more meaningful, nostalgic and hopelessly desirable.

For everything in modern times is exaggerated and intensified until living has become a fever and the throat begins to feel raw and the tongue swollen with the thirst for peace, serenity and a return to dignity. One comes to Francis as to a cooling draught.

The following is not a life of St. Francis of Assisi. It is not even an essay or an estimate. It is a groping for an expression of some of those qualities in him that have touched me deeply in recent years.

Thus, if you will accept this as an expression of what St. Francis means to me, and not what I think he should mean to you, or to any one else, we shall both feel more comfortable on the ensuing pages.

117

Over and beyond the lyric life of Francis and the exquisite poem of the brief span of his years on earth, I am captivated by his unfailing courtesy, his humor, cheerfulness and gayety of spirit, but above all, his deeply satisfying humility.

Once you have accepted a man as a saint, it is difficult to return to the contemplation of him as a man, for custom, time and canonization throw an aura about him. And yet, so many of the qualities of Francis and the things he did that were accounted saintly, were manly too, so warm and earthily human and mortal that one thinks one loves him for this manliness only to find then that they approach the divine because of the manner in which they were used to enrich the world. We are all endowed in some measure with similar traits and capabilities, but only Francis used them to send up a life-long song to his Creator.

For instance, throughout his existence one encounters with a kind of pleased astonishment the constant evidence of his gentle courtesy.

I do not know why one should *not* look for courtesy in a saint, but it does seem foreign to the sometimes chill and austere presence one comes to associate with the Holy. One remembers thunderers, sufferers, fanatics, martyrs, mystics, zealots and benefactors of mankind, but not so many of exquisite courtesy.

Yet the root of courtesy is love. Good manners are founded upon the ardent desire not to offend one's fellows and the experience of genuine regret at having done so. One feels that the engaging politeness of Francis stemmed from his sincerity and the depth of affection he entertained, not only for humans but for every object animate and even inanimate that shared living space with him on earth.

Francis had a relationship to everything, to man, beasts of the fields and forests, the birds, the fish, trees, flowers, even stones, the sun, the moon, the wind and the stars, fire and water, rain and snow, storms, the earth, summer, winter and the tender elegy of springtime. With all of these he dealt courteously and admitted them to the circle of his immediate family, for a man who believes in and loves his Creator with his whole heart must also dignify and love all of His creations.

Many of the legends regarding Francis, his feeling for his surroundings and the living things that populated the countryside, can be misleading, unless one remembers this matter of courtesy towards and fellow feeling for one's lesser neighbors.

There is, for instance, the story of the fisherman who presented Francis with a carp that had just been drawn from the lake. His poet's delight in the silvery beauty of the fish was mingled with pity for its gasping struggles. He returned it to the waters whence it had come. Thankfully, says the tale, the fish followed his boat to the other side of the lake and was waiting for the Saint when he returned.

It is not the legend of the grateful fish that is important, but the release. Do we ever experience the deep sense of kinship entertained by Francis for the other inhabitants of our planet? Have we so much as a moment to spare to try to love, understand or pity what we destroy?

Francis did not preach a sermon demanding that all fish be returned to the sea, or for that matter that we refrain from catching them. But towards that particular one that had swum into his ken he behaved like a friend and a gentleman. There is nothing that Francis ever said or did to indicate that a man need be ashamed or feel guilty because of eating a lamb cutlet, provided he loves the living lamb, or that it is wrong to bring down a pheasant with a fowling piece, if one is capable of humbleness in the presence of such a beauty a-wing.

Francis accepted and lived with the hunter, the fisherman, the farmer, the butcher. He neither humanized nor sentimentalized animals. But he did feel for them, admitting them to their rights of kinship with him and giving them the same courtesy that he bestowed upon his fellows.

119

And if he was sorry for their difficulties in a predatory world he was also keenly aware of the many beauties and blessings with which they had been endowed. What reaches one's heart is the touching simplicity with which he admitted every living thing to the equality of gratitude towards its Maker.

We admire the sincerity that led him to preach to the birds to remind them to praise and thank Him who had endowed them with such lovely plumage, abundant food and graceful power of flight. And it is the gesture of addressing them as fellow creatures that is the wonder of this particular story and not the legendary account of their response at the finish of the sermon. For it is no miracle at all that our animal brethren almost invariably react to true courtesy, kindness and consideration. It is simply that there was and still is so little of it practiced in good faith that when it is tried and found to work, it smacks of the marvel. Francis must have thought it the most natural thing in the world for the beasts to have responded in kind to his politeness and consideration.

We find him experiencing no surprise at the taming of the wolf of Gubbio since he had never believed the beast to be either savage or evil, any more than he believed the bandits he occasionally encountered and turned from their paths to be vicious. The man who can wholeheartedly believe that all things are created by God and that God does not create evil, is freed from many burdens, and one of them is fear.

Many of us are capable of loving a pet, weeping over a run-over dog, or shedding tears over a dead bird, but for the most part we are only mourning the loss of an extension of our own egos. Old dog Tray is always to us what we think he ought to be and rarely what he actually is. Seldom is he or any of his kind admitted to friendship or a place on the hearth because he is after all a relative in the large family of the children of the Creator.

120

ST. FRANCIS OF ASSISI

by Jan Yoors

Francis had pets, a lamb, a pheasant, a rabbit, a cicada, a dog, a wolf, but upon honest and unsentimental terms. For he was as polite and considerate to an earthworm, a slug, a bird, a beetle or a mole, as amusedly tolerant and withal, understanding and warmly loving as one would be to one's brother and sister. Indeed, they were his brothers and sisters. He called them so, not with the pious emptiness the words have come to connote in modern times, but with the deep conviction of the kinship.

It is told of him that he would stoop to remove an earthworm from his path so as not to crush it. One feels that with Francis it was a personal as well as symbolic courtesy to something living he happened to encounter.

There appears to be a touch of the child's world of fancy in this but it is really an intensely practical way of life aboard an overpopulated planet, and what is more, it has the great advantage of beauty over ugliness. Looking back to the daily joy and happiness that Francis managed to crowd into the forty-four years of his life it is not at all difficult to understand that it is better to be kind than unkind and to be generous and accommodating instead of rude and possessive. This is not childish. It is one of the most adult discoveries ever made.

And one notes with equal satisfaction that Francis expected a full return of courtesies, and what is more, he got it. For in that state of Nature which exists in the faith that all is divinely created with love and delight in beauty (and who shall say that a maggot, a spider, a rat or a hippopotamus is not beautiful in the eyes of God) there must be give as well as take.

Thus there is no difficulty in understanding his request to the noisy swallows wheeling, looping, twittering in the late afternoon sky, drowning out Francis's attempt to preach, with their chatter—"My brothers and sisters, the swallows, it is now time for me to speak. You have been speaking enough all the time. Give me leave to be heard."

121

It is recorded that the swallows piped down.

In the same spirit was his request to Brother Fire in the shape of a red hot iron physicians were about to use to cauterize his temples in an attempt to cure his growing blindness late in life:

"Brother Fire, who art nobler and more useful than most other creatures, I have always been good to you and always will be so for the love of Him who created you. Now show yourself gentle and courteous with me and do not burn me more than I can stand."

One can only long for a world in which Brother Fire indeed responds in kind to such a gentle and persuasive plea, for when it was over, Francis said to the physicians—"If that is not enough burning, then burn it again, for I have not felt the least pain."

These are the pictures that uplift the spirit and enchant the heart, a worn and sightless man who through faith and simplicity has found the key to communicating with the universe.

The biographers write that Francis was personally unprepossessing and undistinguished in appearance and then offer usually some kind of apologetic gloss for the fact that physically the gay little tramp of God did not measure up to the standards set by the imagination for the good and the holy.

But it is precisely because Francis was an insignificant-looking little black-haired fellow with a scrawny neck and uninspiring features that I find myself loving him the more and cherishing the figure of him that I conjure up for myself.

Francis's own estimate of his person is indicated by his reference to himself as a "little black hen," thus at once creating an amusing and warming picture in one's mind of a small, dark, busy fellow with an alert and glittering eye, narrow head, thin shoulders and pipe-stem legs, pecking and scratching about his business, poking into everything and never still for a moment.

Almost as captivating is the amazement of brother Masseo, one of his early disciples from Marignano, who one day said to Francis in effect—"How do you get away with it? Look at you, there's nothing to you. You haven't got looks, you don't cut any kind of a figure, you have no learning and aren't even of noble birth to make up for everything else you lack. And yet the whole world runs after you and wants to see you and hear you and obey you. I can't make it out."

Francis replied simply that God had selected him, the poorest, most miserable and wretched specimen on the whole earth to do His work, using Francis as an instrument wherewith to shame the noble, the great, strength and beauty and worldly wisdom, and make it clear that all power and virtue come from Him and not from creatures and that no one can exalt himself before His face.

It is curious that in the old walled city with its churches and squares and crooked, cobbled streets clinging to the side of Monte Subasio, one still feels the presence of Francis so strongly after more than seven hundred years. It is not only that he is remembered spiritually, but here he was born and lived. Every alley, every market square or plaza, every time-worn stone upon which one stands or rests one's eye, once felt the touch of his feet, or the passage of the rough hem of his habit sweeping by.

Here is the house where he first saw the light of day, there the Church where he was baptized; at this fountain he surely paused some time to drink; from that stairway he exhorted his fellows to love their Maker and one another. It seems impossible that he has departed from these houses and passageways and arches, the squares and gathering places that his eyes looked upon, these roof-tops, eaves and tall chimneys and stone towers that listened to his voice rising from the winding streets below in song or poetry, or simple praise from a heart bursting with joy.

There is the feeling that one has but to turn one more corner to encounter him striding along barefoot in his frayed and patched, mud-colored robe, tied at the waist with a piece of rope, black-haired, black-bearded, dirty as a sweep from the task of cleaning out a church, hands roughened, fingernails cracked and blackened

123

by hard work, a busy, bustling man, not loitering, but going somewhere with a kind of zestful excitement that he carries along with him, his expression alive and cheerful and full of interest for everything about him, and yet in the dark, expressive eyes one notes the pervading calm that marks the gaze of those who have conquered self.

Outside the walls too, the market place above the city is unchanged by time, and along the chalky roads that wind about the mountain one looks again to catch a glimpse of the sweet, ugly, unkempt, dusty little man, always a little gaunt from discipline and fasting, always sweat- or travel-stained, pausing perhaps to ransom the lives of two lambs from some peasant leading them to slaughter.

And one feels too that no one ever had to point and say, "There, that little one who looks like nothing at all, that is Francis of Assisi." He was no spellbinder or thunderer with menacing gestures and brazen voice, but only a simple man with an idea in which he believed to the exclusion of everything that was false or mean.

The impact of the saints upon the modern world appears to be diminishing. They are agreeable and stimulating stories in a book, or wood, stone or plaster figures in the niches of old churches staring their supplicants down with painted eyes. Yet no one in history is capable of sending such piercing trumpet blasts down the corridors of time as the meek lowly, the humble and self-sacrificing and the devoted. The soldiers, statesmen and conquerors catch the eye and the intellect, but the lovers of God capture our hearts.

If, in a sense, the saint was often created by the times and the need for him in a sick world, the illness appears to return with cyclic insistence. In such periods, when humanity becomes poisoned by too persistent a dose of its own evil, one is suddenly aware of something golden shining in the darkness that surrounds the human soul. Then is when one presses one's nose against the seemingly impenetrable window panes of the past with an almost juvenile yearning for a share of the spiritual beauty that lies so clearly visible on the other side.

Saint Francis in particular defies the would-be imitator, for his courage was so gigantic, his faith so unswerving, his simplicity so unassailable and his consistency so unique that his like has not been encountered since.

In this bleak, barren era of too much material abundance, one can still warm oneself at the fires Francis kindled seven centuries ago and reduce the growing chill in one's heart at the flame of the example of this man whose entire mature life was nothing but one inexhaustible pouring out of love.

Yet because one is human one finds oneself attracted to the humanity in a Godly figure. I find myself particularly enchanted by the contemplation of this twelfth-century man, inspired by divine fire, equipped with the indomitable will and moral courage needed to pursue the inspiration, who was yet leavened with humor and who had that occasional, impish, small-boy quality that is so endearing when it is found in truly adult men.

For Francis was possessed of the light humor of wit and grace, the heritage of his younger days in Assisi when he was town host, playboy and troubadour. By living and acting as he did he made many other ways of living and acting seem ridiculous. He appeared to be doing what he did with great import and seriousness, nevertheless he had a mischievous and merrily sly way of undermining all the kinds of tyrannies that complicate our lives, such as wealth, birth and ambition.

He was likewise a master of the humor that is directed against that weak and frail vessel—self.

For instance, he had another name for his person, besides the "little black hen," which he applied when he found the spirit more willing than the flesh to endure the hard labor of rebuilding churches by hand. He would refer to his body as "Brother Ass," and order it to do his bidding as one would the little pack animal.

The joke is even more tender than usually imagined, for in Italy, the donkey is less the symbol for stupidity and stubbornness than it is for patience and hard work. For centuries it has been part of the scene, a beast of burden that goes docilely where it is led and does what it is made to do, often staggering uncomplainingly beneath cargoes that appear far too great for its capacity. Like all saints and ascetics, Francis conducted a running feud with his body during his lifetime. But he is the only one who bestowed a name upon his own unwilling carcass that brings a smile to the lips.

With Francis the joke was always upon himself; it was he who was the fool and never anyone else. Hence, more often than not, there were tears mingled with the laughter he engendered. It is a classically comic situation when a pious fellow who preaches abstinence and self-control is caught in gluttony, his features still greasy from the feast. How much funnier, and withal, deeply touching it becomes when it is Francis who, as it were, puts the finger on himself and has himself towed through town on a halter by a disciple, the meanwhile crying "Look here, you people! This is the man who asks you to fast and repent while he himself feasts on a tender bird just because his stomach hurts him a little. That glutton, that reveler, that hypocrite."

His impish and adorable small-boyish quality comes to light in the masquerade he enacted one Easter when the brothers of the convent at Greccio, expecting a visitor of importance, so far forgot the principles of their order as to set a table with cloth and glasses.

Just as they were sitting down to table with the distinguished guest there came a knock on the door and a voice known to them all, but now filled with exaggerated unction, cried, "For the love of God, give alms to this poor and infirm pilgrim."

When they opened the door everyone saw that it was Francis

126

"disguised" in an old hat left behind by a beggar, and with staff and cloak. Bidden to enter by the unhappy brothers, he completed their confusion by taking his bowl of soup and piece of bread and crouching down on his heels in a corner by the fireplace. Here again is his favorite comedy of example.

But one feels that his deepest chuckles were reserved for the divine practical prank he played on the concept of money. Jesus was outraged and angry when he drove the money changers from the temple, but I am certain that Francis was laughing inwardly when he ordered some money that had been left during his absence, to be thrown out onto the dung-heap.

He could have ordered it thrown into the dust at the side of the road, or into the fields, or let it be swept away by the stream, but no. By the dung-heap he designated its merit, quality and value. He labelled it unmistakably for what it is and the place it deserves in the scheme of things. The humor is low, earthy, Italian, but retains that divine directness that strikes to the core.

I come now to that quality of Francis that I love the most and that is his humility and genuine un- or anti-arrogance. He faced up to himself, learned to know himself truly for what he was in relation to his God and the world in which he lived and thereupon he simply shed every arrogance known to man and invited those who cared to do so to join him in doing likewise. He found Paradise on earth and generously offered to share it with his fellows.

It is true, arrogances were fewer and simpler in those days and in the less complex society only recently emerged from the dark ages when man did not have so much to puff him up. There was the arrogance of living on a hill with armed retainers in a stone castle, the arrogance of golden spurs and the arrogance of bulging coffers. There was the arrogance of learning in the days when the ignorant and unlettered were in the majority, the super-arrogance of those who claimed to rule man by divine right, and the arrogance that sometimes went with custody over the keys to Heaven. And with these there was an end to them. A fellow might peacock in fine clothes, or set too rich a table or carry his armor to the inlayers and engravers, but outside of that, man was on the whole not extravagantly pleased with himself.

The indecent and shameful arrogances of our times by comparison almost ennoble those that Francis persuaded his disciples to surrender in following his example. It makes one hark back with longing to a period when ridding oneself of them was no more complicated than selling all of one's possessions and taking to the road, like the rich merchant, Bernardo of Quintavalle, or laying aside sword, armor and war charger to take up the cross like Angelo Tancredi, or hanging up one's lute at the altar and exchanging the parti-colored hose and slashed doublet of the *Troubadour de Dames* for the robe and rope of the *Jongleurs de Dieu*, like Divini, the poet.

Now the roster of the humble has been cut, many more of us live in palaces and eat the food of princes. A fool can make a war and lead a world to slaughter; learning has elbowed its way through the firmament a hundred billion light years closer to God's throne but not one split second nearer to Him in spirit.

All the arrogances of civilization and mechanical progress have been added to the list, the arrogance of the wise-guy and the huckster, of the lucky, the cunning, and the self-made, the narcissistic orgy of a mankind gone mad with admiration for its own cleverness. When the symphony of self-adulation becomes unbearable, the mind is rested in turning to Francis, the humble, unprepossessing little poet of life with the golden heart, the clear, unsullied spirit and the unbelievable courage to strip himself of everything. It is not difficult to understand how in his day, entire villages and communities flocked to this voluntary poor man who had demonstrated the exquisite joy of possessing nothing beyond the sun and the stars, the warmth of fire, the cooling draught of water, the color and perfume of a flower. It was dark in those days too, until Francis threw open the window of his soul and let the daylight in. Taught by the example of Francis many throughout the world for the first time approached some of the beauties of the mind and spirit that are not encumbered by the arrogances of possessions.

I would not have the courage to follow Francis today, but the need for him and everything for which he stood is deeply felt. The higher the civilization, the more brash and insufferable the arrogances, the dearer the longing for the simplicity, peace and humility of which Francis was capable.

For I trust him. Because after he had stripped himself of everything he had, the last shred of clothing, the shoes from his feet, the staff from his hand, the food from his lips, when he had learned to sleep out in the chilling rain with a stone for a pillow, when he could sell even the book of the Scriptures that nourished him spiritually to provide bread for a woman in distress, then it was that this great creative artist of the world's most beautiful poem of living, wrote the climax of his farewell to earthly pride, for he shed even the last remaining arrogance, the arrogance of poverty and humility.

"Take no pride of your voluntary poverty," he counsels the brothers, "for behold, there is a beggar even more ragged, miserable and threadbare than you, and you are in debt to him for everything you have."

He forbids his disciples in their pride of poverty to dare to condemn those who dress in fine clothes and live in luxury and happiness, or to whine, complain, or criticize the rich. As the brothers wander through the world, they shall be mild, modest, humble and friendly to all. They shall not contend with one another, and they shall judge no one. And above all, they must be cheerful.

"Let the brothers take care," he wrote, "that they do not present the appearance of hypocrites with dark and downcast mien, but that they show themselves glad in the Lord, cheerful and worthy of love and agreeable."

This abnegation of the sweets of sacrifice, this joy within joy, was the ultimate in unselfish giving; in the long catalogue of things that Francis surrendered in order to approach nearer to the God he loved, it shines with the purest light through the black centuries of human behavior. This man I cherish. Him I envy greatly for I long for the happiness that was his.

The power to attract and to move the human soul has never left him. That is why Assisi is yet so filled with him that you feel surely at the next square, by that old stone fountain, you will find him striding along, the cowl of his robe thrown back from the small dark head, his voice raised in the melodies and language of Provence, singing from his full and grateful heart the words of praise and thanks to Him who created all things so beautiful.

But more touching than anything is to descend the many steps of the Basilica of his church to reach the crypt where he is buried, and to find his resting place no dark and musty mausoleum but a simple little chamber that is filled with a kind of light and airy grace. The crypt and the tomb itself are echoes of the poverty and simplicity he courted during his lifetime.

For men, moved by what he was and did, have built a chimney to his sarcophagus, an opening that admits light and air, and at night the stars. And in the day at certain times, the sun he loved so greatly sends a shaft slanting down through the opening, and it seems to shine directly into the great heart that is buried there.

The symbolism is inescapable. So shines Francis, the shaft of his being aimed at the heart of a world that grows darker by the hour.

130

The feet of St. Francis must have been, by the time he died at the age of forty-five, a remarkable testimony to his blithe fortitude. They were no doubt gnarled and bitten and criss-crossed by the sharp stones of Spain, the snow of the Apennines and the sands of Africa. The soles of the feet, I imagine, must by this time have become almost insensible, almost a form of leather covering, but this relative immunization to hardship does not occur on the upper skin of the human foot or in its bones. And even on that leathery under-surface, as one sees on the feet of the poor in Asia who have never worn shoes, the marks of the hard road remain incised.

And the road was, I believe, hard. The joy upon which St. Francis insisted throughout the twenty-odd years of his specific mission was natural, arose from his depths, and was his character-istic form of worship; but it was also—and not in the least contra-dictorily—a protection against the hardness of the road. It was not so devised or intended—for who can devise or intend joy?—but it was thus that it worked.

131

Often he must have bathed his feet in the cool Umbrian brooks that were nearest, somewhere in the hills between Assisi and Perugia, and taken delight in the ripple of the water over weary skin and bone. I can imagine him as singing while he did this—singing for sheer pleasure in water, sun, sky and air, the presence of his sisters the birds and his brother the goat. It would have been a lesser delight to do so in the sullen, half-desiccated river-beds of Spain and Africa—excepting, perhaps, the Ebro, which flows with something like his own impetuosity to its mother the sea. And the shallow, tepid water on the beaches near Palermo must have seemed to those feet hardly water at all, but a kind of soup which could never solace the tendons beneath the skin. Although there, we may be sure, he rejoiced in the bluish transparency over the white sand, whatever its shortcomings as water.

What must have been the joy of those feet in the fields of Galilee? The fields and hillsides in Galilee are covered in spring and early summer with a variety of wild-flowers to which I can put no name. Innumerable generations of human beings have been sensitive to the particular beauty of the wild-flowers in Galilee. Lord Wavell, in his biography of the military chieftain who was his hero in youth—Allenby—tells us that the great commander kept careful notebooks on these flowers, as did Wavell himself. If you have seen them at the right time of the year you can never forget them. Whole hillsides sing out in a species of visible rapture not violent in the least, but delicate and temperate as the climate of the spring. Francis, the Little Poor Man, would certainly never have wished to walk upon any of his sisters the flowers, but the fact is that he could not have walked anywhere in Galilee without stepping on them. And once he had done so I believe that they would have come to seem like balsam, the soft and friendly touch of something meant to heal and make happy, the promise of happiness to feet tired of the long road.

Francis went to Palestine in 1219 and returned to Italy in Sep-

132

tember of 1220. His first attempt to go to the crusade (it was the Fifth) ended ignominiously: he stowed away on a boat and was promptly returned to Italy. He did better the next time. He did not have much luck with the Christians, who were too busy carousing in their camps about Damietta to pay much attention to this barefoot mendicant. The inexplicable thing is that he got on very well with the Arabs. It was with the Sultan's permission and safe-conduct that he walked through Palestine to Jerusalem, Bethlehem and Nazareth and returned in safety to the Christian armies.

This, in the midst of a cruel war, would be beyond credence today. The barefoot friar would be shot at once when he passed from one opposing army to the other—and by that I mean, whichever way he was headed. If he were going from the Christians to the Saracens the latter would shoot him; if he were going the other way the Christians would shoot him. It was different then.

All sorts of musings arise about this strange journey of St. Francis to Jerusalem. What about Frederick II, for example? What did he think? I have always believed that this voluptuous but educated monarch, with his wonderful taste in architecture, poetry and art (particularly mosaic), was one of the creators of the modern world as well as of Italian literature and language. What can compare with the mosaics of Monreale and Cefalù? De Sanctis in his *Storia della letteratura italiana* was perhaps the first to give unstinting appreciation to Frederick's part in the origins of the Renaissance. But what did Frederick II think of St. Francis? We do not know. When Francis appeared before him and made his impassioned plea for the protection of certain birds we may suppose that the monarch was astonished, to say the least. He may have supposed that the barefoot little man was insane. But hardly for one second could he have considered giving up the sports of falconry which were the abiding pleasure of the court at Palermo.

Then, when Frederick was commander-in-chief of the Fifth

133

Crusade, combining with this activity all sorts of political pre-occupations about Germany, Italy and the control of the Mediter-ranean, not forgetting his complicated relationship with the papacy, this absurd but irresistible mendicant crops up again, preaching the New Testament in the most literal way imaginable, and goes off to the enemy army and the enemy territory without a qualm. Did Frederick know anything about this, think anything about it, do anything about it? Did he even know, really, who St. Francis was?

We might similarly enquire about Pope Innocent III if we did not possess, in this case, some information. Innocent III was one of the greatest of popes in the historical sense, a man of brains, courage and vision, whose influence upon the development of the age was immense. As a philosopher and scholar he made his mark early, and although he was not even an ordained priest in January, 1198, when he was elected pope at the age of thirty-eight, his fellow-cardinals appear to have had no doubt that he was the one man who could lead the Church out of confusion and weak-ness into strength. He did so. His ordination to the priesthood came over a month after he was elected pope; his consecration as bishop followed the next day. But we may doubt if he ever in his heart felt himself to be a priest. He was the guardian of the Church. He himself said: "I have no leisure to meditate on supra-mundane things; scarce can I breathe. Yea, so much must I live for others, that almost I am a stranger to myself." How he dealt with all the states and princes of Italy and Germany is no part of our concern, but his pontificate left the Church firmly established as the strongest power of the western world, holding together the thirteenth century in that unity which was never afterwards to be restored. Innocent vanquished largely by spiritual means, by in-telligence, authority and religion combined: he attacked the princes through their moral shortcomings, and thus had no need of violence. It was by such means that he brought into being the reality of a papal supremacy which had only been theoretical before. During the eighteen years of his reign every sovereign of consequence in Europe, from Norway to Bulgaria and from England to Sicily, surrendered his crown to the Pope and received it back again in feudal fief to the Throne of St. Peter. (King John of England was stubborn but had to yield to the interdict: and Innocent's legates played an important and sometimes decisive part in England.)

This great artisan of the marvelous thirteenth century was, although perhaps not a priest in the deepest sense, yet truly saturated with religion. Every act of his life seems to have a religious purpose, motivation and even method. His achievement may be called largely secular in all the senses of that word, but it was founded on the religion which, it must be remembered, the overwhelming mass of Western mankind felt as a living truth at that time.

The dying Constance, widow of Henry VI, left her infant Frederick II to the guardianship of the Pope. We can imagine that she did so in sheer despair; the conflict of empire and papacy had become almost a condition of life, and therefore of her own duty, but what else could she do? There were rival claimants and the Two Sicilies were not safe for a baby king. Thus within the very first year of his pontificate Innocent III obtained everything that his predecessors had struggled for in vain.

This great Pope had been puzzled by Francis of Assisi, and it seems that at the time of their first conversation (1210) he did not wholly surrender to the little man. It was the influence of a dream —a dream in which the barefoot man with burning eyes was seen to be the bulwark of the Church—that made the Pope give Francis the first promises of approval and support. The promise seems a bit cautious as we read it today—knowing, as we do, the whole historic depth and strength of the Franciscan revolution—but we have to remember that Francis was practically unknown and untried, that the Pope had enormous responsibilities for the entire

135

world, and that there was no possible means of knowing that Francis was initiating a movement which would rejuvenate Christianity to its marrow. The Church was already very old and had known many vicissitudes. It is not surprising that the Pope was reluctant to engage himself without reserve in support of so novel an experiment as the effort to live literally by the Sermon on the Mount.

All that had happened years before and now the great Pope was dead. Innocent III had preached many crusades, not all against the Saracen. His last was the Fifth Crusade, proclaimed to the Lateran Council in 1215, the year before he died. This was the most unified and organized effort of them all. It is recorded that the Council hardly discussed anything: it did little but register the decrees of the great Pope, the undisputed master of the time. Young Frederick II in Germany took the cross. The Truce of God was proclaimed for all Europe to last for four years from the year 1217, when the Crusade was to begin.

Now, a man like Innocent III could not possibly have beheld the Little Poor Man of Assisi, and given him support and sanction for five or six years, without having a very special feeling in his regard. Young Frederick must, really, have felt something too, for he was sensitive as we know, and the young are impressionable, and Francis must have been a pretty startling apparition at an imperial court. In the case of Innocent we have the further human supposition that he, who was not a priest except as an indispensable and belated adjunct to being Pope, felt particularly drawn to the little man who was also not a priest and yet burned with undeniable religious genius. Furthermore, the obsession of Innocent's life was Jerusalem. He could never forget it although he had never seen it. That was the real explanation of his crusades, which were less political than almost any other in origin.

And Honorius III, his successor, a man of learning and piety, seems to have wished above all to carry out the wishes of the great

136

Innocent. In a sense, Honorius inherited Francis of Assisi. It was Honorius who gave the final paper approval to the Franciscan Order in 1223. Honorius devoted himself to the Fifth Crusade, to pacifying Frederick II, and to the final purpose of unity which animated Innocent's life—that is, unity of the Western world and if possible reunion with the East. Honorius was Innocent's posthumous legate in all these momentous concerns.

Now, it is my considered opinion, based upon what is universally known of human nature, that Francis on his strange journey to Palestine had the benefit of august protections. Emperor and Pope watched over him, perhaps very secretly and indirectly, perhaps by absolute orders. Who can tell? The early biographers of Francis were saints themselves, unworldly creatures, and what could they know or guess about emperors and popes? Francis was willing to talk to an emperor or a pope about what concerned him deeply, such as his barefoot brothers the *Jongleurs de Dieu* or his sisters the birds, but he could have had no real conception of what such men were up against, the weight of their preoccupations, their methods of work, the breadth and complexity of their daily tasks. It probably never occurred to him that either Innocent III or Honorius III watched over him from afar, and least of all that the brilliant young Emperor should have given him a thought.

And yet, regardless of documentary evidence, is it humanly possible that they should not have done so? Arguing simply from the experience of life, is it conceivable that Francis of Assisi could have been, by 1219, in any way obscure, unknown or disregarded? I think not. And I think it would have been downright silly of Frederick II, whether he was in Germany or in Palermo, not to request and obtain dispatches from his crusading armies about this strangely powerful little man who had come among them. Orders he *must* have given; and these must have been orders for protec-tion. That they do not survive and that we know nothing of them hardly matters one way or the other. If we know anything about human nature at all we must see that Francis, after almost twenty years of journeying up and down Italy and Spain and Africa, was fully recognized as one of the phenomena of the time and perhaps already of all time. Frederick II was not stupid and neither was Pope Honorius III, who explicitly sanctioned both St. Francis and St. Dominic and thus simultaneously proved his sagacity and his catholicity.

Furthermore—I continue the hypothesis without worrying about the absence of proof—the Sultan Malik el-Kamil must have known all this. The Ayyubite kings were capable, astute, educated and humane. This particular family—Saladin and his brothers Malik el-Adil and Malik el-Kamil—were the pride of their race. We in the English-speaking world learn as children that Saladin, the pattern of the "noble Arab," even though of Kurdish origin, was recognized by the Lion-hearted Richard as a knight of chivalry. The behavior of Sultan Malik el-Kamil towards Francis of Assisi convinces me not only of his courteous and noble personality (of which there has never been any doubt) but, what is more, that he knew all about St. Francis before he ever set eyes on him.

In other words, what I propose as a reasonable hypothesis based upon what we know of human beings is this: that Francis was protected not only by that which was innate in himself, not only by the awe with which all men regard the true and the good, not only by whatever one may feel to be the spiritual powers of the existing world, but also, and quite, quite simply, by the authority of Pope and Emperor and Sultan, all three. This has never been suggested before in works known to me, and I cannot imagine why. It seems that scholars and historians think nothing true unless it be supported by documents of unquestionable authenticity. Such caution is laudable where facts are concerned; but here there is no question of fact. We have the facts. What is lacking is a plausible or acceptable explanation of the facts. How can a barefoot little man, not only unarmed but with no possessions of any sort, begging for his bread from the soldiers of all nations, pass between opposing armies in a time of war and return again unharmed, untouched, after a sojourn of months in the land he called holy?

The protection of Pope, Emperor and Sultan would not be enough in itself to ensure the immunity of the little man at all times and places. The crusaders were rough fellows and did not take too kindly to any effort made to convert them to their own religion. Most of them thought—and indeed it was the idea of the crusades—that merely by going to Egypt and besieging the port city of Damietta they were satisfying the requirements for eternal salvation. Did they not wear the cross? Why then should they bear it as well? Francis talked to deaf ears.

And yet these rough fellows who had left their homes to redeem, as they said, the Holy Sepulchre, and who thought themselves entitled by the crusader's indulgence to sin at will, and who did not like the climate of Egypt anyhow, could not have been hostile to Francis. We have no indication of hostility towards him on the part of any human being or animal after his twenty-first year. They probably regarded him principally as a bore—disquieting at times, particularly with those burning eyes that seemed to look far beneath the surface when he regarded you straight, but a bore and a chatterbox just the same. I imagine that they gave him bread, wine and pity, and thought of something else.

But the Arabs were not crusaders: they were merely defending their territory against invasion. They had no indulgences and they were then, as now, a people with no repulsion towards violence. Why did they spare the barefoot Italian, the Christian preacher, who walked through their armies begging, talking, singing, mad as a hatter no doubt, but also in all probability a spy for the Frankish troops?

They spared him first of all because he had the safe-conduct of the Sultan Malik el-Kamil, a written guaranty of safety in all Islam. Furthermore I have no doubt that the Moslem prince watched over him all during his months in Palestine, sending guards to follow him and protect him wherever he went. Francis would never have known. He was too entranced with the dream-journey. As he walked singing on the high road to Bethlehem I can imagine the shadows that came and went along the road, making sure that he was safe. In the dark ways of Jerusalem at night they may have come to him sometimes and said: "Go home, little brother, the city is not safe tonight. And when he walked from Jerusalem up the road to Tiberias and on to the Galilean hills there were always in his neighborhood, if I am right, some agents or emissaries of the Great King, and every village elder was aware of his passing.

At this time we can see the studious Pope Honorius toiling at his desk late at night, reading reports and writing answers: this for Norway and that for Spain. We can see him lift his head in the candle-light and look into the shadows of the vast room in the Lateran and say to himself: and what of that Little Poor Man? What is becoming of him in the land of the heretic and infidel? And he writes to the Cardinal-Legate Pelagius, field commander of the Christian armies before Damietta, to enjoin care and ask for information.

Frederick II stands in a sort of perpetual tapestry, a handsome young man in *pourpoint vert* with a falcon on his wrist, two mistresses at either side and four pageboys at his feet, while the troubadour sings to his lute in the Provençal language and the business of the empire waits round the corner. He is too young to care much about the Crusade, even though he wears the cross. He has promised over and over that he will go to Egypt to command the armies, of which he is officially commander-in-chief, and he does not go. But his mother Constance was Italian-born, and he feels himself to be Italian, and king of Italy like his father before him. So he, too, says: Where is the little man? What has become of him? See that orders are given in Egypt.

140

Meanwhile it is easy to imagine Francis sitting cross-legged on the shore of the Lake of Galilee, at Tiberias for instance, rubbing his tired feet while the Arabs push food into his mouth in their perennial manner and ask him polite questions. He must have picked up a little Arabic rather soon, for he had a great gift for speech (his French and his Provençal were quickly acquired too). He would have tried to speak to them of his pilgrimage and its reasons, of the great image he bore in his heart, that of the Lord Jesus, and of the desirability for them to abandon their own religion and adopt his. They would have been eminently courteous and kind, but he could have made little or no progress. The very fact that the Prophet Mohammed (Upon Whom Be Peace) revered the Christian religion and taught so much of it has always been a stumbling-block for those who wish to make it exclude all others. Francis must have looked across that lake at the blue hills of Moab and wondered. What had become of his brothers the *Jongleurs de Dieu?* He had left them partly through longing for Galilee and partly because the growing multitude of his followers had begun to oppress his spirit. He could not govern; he could not administer; he could not lay down the law. He was a follower himself. When the follower is followed what does he do? It was soon after this that Francis gave over all responsibilities for the Franciscan Order to others.

The fresh fish in baskets by the shore at Tiberias are cooked over the fire and the Arabs squatting under the lean-to of woven palm-leaves thrust them into the visitor's mouth as an earnest of hospitality, urging him thereafter to help himself. Francis, musing over his brothers the infidels, undoubtedly wondered at their courtesy and grace, their solicitude for his comfort. He had not expected anything of the sort: he had expected, hoped and longed for martyrdom. He had prayed for it repeatedly, had sought it in Spain and Africa. He would preach the Cross to the ferocious heathen and they would kill him for it. But instead of this result, what did

141

he find? Not only no hand was raised against him—the Sultan's orders may well have caused that: everything was consideration and kindliness equal to his own. Why should anybody have killed St. Francis? Even when he urged his hosts to abandon their own religion, held by their fathers for five or six hundred years, he did so in the terms of gentle courtesy native to him and explicit in every word he left behind him. So that, in addition to the safe-conduct from the Sultan, he had also this most powerful force, the force of innocence and good will.

And as he saw, here and in Jerusalem and everywhere along the way, that martyrdom was not for him—although several of his own followers had already braved it and suffered it—he must have cast his mind back to that strange interview with the Sultan Malik el-Kamil, the brother of Saladin. He had been taken prisoner (by design of course, although we do not know the details) and went into the tent of the Great King ready for death. We may suppose that the tent was of some rough, heavy cloth like canvas on the outside, but hung with silks and spread with carpets inside, and quite possibly with flowers and scents as well, even though this was war. The Saracen ruler was not far from the front lines, some-where in the Isthmus of Suez. Francis began to speak to him in French, which the Sultan spoke well, and without any hesitation delivered him the admonition to abandon his own religion, take the cross and surrender Jerusalem. It is recorded that the Sultan listened politely, asked courteous questions, elicited the information that the little man wished to walk though the country to Jerusalem, Bethlehem, and Nazareth, and forthwith granted him the permission and wrote out the safe-conduct. What Francis was too unworldly to know is that the Sultan could have sent orders to every official in the whole country between the Jordan and the sea to let this man pass in peace and watch over his safety. There were many Christians in Palestine—indeed there have been for two thousand years up to just now—but they were natives of the country: this was possibly the only pilgrim from Europe between Suez and the Hellespont.

So he was safe and, although grieving over the denial of his desire for martyrdom, must have been grateful in his usual sunny way to those whom he met along the road. There at Tiberias, with the silver fish jumping in the wicker baskets and the warm air tempered by the palm-leaves overhead, he may even have been happy. And when he arose to go who can doubt that he offered the Arabs his prayers, as they offered him theirs, even though in divergent forms?

So he took the road that leads up past Magdala, the village where there was a woman with long hair, hair long enough to dry the feet she had washed. From there on the road rises through the exquisite hills of Galilee, and at this turn or that you can glimpse the lake. Francis would have gasped at the flowers. The wild anemone in all its range of beauty is perhaps the chief of these, but there are many others, many I could not name at all. Then you get up into the interior to a higher and cooler region where, at last, on a high part of the great slope, is the village of Nazareth.

This was for many centuries, until only about three years ago, one of the few entirely Christian villages in that or any other part of the world. In the time of Francis there would have been the same small but homogeneous community that has been there for almost two thousand years. There were, of course, no Franciscans then, as there are now. (The Franciscans at Nazareth, at Gethsemane and at Bethlehem, as well as in Jerusalem, were no part of the vision of Francis so far as we know: they came by themselves.) It has appeared to me that Nazareth alone, in a land of unceasing bloodshed, speaks of peace, breathes peace, in a manner unknown elsewhere. We may assume that the Little Poor Man felt this, too, among other things, as his feet pressed the anemones.

The exact sequence of his journey is not known. He could have continued through Galilee from Nazareth and returned down the

143

coast to the Sultan at Suez. He could equally well, and I think it psychologically more probable, have turned back the way he came and revisited Tiberias on the road to Jerusalem. He would probably have wanted to return to Jerusalem once more before taking his leave. It might be a little longer, but it would have suited him better. He could memorize every cobblestone in the street called Via Crucis, leading from the great Mosque (where there is the Rock of Abraham's sacrifice) to the basilica and crypt of the Holy Sepulchre. The street at the top of the hill, alongside the Holy Sepulchre, has been called the Street of the Christians for many centuries. (It was almost destroyed by bombardment three years ago.) Francis probably lodged there with some Arab Christian family or priest. We know none of these details. We may, however, be quite sure that he felt to his depths the beauty of the summer stars over Jerusalem, since he probably slept on the roof (as most do) and touched their nearness with his wondering eyes.

It is traditional that he prayed often and much in the Garden of Gethsemane, across the valley from the great Mosque. The Franciscans have had this place in their special care for centuries: two of them suffered martyrdom there at the hands of the Zionist terrorists four years ago—the martyrdom that Francis sought in vain.

So he returned to the Sultan, who listened to him politely and saw him safely transferred to the Christian lines; and the Christians sent him back to Italy, no doubt with a great sigh of relief.

Francis had not much longer to walk the roads. First he had to get rid of the troublesome details of administering an enormous organization. He had never intended any such thing. When people came to him and said they wanted to do as he did and take the vows of poverty, chastity and obedience, he did not feel entitled to refuse. Years before it had been by ones or twos that they came; now it was by the thousands, and he was appalled. His idea of a vast assembly of the brothers was that they should simply come to the Porziuncola, and nothing further in the way of organization

144

was required: food, drink and shelter would be forthcoming some-how. (It was: the whole population for miles around provided it.) It is easy to imagine how this impracticality stunned St. Dominic, who attended the meeting *à titre d'information*. Dominic's great-ness was of another kind.

The fact that Francis abdicated all control of the revolutionary society he had founded has been much discussed in literature, but what seems to me most significant about it is that it came imme-diately upon his return from Palestine. We may speculate as we will as to the effect of Nazareth, Tiberias, Bethlehem and Jerusalem on his humble heart. What we know is that as soon as he got back to Italy he gave up every vestige of authority over other human beings. His words at the great assembly were:

"Lord, I give Thee back this great family which Thou didst en-trust to me. Thou knowest, most sweet Jesus, that I have no more the power and the qualities to continue to take care of it. I entrust it, therefore, to the ministers. Let them be responsible before Thee at the Day of Judgment, if any brother by their negligence, or by their bad example, or by a too severe punishment, shall go astray."

He was free again to heal the sick, to tend the leper, to walk the roads and sing. Two years before his death he went up to Monte Alverno and undertook to fast and pray for forty days, after which he had his great vision and experienced the Stigmata. His feet had been crucified for many years; now they showed the signs.

A flower grows beside the Basilica of St. Francis at Assisi. I think it is a white rose: I cannot find out just now without disturb-ing people who have other work to do. The books accessible to me do not mention it. It is in any case a white flower which blooms unseasonably, all the year round as I remember. It may be a de-scendant of the anemones of Galilee. At any rate it was blooming, and most unseasonably, on the wintry day when I last visited Assisi.

145

ROBERT FARREN

*

St. Thomas of Aquin

We could in a way more properly speak of Juvenal Aquinas than we can of Thomas Aquinas, for the satirist *was* born at Aquino while the philosopher was not, though the latter's surname derives from the name of the town. It was Roccasecca, a few miles further north in the Kingdom of Naples (now the Abruzzi region of Italy) that was Thomas's actual birthplace, but Aquino was the town which gave his father his title, Count of Aquin. The birthplace is certain, the year of birth—1225—only probable. Landulf was his father, Theodora (in her own right Countess of Theate) his mother. The boy, then, the seventh son among possibly eight and possibly twelve children, had Norman blood from his mother, Italian and imperial from his father—for Emperor Frederic Barbarossa's sister Francesca was Landulf's mother. Supposing Thomas to have been born in 1225, he appeared in the year before St. Francis of Assisi died, the year in which St. Louis of France became king.

When he was five, in 1230, he was sent to Monte Cassino, the famous Benedictine monastery, to begin his schooling. It was near,

146

it was celebrated, his uncle Landulf Sinibaldi was Abbot, Count Landulf wished to make peace with the Benedictines, and Count Landulf was ambitious for his sons. As to the making of peace, the Count had a while before assailed the cloister with arms. As to the ambition, Thomas was a second venture where a first had failed. Giacomo, the second son, had been elected Abbot of the Church of San Pietro di Canneto, but papal prescriptions had been unobserved and the Pope had annulled the election. It was the age of the "benefice," with or without the "cure of souls": by no means all of those who lived by the Gospel did so because they preached the Gospel or were ordained to do so; it took a long time to make dues and duties go together, to restrict Church revenues to men who earned them by ministry; and meantime the Landulfs looked for their share for their sons. Thomas would be Abbot at Monte Cassino and in consequence the equal of many a temporal lord.

He was well taught and they say he learned well; but of the nine years he spent there only one story is told. It is that he used to ask his teachers "What is God?"

He was about fourteen, in 1239, when his uncle Barbarossa's grandson, Frederic the Second, invaded Monte Cassino and expelled the monks; Thomas of course was sent home. According to his contemporary biographer, Peter Calo, the Abbot, his uncle, wrote to Thomas's father to advise further schooling; he should be sent to Naples, Landulf Sinibaldi said, for it would be a pity that a boy of such talents should be left in obscurity. Naples, besides, was another family place, for Emperor Frederic the Second, who had cut short Thomas's schooling at Monte Cassino, had founded a university (or *Studium Generale*) in Naples in 1224, a year before Thomas was born. So to Naples Thomas went, in the same year, 1239, as he had left Monte Cassino.

Two things happened to the boy in Naples, two seminal things for Europe and the Catholic Church. In the city of *Stupor Mundi*

147

(for so they called Frederic) Thomas met the Dominicans and for the first time heard of Aristotle.

William of Tocco, an early biographer who heard and saw Thomas at the height of his fame, is one of those who tell us the story about Naples. They tell us that Peter of Ireland, one of Thomas's masters, had a profound knowledge of the teaching and writings of Aristotle, having composed commentaries on some of the books of the Greek, and that he communicated to Thomas his passion for the master. If ever Peter encountered Albert the Great, the midwife of Thomas's thought, the two old men must have wondered at the child of their schools.

The Dominicans were in Naples. In 1231, eight years before Thomas came to the University to study in the Faculty of Arts, they had founded a school for theology which was incorporated with the University; and not far away from the latter was their Church of San Domenico Maggiore. A child who persisted in enquiring "What is God?" might easily grow into a boy attracted by a school of theology; but we do not know anything which shows that the school drew him on. We know, on the other hand, that he used to pray in San Domenico, as he naturally would, and we know that he and some of the Friars Preachers noticed one another. The Dominican order very justly sees the hand of God in the boy's inclination to join them, and the Church as a whole very justly allows that his subsequent life is evidence for that belief; but simply on the plane of ordinary human psychology we may see a romantic motive in the boy, and a desire for the enrichment of the talent of his order in the priest who encouraged him—Friar John of St. Julian it was, according to the old Life by William de Tocco. On the boy's side there was the strangeness and the queerness of the Mendicants, with their tart appeal to Gospel poverty, which was setting on edge the teeth of many upright Churchmen, and on the priest's side there was divination of extraordinary temper in the boy. Boy and priest understood one another and Thomas be-

148

came a Dominican novice and received the habit. The year is uncertain; it is given as variously as 1240, 1241, 1243 and 1244; but April 1244 has strong support, and Thomas's age at that time (he would be nineteen) would be sufficient to make the serious decision possible. Dr. Grabmann says it was in San Domenico Maggiore, and at the hands of the Prior, Thomas Agni, that the habit was received.

The Dominicans rejoiced and Thomas's relatives were horrified: we have the witness of the time in the very words of the time. "The friars of the aforesaid Order," says William de Tocco, "exulted in the Lord, because a youth so well-born and so admirable was theirs by divine destination: one for whom they hoped already from the clearest signs the attainment of the summits of achievement."

The horror of the relatives is easy to comprehend; the Catholic family does not always welcome its members' vocations, more especially when the family is propertied, powerful, and thirsty for further aggrandisement, and still more especially when the vocation is, although acceptable to the Church, in some sort unconventional. Young Thomas's people had something of this character in them; and Thomas had chosen the barely respectable mendicants, the Beggars. Landulf and Theodora had nothing against a vocation; they had prescribed a vocation for Thomas, when Giacomo had failed; but a vocation was one thing, and social dereliction another: the ancient and encrusted splendour of the Benedictines was not to be given up for a beggar's coat. Thomas's people were horrified: they could scarcely have been more so had their son changed Bible for Koran, declaring for Allah and Mohammed and a Paradise of Houris.

Norman mettle is prompt and definite in action. Theodora sent word to others of her sons, who were serving with the Emperor in Tuscany, to fetch back Thomas; and they, riding out, apprehended him at Acquapendente on his way to Paris, the Master-General himself (called John the Teuton) having taken the novice in his personal charge to hurry him beyond the clutching hands of his relations. (The Mendicants, no doubt, had been forced to develop such arts; and remember that Thomas was of an age to make his own choice.) Rainaldo the poet and the other brothers brought Thomas home to Theodora, and the runaway was clapped in one of the family fortresses, the Castle of Monte San Giovanni, not far from Roccasecca. That was in May 1244, and they say he was jailed for a year.

The Dominicans did not give him up too easily. They appealed to Pope Innocent IV, who ordered the Emperor to seize the captors, which he promptly did, requesting the Dominicans to advance their complaints against them. They, however, "for fear of scandal," we are told, "and because they had learned that Thomas still wore the habit," desisted. They found means to bring him new habits also, his sister saw that books were put on his table, and with iron placidity he read and practised his Rule. The books—the Scriptures, the *Sentences* of Peter Lombard and the *Metaphysics* of Aristotle—continued the line of his instructors so far; the habit asserted his vocation visibly; and the practice of the Preachers' Rule formed him interiorly. Prison was not to interrupt this plan, which was Thomas's and God's.

Force not succeeding, the family attempted persuasion. Marotta, his eldest sister, argued with Thomas, endeavouring to reason him out of his obsession with the Beggars; but instead, with his assistance, she reasoned herself into another vocation and became a Benedictine nun. Marotta did not know (how could she?) what a work she took on; one does not suspect one's young brother of a mind like a star.

Persuasion failed and the family tried degradation. Tocco's chronicle, with genuine Biblical bluntness, tells us the story. A girl, whom with medieval justice the friar's text allows to have been very beautiful (*puellam pulcherrimam*) was sent to Thomas in the room in which he slept; she was decked in her fancy-woman's finery (*cultu meretricio perornatam*) and her orders were, by look and touch and toying and whatever other means might occur to her, to incite him to sin. These Aquinases, like the Borgias in a later time, could fashion all manner of men; in the one Latin family were material and impulse towards saint, robber baron, poet and unprincipled ruffian. For freezing viciousness, for a prime sample of what "the martyrs call the world," this effort to savage innocence and thereby break the wing of spirituality could hardly be bettered: one's flesh grows antic, so pitch it down in the sty. Beyond her probable trade and her beauty we know nothing of the girl, but she must have been innocence itself compared with the Aquinases—and anyway she got the fright of her life from Thomas, which may have done her good. She showed herself as bidden, but her looks were all she was given time to employ. Thomas, of whom so far as I know no other violent action is recorded in the whole of his forty-nine years, pulled out a brand from the fire and ran in a blaze at the girl. She vanished before the enormous man with the fire in his hand, and Thomas charred the door with the sign of the Cross.

We are told he never afterwards suffered temptation against chastity. Neither did he suffer any more from his obstinate family, and in Dominic's family he proved a model of obedience. They let him go from his first to his second family: in a basket down the wall of San Giovanni, if the story is true; and Peter Calo says he had taught himself in captivity as well as the *Studium Generale* could have done it in freedom. But that may be partly the Friar Preachers' humility, for the order had a teacher to offer who was worthy of the pupil, and whose name indeed does not die in the greater light. For even a Thomas Aquinas was not too good a pupil for an Albert of Swabia, who was given the uncommon honour among medievals of being actually named in the philosophical texts of his time (*Albertus* they said when quoting or referring to him, whereas almost every other philosopher was simply *quidam*: a certain man); who fathered scientific observation for modern times; and who was one of the foremost of Aristotle's sponsors, in the West. Albert also, we may say, made the Friars Preachers a philosophizing order, declaiming against the know-nothings who "fight against the study of philosophy, and chiefly among the Preachers where there is none to resist them, even as brute animals blaspheming what they do not know."

Released from San Giovanni, his vocation ratified after interrogation by Innocent IV in person, Thomas resumed the interrupted journey to Paris, again accompanied by the Master-General, John the Teuton of Wildhausen. It was in 1245, in the autumn, that Thomas came near Notre Dame; from that year until 1248 he studied under Albert in Paris; and when Albert went to Cologne to found its *Studium Generale* Thomas went with him, and was taught until 1252.

The picture of Thomas in Albert's classroom is ancient, attractive and well known. To those who restrict the Italian racial types to lean, small darting bodies and machine-gun tongues he must seem as Germanic as his master, a looming, corpulent man, deliberate of pace and silent as a stone. The school, like all schools, was aflow with animal spirits, there were nimble talents and slick tongues there, and catching the master's attention and guying the dunces was as prevalent as anywhere that chalk-dust flies by a blackboard. Nicknames abound among students and Thomas got his own, his being grandnephew to the Emperor adding extra spice. *Bos Mutus* they called him in Latin, or in English the Dumb Ox. Thomas didn't mind, even if he knew what they called him. He didn't mind either when a compassionate co-scholar tried to help him with a lesson. And when the co-scholar bogged in the tuition Thomas took it up, and even added points which Albert hadn't taught them at all. Albert was told of the spark in the stone, and there is a story of his eavesdropping happily and another of

ST. JOHN OF THE CROSS

by Salvador Dali

his reading a purloined notebook of Thomas's; but the famous
story concerns his getting speech, almost as though it were blood,
from the stone. He kept Thomas talking and "disputing" in front
of the class for quite a time one day, and burst out with the
teacher's special joy: which is the joy of drawing out the dunce to
put manners on the smart ones. "We call him the Dumb Ox," said
Albert—and you can see him beaming and shutting the book with
a bang—"but some fine day the Ox will let out such a bellow of instruction, that it will sound to the four corners of the world."

Apart from his ripening in the summer of Albert's content we
know at least four things that happened to Thomas in Cologne.
He heard that his brother Rainaldo the poet had died. He saw on
August 15th, 1248, the beginning of the building of Cologne
Cathedral, for which Albert (they say) had drawn up the plans.
He saw, on January 6th, 1252, William of Holland, King of the
Romans, come to visit Albert the Great, Thomas's master. Most
important of all, Conrad of Hochstaden, Archbishop of Cologne,
ordained Thomas priest, probably in 1250, when he was twenty-
five, and he began to celebrate that *corporis mysterium* of which
he would later cry *Pange, lingua* when he came to write the liturgical office for the Feast of the Body of Christ.

It was Albert again who put him in the middle of things. The
Order had to name a "Bachelor" for its House of Studies at the
Convent of Saint-Jacques in Paris; Albert said Thomas was the
man; the General hesitated; Albert canvassed the Papal Legate
who was luckily in Cologne, and Thomas went to Paris. From
1252, at twenty-seven years of age, until 1259 at thirty-four, he lec-
tured and taught in the city of philosophers; but right off the reel
his line got tangled in the weeds. There was another Paris philosopher, impressively but inappropriately known as William of Holy
Love, who was one of the worst of the weeds. The trouble was the
rivalry of the secular clergy with the regulars. The seculars tried
to have it ruled that a religious order might not occupy above one

153

chair of the Faculty of Theology: but this special constitutional plea was put in the shade by a general assault on the religious state as such; and these professional and ascetical disputes were embittered further by a student broil with the City's night patrol, and by the issue of the broil:—one student dead, one mauled and jailed; friction between University and Civil authority; a strike of protest at the University Dominican and Franciscan professors lecturing away and capturing the students. Aquinas did not broil and neither did he wrangle about strikes or chairs; the defence of the state of the religious was the high theme and the speculative one, and on this he debated. William of Holy Love (it is perhaps unfair to translate his name: Guillaume de Saint-Amour they called him in Burgundy and Paris and it sounds less ironical) smote the regulars with a tract, entitling it as his sort commonly do *The Modern Peril, De periculis novissimorum temporum.* Aquinas replied with another, *Contra impugnantes Dei cultum. De periculis,* in the event, was condemned, and William banished, but Thomas's admission as a master of theology was delayed by the quarrel, in which as a Dominican he was willy-nilly involved.

He had, however, begun that inky flood of his writings which is one of the great rivers across time, and he sat from 1256 to 1259 in one of the Dominican chairs at Paris, urbanely and undesigningly charging his name with renown, by teaching well. He was far from "bellowing," but his voice began to go about; Paris, so long ago, herded to his lectures as it did before his day to those of Peter Abelard, as it did some decades since to the lectures of Henri Bergson. The fame had started; Albert was beginning to be proved a prophet.

And here, as we watch his fame begin, a word may be said. Aquinas was not an academic thinker, but a new thinker. He was not praised in his day for being safe and orthodox. Many, in fact, did not praise him but denounced him; for he excited consternation as much as he did admiration.

Aquinas, it is true, was a managed man, which every man with a vow of obedience must be. They said, "Come to Paris" and he came, they said "Go to Rome" and he went, they required him to compose a book for the mission to the Moors and he wrote it like a boy doing sums. He was, even in the thick of controversy, a peaceful man, mild almost to the point of insipidity. But he was not conventional, safe, old-fashioned or academic as a philosopher. For the thing which made him famous *and* notorious was his new-ness, which is to say his originality. We had better have Tocco's own words, or as near as the English will go to them. "He raised new issues in his lectures, instituted a new and perspicuous method of discussion and solution, and employed it to demonstrate fresh and original ideas; so that none who heard him teach new things, and with new thoughts put an end to uncertainty, could doubt but that God had illumined him with rays of new light.

But now, having made this point, we return to his life. In 1259 leaving Paris, Thomas attended the General Chapter of his order at Valenciennes, and collaborated with Albert the Great and Peter of Tarentasia (afterwards Pope Innocent V) in formulating a system of studies (including the "profane" or secular sciences)—which system, a Dominican author tells us, is substantially preserved in Dominican centres today. At this same Chapter Raymond of Pennafort set Thomas to the writing of one of his major books, the *Summa Contra Gentiles*, the work for the mission to the Moors.

For almost ten years he lived in Italy. "He was certainly no gadabout," says Father Martin D'Arcy; to which I answer he was certainly a Peripatetic. Roccasecca, Monte Cassino, Naples, Rome, Paris, Cologne, Orvieto, Viterbo, Anagni—Aquinas lived in them all, choosing none of his own will but each at the will of another. The will of one Pope after another attached him to Papal Courts and schools, and he taught, preached, counselled and wrote for ten years in the light or shadow of the *Curia*. What they thought of him may be inferred from Clement IV's offer of the Archbishopric of Naples (which Thomas refused), from his being chosen by Urban IV to write the Office for the new feast of Corpus Christi, and from these words of Henry the Poet of Würzburg, which Monsignor Grabmann believes to refer to Aquinas:

"There [at the house of the Pope] is one who would become the founder of a new philosophy, if the old philosophy were lying in ruins; As a new builder he would rebuild it in better fashion."

He was *at* the centre and *of* the centre of the Catholic and European world, a witness of momentous outward acts, and as far as he cared or was obliged to be, a participant in them and a shaper of them. But it mattered more to Thomas that he had leisure for writing, that he met in the *Curia* William of Moerbeke, and that they gave him Reginald of Piperno as secretary and companion. He wrote of course mountainously, though serenely and without scamping; tens of millions of words can be proved to be his; and in this time of his life he worked on his masterpiece, the *Summa Theologica*. There is a story that he dictated to three secretaries at the same time . . . Bound up with his thought and writing was the work of Moerbeke, who was precious to Thomas for his proficiency in Greek, and who, urged on by Thomas, made precise Latin versions of some of the works of Aristotle to replace the suspect and tainted Arabian versions. Thomas's close knowledge of Aristotle may be traced to Moerbeke, as well as to Albert and to Peter of Ireland and to his own investigations. Reginald of Piperno became his dear companion: they say he was like eyes and hands to Thomas—his relict (so to speak) in the common daylight when Thomas was "deep down things," withdrawn distantly from sense in the mines of his thought—and they say that Reginald sat with him at table and was careful of what Thomas would eat. Thomas, at the same time, was none of your thinkers of Laputa in Gulliver's fable; they did not rap him gently with a bladder full of peas to prevent his feet stepping over the edge of the world; Father D'Arcy reminds us that he was punctual in observing the appointments of his Rule, and that so also do not the mere wool-gatherers. When a mind is such a mind, and goes about its lawful occasions, then that mind has its leave of absence from wine and bread.

In the autumn of 1268, according to Grabmann, but in the beginning of 1269 according to others, Aquinas returned to Paris as professor, being then about forty-three. Only one other Dominican master filled a Paris chair a second time, and Thomas owed his return to the need which was felt for his presence at the time. For the divines and the dialecticians were still divided, and now their quarrels went down to the groundwork of thought. It was, as the late Father Arthur Little has well said, "one of the decisive battles of the world, on which far more depended for the health of Europe than ever depended on Waterloo."

Aristotle was the ultimate cause of the battle.

Aristotle reached the Scholastics originally through the translations and commentaries of Arabian philosophers. Of these philosophers (who were of course Mahometans) Averrhoes was the chief at the time; and his heresies, conjoined with Aristotle's own paganism, were bound in that age of Faith to make all of Aristotle suspect. The suspicion was aggravated among the conservative thinkers by the disrespect which (according to the conservatives) the Aristotelians showed to St. Augustine, who was until then the chief of the Fathers and the first of Christian philosophers. Thomas's task was threefold. He had first to cut away the Arabian additions to Aristotle; he had next to correct the errors of the master himself; and he had finally to reconcile Augustine and Aristotle—the former's philosophy being bound up with that of Plato, which of course had been criticized by Aristotle.

It was a delicate task, especially as the public and private teaching of the works of Aristotle was officially prohibited by the Church; though it seems that duly qualified persons were left free to study him in private, as Albert and Aquinas and scores of others did, without interference.

157

It is important to grasp the point of this censure and to know how it came to be made. There was (chiefly in Paris) a party which worshipped Aristotle: for them he had proved conclusively everything he held, and to go against him was to go against reason itself. The worship, to make matters worse, extended to Averrhoes, who had taught them to know what Aristotle himself had taught. Between them they described the whole perimeter of truth. Differ from these two and you differed from truth and reason, even though infallible Faith could not be wrong. No wonder the Church was on guard.

For Thomas the Faith and Revelation were divinely attested, and no philosophy was true if it went against them. But in its own sphere reason had its rights, and Aristotle's thought was natural wisdom of the first water, which must be saved for men. We may state his task once again in the light of these tenets, and see it more clearly.

He had to show that Greek came before Arabian: that even if Averrhoes were wrong, Aristotle could still be right. He had next to show that in most of his main propositions Aristotle *was* indeed right. He had then to correct him where he contradicted the Faith, but even in so doing he must not bring its teaching into play, except when the problem was demonstrably insoluble by reason. He had lastly to accommodate his position with that of the Old Augustinian thinkers.

Siger of Brabant was Thomas's principal opponent among the Averrhoists; a subtle-minded, complex man who by his skilful writing and striking character made himself the pivot of a numerous and influential party. It has been charged against him that he held there were two truths, the truth of reason and the truth of faith, and that the two could co-exist and exact assent even when contradictory. The authorities do not all accept this charge as proven, but what is certain is that he charged the air of philosophy with equivocation, that he supported a corrupting ambiguity at the heart of human thinking, that his expositions of others' false reasoning were not sufficiently countered by him when he subjoined to them bare statements of dogma, and that with hints and modifications and counter-statements he was shifty at the best. Thomas fought against him for the purity of unequivocal truth and for a fully candid and consistent doctrine of the complementary relations of reason and revelation. The extent of Thomas's success is nowhere better shown than in Siger's own writings, in which, whether because he had honestly yielded to high arguments or because he feared discipline, he gave ground more and more, reaching finally a largely Thomistic position. He did, in the end, come under heavy censure; he left Paris for Italy and died about ten years later.

Thomas had defeated the Averrhoists philosophically, and both by his work in Paris and his writings in general he attained his other aims, but only the defeat of the Averrhoists was generally allowed to him. Many still deplored his Aristotelian doctrines and his alleged abandonment of Augustine; when in 1277 (three years after Thomas's death) Averrhoistic propositions were condemned by the Bishop of Paris, several of the teachings of Thomas were included in the list; and these were only withdrawn from condemnation fifty-one years later, when Thomas was declared infallibly to be a saint. Even after the canonisation, opposition to Thomism continued for many a long day, but its champions were always many and finally prevailed.

In 1272 Thomas's superiors called him away from Paris and replaced him with a more Augustinian thinker; the Paris professors petitioned the Dominicans to have Thomas sent back, but they were refused. There may be several explanations, but we need not seek them; they do not matter greatly, for two years later Thomas Aquinas was dead. He was forty-nine when he died, and was on his way to the Council of Lyons, to which Gregory X had summoned him. It was at the Abbey of Fossanova, between Naples and Rome, that he took ill, and the Cistercians tended him in the last weeks of his life, distressing his humility by their loving care of him. They knew him for a saint and the whole world knew it very soon.

You cannot put such a life into a dozen pages; you can simply suggest what it was and send readers further to adequate accounts. But much less than tell Aquinas's life in these pages can I say what his work was and how significant it is. One can hint at it by saying that he is the prince of theologians, the great master of Christian philosophers, the reconciler of the Greek with the Hebrew and the Latin genius; and one can say that the Popes praise him in a tireless succession of words. One can say that the hand of Thomas is discernible in every orthodox theologian, and that the other day, when Pius XII spoke about the age of the world to the Pontifical Academy of the Sciences, the bone of his discourse was an argument which Thomas perfected. One can say that the revival of his thought in the past fifty years, after centuries of neglect and contempt amongst most intellectuals, is one of the chief facts of our time. One can say that the dignity of the Catholic intelligence, its superb comprehensiveness and penetrating clarity, are manifested and sustained in him unassailably and fructifyingly. And after ejaculating in this fashion, unsatisfactorily, one can first thank God abundantly for Thomas and then go and read him, the Perennial Philosopher.

BARBARA WARD

*

St. Thomas More

In this troubled and angry world one of the great difficulties in approaching the saints is to be able to believe in their relevance. The title "saint" suggests the nun withdrawn in her cloister, the priest wholly dedicated to the service of God, the mystic, the ascetic—the works of Mary, not of Martha. The citizen of the twentieth century, struggling with income tax or the bill for his children's education, earning a living in the competitive world of law or commerce, or engulfed in the frustrations of government service, pays, no doubt, his tribute of respect to the idea of holiness—he is less likely than his grandfather to dismiss lives wholly consecrated to God and to prayer as "escapism"—but there is no change in his conviction that the daily business of living in office and home is what "real life" is about.

The most remarkable fact about St. Thomas More may therefore be the bare outline of his biography, which reads very like a modern entry in *Who's Who*. He was born in the City of London of a family prominent in the law and city affairs—his father, Sir John More, was a judge on the King's Bench. Thus his young son

161

grew up with the law and the city in his bones. After reading classics at Oxford—in fact only Latin, Greek came later—he began his law studies at New Inn and Lincoln's Inn, was called to the bar young but already with a great reputation for scholarship, and quickly built up a very large and profitable practice as a result of immense knowledge and industry, equal speed and complete integrity.

As a rising young lawyer, he soon came to the notice of the City Fathers and was chosen as one of the burgesses—or members of parliament—for the City. In parliament, still a very young man—in fact, twenty-six—he made his mark at once, particularly in debates to reduce the Government's demands for fresh taxation. The City rewarded its able young burgess. At the age of thirty-two he was appointed Under-Sheriff, an office which made him the permanent legal officer to the Mayor and Corporation.

Meanwhile, More had married a Miss Colt of Netherhall in Essex. Three daughters and a son were born to them, but Mrs. More died only five years after her marriage. More then married a widowed lady, Mrs. Alice Middleton, who survived him.

The reputation which More had earned not only as a lawyer and a man of learning but also as an active politician in city affairs marked him out for further promotion. While still Under-Sheriff he was invited to take part in some difficult commercial negotiations with Britain's most important trading partner, the Netherlands, and it was during the months of discussion in Flanders that he found time to write his book *Utopia*, which at once became a best-seller throughout Europe. His contemporaries counted him, with Erasmus and Budé and Vives, the foremost scholar of his day.

The trade mission also enhanced his reputation for public business. A year or so later, promotion came again in the shape of an invitation to join the government. He was appointed to the Council, on which he served for eleven years. During this period he acted as Under-Treasurer, as Speaker in Parliament, as Chancellor of the Duchy of Lancaster and as High Steward of both Oxford and Cambridge Universities. At the same time his missions abroad continued, and he had the delicate and ungrateful task of retrieving what could be retrieved for England at the Cambrai Peace Conference. This high career of service was crowned by his appointment as Lord Chancellor—or as we might say now, Prime Minister.

So far, the biography reads like a typical success story in twentieth-century political life—the usual beginnings in the law, the gaining of reputation in local politics, promotion to the national scene, ending with the highest political position in the land. Admittedly one has to turn to Mr. Winston Churchill himself to find some analogy with More's combination of statesmanship and great literary gifts. Nevertheless, this scholarship apart, his career is not untypical of the leading men of our own day. For the last years, however, we have to turn our eyes from modern London—or modern Washington—to post-war Budapest or Warsaw or Prague.

Faced with the Government's increasing claim to total power, More resigned his Chancellorship. For a year, he is allowed to live at peace in his own home. But the insistence on submission and on uniformity of opinion seeks him out in retirement. He is told to seal with a public oath his complete acceptance of the "new order." His refusal is followed first by fifteen months' imprisonment without a trial, then by a mock-trial of complete illegality. The death sentence is passed and More is executed as a traitor to the state.

The impression of modernity is surely remarkable. Yet once the dates are filled in, More slips back again into the mists of the past. Born in 1478, we read, member of parliament in 1504, married in 1505, Under-Sheriff in 1510, called to Henry VIII's Council in 1518 and served there until 1529, Henry's Lord Chancellor until 1532, executed by the same Henry in 1535. Back flows the unreality of historical picture-books—the gold chains and fur tippets, the rush-

163

strewn floors and household jesters—More had one, Henry Patenson, to whom he was greatly attached—the odd language: "deus bone, deus bone, man, will this gear never be left?"—the overwhelming authority of the King's good grace, the pageant of chivalry and medieval magnificence of that Field of the Cloth of Gold which More himself attended. It is all very splendid and even moving, but it is infinitely remote. Looking at those men in their velvet caps and the women in their stiff Tudor snoods and wimples, we feel that the troubles which beset them, the issues they faced and the decisions on which they acted are as outworn as their headgear. Let us admit that Thomas More was a great man and a saint, but how can this be relevant *now* in times so different from his own?

In fact, however, the startling thing about Thomas More's career is the extent to which his life, both public and private, belongs as much to our times as to his. This is in part to say that the deepest experiences of mankind are timeless. More's enchanting household at Chelsea belongs to every age in which men and women love each other and bring up their children in peace, affection and loving discipline. The fact that More gave his daughters the same education—in Greek, Latin, logic, philosophy, theology, mathematics and astronomy—as to his son surprised his contemporaries more than it would us. Nor need we suppose that More knew only the joys of loving companionship and gay goodness in his family circle. He felt all the anxieties of any modern head of the house, making both ends meet on an inadequate salary. Like many a man today who has gone from private to public affairs in London or Washington, More suffered a severe loss of income in giving up his private practice and City connexions and entering the King's service. He writes from Flanders that he is hard put to it to keep two households in being at once. Later, on his resignation from the Chancellorship, he refused all financial aid save his pension, and hard times and fuel shortages came to Chelsea, where his wife

164

and grown-up family had to gather in the evenings round a single fire of peat before retiring to their cold, unheated bedrooms.

There was worse to come. We may wonder how many men in Eastern Europe today as they lie in Communist prisons are tormented most of all by the knowledge that they leave their families in desperate want and danger. More knew this quite "modern" agony and wrote to his daughter from the Tower that the "danger and great harm" in which his family were placed was "a deadly grief unto me and much more deadly than to hear of mine own death."

All this, both the joys and the sorrows, belongs to the ages, and we are not likely to be surprised at the continuity of deep and loyal family affections. The surprising fact is that it is in the sphere of public affairs, the very sphere in which we expect, our minds coloured by the romantic legends of the much-married Henry VIII, to find the greatest differences, that More's experience and our own seem most strikingly to converge. In general terms, the sixteenth and the twentieth century can both bear the name "ages of transition." The discovery of the New World then was as momentous as the mastery of the air today. The new learning of the Renaissance was as intoxicating as modern scientific advance. Men were as troubled in 1530 by the division of Christendom between Catholic and Protestant Christianity as they are now by its division between Christians of all communions and the militant force of Marxist atheism. Change, violence, division were in the air More breathed—as they are in the storms of our own day.

The resemblance is more than a general one. In politics and in economics More wrestled with dangers that are still with us, either recrudescent or never really dead. Tudor government represented a violent break with the constitutional mind of the Middle Ages. To the burgesses of the City of London, to the lawyers who had grown up after Bracton, it was a commonplace that "the King is under God and the law." In other words, the monarchy, though immensely powerful, was a monarchy limited by law, by custom and by the established rights of nobles, clergy and commons. Moreover, there was in the local state and in all Europe a plurality of power—the state representing Caesar and receiving the things that are Caesar's while the Church represented God upon earth and maintained its own independent spiritual authority.

The essence of Henry VIII's political revolution after 1529 was to destroy this double web of constitutionalism and divided power. He concentrated all power, secular and spiritual, in his own hands; he overrode all traditional rights and safeguards and judicially murdered those who sought to keep his will within limits. In fact, he and his creature Thomas Cromwell were students of Machiavelli, who taught that a prince must not ask what he *should* do but what he *can* do. Henry accepted the counsel, and not until the English Civil War was fought a century later could the threat of arbitrary despotism be razed from English society.

The Machiavellian dispensation prevailed, too, in foreign affairs. Far from pursuing the unity of Europe, threatened mortally in the early sixteenth century by the advance of the Turks, Henry and his first Chancellor, Wolsey, deliberately plunged England into a series of wasteful and useless European wars. The attacks on France were in part launched in support of the Papacy, which under the worst of Popes—the dissolute Alexander and the warlike Julius—was risking the loss of spiritual power by appearing more and more in the guise of a mere secular Italian principality. But personal ambitions—Henry's desire to rule in France and Wolsey's desire to be Pope—played their part in a policy which tore up the garment of European unity and ruined England in the process. Such was the political background to More's public life—the struggle against totalitarian power within the state and against the pursuit of nationalist ambitions of aggrandisement abroad.

He had to face as lawless a revolution in economics. In the Middle Ages, men's love of wealth and acquisitiveness had been

166

to some extent checked by the ideal of voluntary poverty, by the traditional rights of the peasants to common lands and open field, by the extent of monastic wealth used in part on hospitals and charity, and by an infinite number of bequests and charities to schools and hospitals administered by the Church—such, for instance, were the four great hospitals of London. If, however, the prince—Henry VIII—might now do what he could and not what he should, the existence of so much wealth was tempting indeed, and there were men behind Henry very ready to share in the temptation and the plunder. Abuses in the Church provided the excuse, but the real aim was private acquisition. The peasants' lands and the Church's charities vanished together into the greedy hands of Henry and his followers in the violent, unrestrained beginnings of modern capitalism.

All these revolutions—in despotic government, in international lawlessness and in economic upheaval—came to a head in the years of More's Chancellorship, and it is the measure of his greatness that he alone, with one saintly bishop, of all the leading men of the time, saw the drift of these revolutions and was prepared to die rather than to conform to them.

We need not suppose that their meaning was easy to discern. Like most great upheavals, they came masked in a mass of irrelevances and cross purposes. On the face of it, More died for refusing to accept Henry's divorce from Katherine of Aragon and remarriage with Anne Boleyn and also for rejecting Henry's claim to supremacy of the Church in England. The argument turned on the Papacy, since the Pope would not declare Henry's first marriage null and void and since the Pope, not the King, was in More's eyes the spiritual head of the English church.

Yet the Papacy was making itself a dubious enough force in More's day. He had resisted for twenty years Henry's addiction to European war in the wake of warlike Popes, seeking to preserve their papal states. Why should he now defend the Papacy when

167

he had actually warned Henry against its secular policies only a few years before?

The same ambiguity hung over Henry's economic "reforms." They were done in the name of abuses in the administration of the Church charities—abuses which More admitted and himself denounced. Here was a maze of good and evil intermingled. Certainly it bemused most other English minds.

The supreme value of More's resistance was his perception of principle under the tangle of politics and conflicting interests. He saw that the King in claiming his divorce was putting the will of the prince above the moral law. If there, why not elsewhere? The shadow of future totalitarianism lay over this return to despotism. More saw, too, that Henry in breaking the spiritual link with Rome was undermining Western unity—with the Turks at the gate—just as the Popes, by their wars, had earlier risked the same calamity. He foresaw the result. The intransigence of the King and the bellicosity of the Popes would destroy all trace of European unity and hasten the coming of the lawless, selfish sovereignty of the new nation-state.

Equally, More could see through the cynicism of an economic revolution which, in the name of reforming abuses, was grabbing the poor man's patrimony. He saw "a conspiracy of rich men procuring their own commodities under the name and title of the Commonwealth," while destitution spread and labourers were turned from home and land "whom no man will set to work, though they never so willingly offer themselves thereto."

We must be honest and admit that these evils—of despotism, of international lawlessness, of economic injustice—are with us to this day. They appear now in the aggravated threat of totalitarianism—in the Communist claim to total conformity, in the cynical opportunism and ruthless self-interest of Soviet foreign policy, even in the deceit of "Soviet full employment" which masks the millions labouring in Arctic slave camps.

Nor can we forget our own part in the totalitarian development. In the West, we have kept faith with constitutionalism and with the division of power. More, today, would applaud our rule of law and the parliamentary institutions for which, as Speaker in 1523, he was the first to demand complete freedom of speech. But arrogant national interest wrecked Europe again and again before Bolshevism was heard of, and even today, the Western powers have yet to find ways of creating lasting unity before the threat from the East.

In economic life, too, Western industrial capitalism for a time was fully as ruthless as its Tudor origins, and too many of the poor and the workless—whom More in his day longed to help and employ—turned to Communism in default of Western aid. Even now, in spite of many generous reforms, we still fall far short of the corporate and neighbourly responsibility which More looked for, with the common work and property of the monastery as his ideal.

In the development of ideas, four centuries is only a little space. Today, facing Soviet totalitarianism, seeking for a unity that still eludes us, compassed about with problems of economic justice— we in the West stand at the end of a revolution at whose terrifying beginnings More assisted. The issues have not changed, but we with all our hindsight still lack his prophetic clarity.

Will anyone now maintain that St. Thomas More has no relevance to our day? He lived in the middle of secular affairs— a lawyer like numbers of our own contemporaries, like them going first into Parliament—or Congress—and like them rising higher and higher in public life until the greatest issues of foreign and domestic policy are in his hands. And these issues are our issues, the issues of liberty and the rule of the law, the issue of totalitarianism, of unity and honesty in foreign policy, of justice and brotherhood in economic life. It is hard to picture a man more fully contemporary with ourselves or a man whose life and death are more relevant to our own struggles.

But, the critic will say, what has all this to do with sanctity? You have spoken of the layman, the father of a family, lawyer, statesman, martyr for liberty, prophetic interpreter of the modern age. But has all this any bearing on the fact that he is called a saint? You have shown him immersed in secular affairs and deciding great secular issues. You have not shown that his sanctity was relevant to either.

In fact, More made the stand he did because he was the man he was. We have always to remember that in his protest against arbitrary power and the abrogation of the moral law he was almost alone. There were many men of equal learning and brilliance to face the issues raised by Henry's despotism. We cannot understand the difference between More's clearsightedness and their lack of ability—or of desire—to understand the principles at stake unless we know what manner of man he was and what were the sources of his insight and his strength.

He was, first of all, a character of complete integrity. Even at his trial when no effort was spared in the attempt to defame him, nothing could be found in his record, as lawyer and statesman, save absolute honesty, endless generosity and complete discretion. In such matters the popular legend left behind by a man usually does not err. In his beloved city of London, a century of anti-Catholic propaganda could not wipe out the people's memory of More as a just, great and merciful judge. In the fragment of the Elizabethan play *Sir Thomas More* of which Shakespeare is part author, we see him as London saw him—"the best friend that the poor e'er had."

Londoners were shrewd in their tradition. If one thing more than another distinguishes More, it is his capacity for friendship and affection. We have seen him already, the devoted father of a brilliant family, with sons- and daughters-in-law who love him with filial warmth and indeed follow him—one to death, many to prison, all in exile. But this inner family circle had around it a group of friends which included the finest minds in Europe. For Erasmus,

170

after a friendship of thirty-six years, it seemed that "in More's death, I. . . . have died myself; we had but one soul between us." Vives, another great humanist, was his guest at Chelsea. The great Holbein found his first patron in More. Nor was More's love only for the talented and the notable. He was indeed "the best friend the poor e'er had." As a young lawyer, he handled all poor men's suits for nothing, and it was in the Court of Requests—the poor man's court—that he gladly served when he first joined the King's Council. Love for the poor stirred him to bitter anxiety over the fate of the labourers turned from their homes and lands, a change which others were welcoming in the name of progress. We know that in his own house, the poor of the neighbourhood were regularly feasted, and Margaret, his daughter, had special charge of the almshouse he had built. And we have a letter from More to his wife, Dame Alice, after a fire had destroyed one of their barns, telling her to pay full compensation to anyone who might have suffered as a result, "for as I should not leave myself a spoon, there shall no poor neighbour of mine bear no loss by any chance happened in my house."

Integrity, affection, friendship, intense personal love for the poor —these are great qualities, yet other men had them in More's day and still they did not see the issues clear. These admirable natural virtues take us no further than the outworks of More's character. Whatever it was that gave him his keener vision and his deeper understanding must lie beyond.

One of the great difficulties in finding one's way to the inner citadel of a man's being is that, if we already know his life, we assume that it was quite inevitable that it would always have developed in just such a way. It is as well with More to realize that quite the opposite is the truth. If there is inevitability in human affairs, then inevitably More should have ended not on the scaffold but as Duke of Chelsea, and no doubt Grand Old Man of the Elizabethan settlement.

He was born to be spoilt. He had all the gifts most likely to

171

commend him to a vivid, intellectual, pleasure-loving Court. He had a legendary wit, he was extremely attractive in appearance—indeed, in his youth young women had thrown themselves at his head. His learning was unequalled, and he had in addition the warm, loving personality which drew all to him. Moreover, he was not rich. He had his way to make in the world. Can one picture any combination of circumstances more likely to catch a young man by the throat with ambition and lead him into the scramble for wealth and honour which a vast majority of his fellow courtiers were pursuing successfully all round him?

We know that the King's good yet terrible Grace, Henry, conceived the warmest love for More. For weeks on end he would detain his friend at Greenwich to keep him company after the royal supper. Henry would delight in arriving unexpectedly at Chelsea, and one evening he walked for an hour beside More with his royal arm round his friend's neck.

Yet after this touching proof of royal favour More remarked to his son-in-law: "Howbeit, son Roper, I may tell thee I have no cause to be proud thereof, for, if my head would win him a castle in France, it should not fail to go." And we have Erasmus's evidence that More struggled as strongly to keep away from Court as most men to go there.

He was not spoilt—in the most spoiling of ages. He was not ambitious—in a most striving and ambitious time. He could still distinguish between the King's will and the moral law—when most courtiers had forgotten the distinction. Why?

There is no secret about it. More was from his first youth a man of prayer. While he studied at Lincoln's Inn he lived a life of complete austerity with the Carthusians, working and praying nineteen hours a day and sleeping on a board with a log for a pillow. Even when he found his vocation in marriage, the prayer and the austerity continued. He rose at two in the morning and worked and prayed until seven. He wore a hair-shirt all his life and took the discipline. Should we think this a commonplace of those rougher days? On the contrary, his wife was so horrified that she tried to have the hair-shirt banned by his confessor, and his merry little daughter-in-law, seeing a corner of the shirt sticking out as he sat at dinner without his ruff, had an uncontrollable fit of laughter. To live in such austerity was as unusual at Henry's luxurious court as it would be today.

Here, then, is the source of More's discernment. Ambition, the grab for wealth and power, meant nothing to a man whose life was steeped in prayer and austerity and whose ideal remained— as we see in *Utopia*—the simplicity and common life of the Franciscans or the Carthusians. As he said to his children: "We may not look at our pleasure to go to Heaven in feather beds." Not all the power and glory Henry could offer—and he offered much —corrupted a man who looked to follow his Master in the way of suffering. "To aim at honour in this world," said More grimly, "is to set a coat of arms on a prison gate."

So it was with his death. Once again we have to think away our idea of his martyrdom as inevitable. More knew what he believed to be his weakness—there was never a more humble soul. He saw good and learned clerics like Dr. Wilson and Bishop Tunstall hesitate before the final threat of death. He feared to the end that, confronted with torture or the traitor's death of disembowelling, he might falter. So, in his prison, he turned to the contemplation of One who, faced with agony and death, sweated blood and prayed that the Cup might pass. In his Treatise on the Passion, More wrote: "He that is stronghearted may find a thousand glorious valiant martyrs whose example he may right joyously follow. But thou now, O timorous and weak, silly sheep, think it sufficient for thee only to walk after Me which am thy Shepherd and Governor and so mistrust thyself and put thy trust in Me."

Here is the inner citadel of St. Thomas More. Throughout a life set in the hubbub of law and public service, among the temptations of courts and princes, surrounded by men straining after new honours and new wealth, he walked with God, and to all his earthly occupations brought the vision and insight of eternal things. He is timeless because he lived timelessly in his prayer. He served the moral law, and the interests of peace and unity and love and compassion because he lived these things all the day in his soul. And because his whole life was centred on God, he could distinguish the things of God from the things of Caesar and could die at last on the scaffold

"the King's good servant, but God's first."

JOHN FARROW

*

St. Ignatius Loyola

He died nearly four hundred years ago, yet few men are as alive as he today. Since stone and metal could be shaped, men have sought permanence with structures to defeat time. St. Ignatius Loyola has a full share of buildings and statues to perpetuate his name, but his true memorial is that determined company of men who live as he lived, who today follow his unchanged discipline and high inspiration, preaching and teaching, living and dying for the glory of God and for the betterment of their fellows.

He was born at a time when corruption was ordinary among the secular clergy and not uncommon in the cloister, when heresy, along with vice, was threatening Rome itself. With some truth, if not with remedy, the rebellious monk of Wittenberg could shout his rude comparisons between Babylon and the Eternal City. Scandal and abuse seemed everywhere, but conditions breed their own antidote. Evil was met by virtue. It was as simple as that.

The heroes of the Counter-Reformation were on the march,

175

gigantic in sanctity, sacrifice and action. Ignatius was of this bright legion. He had the inspiration of his high destiny, but what alchemy produced the genius that left so permanent an imprint upon his own generation, and on his followers through the centuries? No special spiritual nurturing was his during childhood and adolescence. His family was Christian enough, no better nor worse than others of their rank, noble in status, strong in belief perhaps, pledged to the Cross by birth and by fierce vow, but often weak enough in actual practice. Don Beltrán Yañez de Oñez y Loyola gave his seventh son the name Iñigo. Later on it was changed, after the name of the saintly Bishop of Antioch, to Ignatius. He was the youngest of a family of twelve or thirteen, and in addition to these brothers and sisters there were the bastards of the family to frolic with him in the courtyard of the castle at Loyola.

In a large family the choice of career is always a problem for the youngest son. There were undoubtedly long discussions on the subject by his elders. The Church seemed the easiest course, not only for Iñigo but also for one of his brothers. The family had relatives and influential connections in high places. Rich benefices should not be too hard to obtain. So, at an early age, he was given the tonsure. But there it ended, for the lad had other ideas. The high chivalry of Spain was then in full flower. Columbus had splashed his anchors in the waters of the New World a year after the boy was born. All Spain echoed with tales of adventure and opportunity. There were princes to be served and courts to be attended. There were riches to be won and high-born ladies to be courted by him who wore a sword and had no fear to flash it for fashion or for whim, for passion or for gold. Thus the young nobleman thought, and apparently his guardians agreed, for off he went to serve his apprenticeship in the household of the majordomo of Queen Isabella. Barely able to read or write, he quickly grew adept with dagger and sword and in all the graces and tricks of the courtier. The excitement and chances of war, the pursuit of a comely miss, these were for him, who remembered the tonsure only when it became convenient to plead clerical immunity. This he did when he was arrested and charged before a civil magistrate. On a return visit to his birthplace there had been a celebration and then a nocturnal brawl. Apparently, with much wine, some blood was spilled. The precise nature of the crime is not known, but it was serious enough to cause the arrest of Iñigo, and also to involve his priest brother. The young cavalier claimed his immunity, but ample evidence was given that he had never worn the tonsure or donned a cassock. The case dragged on, and he seems to have evaded justice, for he was returned to the Royal Treasurer's service. But not for long. He was now old enough to take to the field.

We find him at twenty-four in the service of a kinsman, the Duke of Najera, a full-fledged soldier, eager in battle, enjoying life just as he wished it, dressed extravagantly, dreaming of romances and seeking them with ardor, brawling and dueling, ever jealous of his honor. "I saw Iñigo with my eyes," said the Bishop of Salamanca, "pass a line of men in the street, one of whom unfortunately shoved him against the wall, and he took after him with drawn sword to the end of the street, and had he not been restrained, would have finished by committing murder."

France and Spain were at war. A Spanish citadel had been erected at Pamplona in Navarre, and behind its thick walls came the end to Iñigo's dreams of martial glory. The French besieged the fortress. There was heavy fighting. A cannon ball felled Iñigo, breaking one leg and wounding the other. The French overwhelmed the defenders, but so struck were they by Iñigo's fierce bravery that in the chivalric manner of the age they imposed no penalty, only did him honor. A physician was appointed to attend his wounds and a litter was provided to carry him to his ancestral home.

177

His right leg set badly, and it was deemed necessary to break it again. It was a painful process, and he became grievously ill. The leg finally healed, but it was shorter than the other and terribly misshapen, a piece of bone protruding from below the knee. This was unbearable to him, for these were the days when curve of calf, the fashionable boot, were all important to a gallant. He called for the doctors and demanded that the bone be sawn off. They told him the agony of pain that would be his if he persisted, but persist he did and the bone was hacked. Then, in an effort to lengthen the limb, a clumsy device of weights was rigged to stretch it. So, in the interests of vanity, a long torture began, and so too commenced a miracle, the sustained miracle of St. Ignatius, the miracle that was to survive his grave, the miracle that was to breed a never-ending procession of saints and martyrs, the miracle that was to cradle the Society of Jesus.

To ease the ache and weariness of convalescence he called for books, stating a preference for chivalrous romances. But all that was available in the castle was a Life of Christ and some stories of the saints. He read, and he who was already judged a hero became deeply impressed with far greater deeds of heroism. Gradually it came to him, the high inspiration, the spiritual light that never was to dim, the true sense of right and wrong, the knowledge of the real goal to be achieved. He had a vision of Our Lady with the Holy Child, and from then on "every unclean imagination seemed blotted out from his soul, and never again was there the least consent to any carnal thought."

At first he did not say much, but the change in Don Iñigo was of course noticed by his family. There was murmur and conjecture, and one alarmed brother advised him not to make any rash or sudden move. But Iñigo had already made his decision, even though he did not know where the course would lead him. As soon as he was able to leave the sick-room he departed for the shrine of Our Lady of Montserrat. To avoid family objections he pretended he was visiting his patron the Duke of Najera, and therefore he began the journey in the elaborate style and garb of his rank. It was not only the external signs of his late calling that remained unchanged. He fell in with a Moor. There was religious discussion, and while admitting the truth of the Virgin Birth, the Mohammedan expressed doubts as to Mary's chastity in her later years. Iñigo flew into a rage, and his hand closed on the hilt of his dagger. The frightened Moor applied his spurs and galloped away on a side road. Here was test indeed for the new Iñigo. Should he as a knight avenge the insult to the noblest of women with blood or should he act as Christ had taught? Sorely troubled, he thought to appeal to a higher, or lower, reason. Abandoning the reins, he let his steed take its own direction. If towards the Moor, then there would be a dead infidel and Our Lady's honor avenged. But the animal turned towards Montserrat, and surely in heaven Our Lady must have smiled, for Don Iñigo had thus, helped by a mule, mounted the first rung of the ladder that led him to sanctity.

At Montserrat, under the guidance of a wise Benedictine, he made a long confession that was preceded by three days of rigorous self-scrutiny. His sword and dagger felt his grip for a last time when they were hung before Our Lady's altar. There, on the eve of the feast of the Annunciation in 1522, he went to his knees and spent the entire night in vigil. He had dispossessed himself of his rich clothes and money, and now he wore the meanest of robes. After the night of prayer, he left Montserrat, and without any definite direction in mind, wandered across the countryside until he arrived at the little town of Manresa. Here he lingered and embarked upon a prodigious program of prayer and contemplation, austerity and works of charity. When the harshness of his many penances caused his health to falter, the Dominicans gave him refuge. He appreciated the ordered life of the priory and in particular was glad to rise at night and assist at Matins, but he made

179

no attempt to take the habit. His tortured conscience made him think he was unfit and unclean, nor did absolution seem to bring him peace. Remorse for his past sins sank him into an abyss of despair until he was almost driven to insanity. He discovered the *Imitation of Christ* and devoured it word by word, seeking by prayer to thrust his soul upward, to follow and join with his Master.

It was at this time that he began to make notes of his attempts at ascent towards God through prayer, and from these notes written by a man as yet with scanty education, came a little book called *The Spiritual Exercises*. A book not to be read but to be lived, it is the most important of its kind ever written, a guide to the achievement of closeness to God and absolute negation of self. With his genius for order and discipline, Iñigo was able to put on paper, step by step, well-defined instructions and regulated meditations that would carry the exercitant from stage to stage in the control of his senses and the mystical conquest of his soul. The manual is as practical now as it was then and is surely one of the many elements which sustain the flame of immense vitality that characterizes the Society of Jesus.

Early in 1523 Iñigo commenced his famous pilgrimage to the Holy Land. The journey was an ordeal of hardship and physical suffering, but it was also a spiritual feast for the pilgrim, who now, although but dimly, began to realize the direction of his vocation. In order for him to be of value to others, the deficiencies of his education would have to be corrected—no easy task was this for a man of his age and meagre schooling, but he undertook it with characteristic will and zeal. For eleven long years, living the life of pauper and beggar, he bent to books and listened to lectures, at the University of Alcala, at the University of Salamanca, and at Paris. His views on education, along with a life of prayer and penance, gradually gathered sympathizers who, owing to his gift for leadership, became followers. But the same

180

unorthodox views also brought violent opposition of every kind. Iñigo was ridiculed and harassed, beaten and even imprisoned. With his fiery zeal for reform, he was suspected in many quarters of being a possible heretic, but Iñigo thought only of truth and the means to preserve it.

The life became too hard for his first companions, but as he persisted on his way new admirers came to join the little band that veritably was the core of what might be called the shock-troops of the Counter-Reformation. In these early days they adopted a common dress, followed the *Exercises,* studied hard, and accepted the many oppositions as mortifications to be sought and desired.

Iñigo's first intention was to take his yet unnamed group to the Holy Land when their studies were completed. There, on the soil that Christ had trod, they would try to lead the perfect life, doing works of charity and converting the infidel. If circumstances, such as war, prevented them from going to Jerusalem, they would place their destiny in the hands of the Pope. On the 15th of August, 1534, they made this intention a solemn vow, along with the vows of poverty and chastity. One of them, Peter Faber, was already a priest, and he celebrated this historic Mass, giving Holy Communion to Iñigo, Francis Xavier, James Laynez, Alonso Salmerón, Nicolás Bobadilla, and Simón Rodríguez. Not long after, these dedicated pioneers were joined by Claude Le Jay, Jean Codure, and Paschase Broët, who made similar high pledges.

The Society of Jesus was already in existence, even though yet without name and not formally inaugurated. It was an opportune moment for the little band. The Church was in desperate need of warriors to defend the faith against the disorders and feuds that were following in the wake of Luther's revolt. The year that Iñigo knelt before Peter Faber at Paris was the year that the enfeebled Pope Clement VII died, leaving a woeful legacy to his successor, Paul III. Not only was the fabric of Christendom being rent in a spiritual sense, but there was the curse and sorrow of widespread

war. Spain and France were in conflict, and Mohammedan buc-
caneers prowled the Mediterranean at will. Lateen-rigged craft,
sails emblazoned with the Crescent, cruised off the coast of Italy.
The Turkish Sultan boasted that he would move his harem to
Rome, and the wail of muezzins could be heard in Hungary and
Austria. Factious princes were utilizing the ideas of Luther to
unfetter themselves from a higher authority; Protestantism was
engulfing Switzerland and the Scandinavian countries; England
saw the birth of a national church which denied the supremacy of
the Holy See. A whole crop of saints and martyrs gives luster to
the story of the Counter-Reformation. Women and men rivalled
each other in the great combat. The older Orders were quick to
show initiative and example in reform, and inspired warriors
formed new Orders. The Pontificate of Paul III witnessed the in-
auguration of the Council of Trent, which gave the sturdy bulwark
of clear definition to the preservation of the treasures of faith and
true reform.

The ex-soldier could not have realized, as he knelt before Peter
Faber, the illustrious role that he would play, the immense share
that would be his in the titanic struggle that was taking place. Yet
he was gradually moulding his followers into an organization that
was ideally suited to combat the new doctrines and to correct the
old abuses. These disciples of his were to be ascetics, but their
work was to be in the world, not the cloister; they were to be
teachers and preachers; they were to be trained scholars able to
meet argument with better argument; they were to be true practi-
tioners of poverty; they were to renounce all rank, temporal and
ecclesiastical. And they were to live under the intense discipline
which has always been their distinctive characteristic. The ex-
soldier insisted on and founded that system of undeviating obedience which has been misunderstood by friend and foe alike,
the indestructible species of obedience which from its inception

has surrounded the name of Jesuit with hostility and suspicion, admiration and love.

The plan on which Iñigo resolved, to lead his disciples to the Holy Land, was doomed to failure. After many reverses and slow travel by way of Spain and Bologna, he gathered his group in Venice only to find that transport was impossible because of the Turkish war. Rome was the alternative, and to Rome they eventually went. By this time they were priests, for permission had been given them to be ordained. In the second and third weeks of June, 1537, Iñigo and six of his friends received minor orders and the subdiaconate and diaconate, and on the Feast of St. John the Baptist they were given the priesthood. But even though his hands had been consecrated, Iñigo did not feel it was time for him to raise the Chalice. A year and a half was to pass before he dared to approach the altar and celebrate the solemn Mystery.

In Rome the group met with the Pope's favor, but also incurred the slander and suspicion that has ever been the lot of the Society. It was about this time that they became known as the Company of Jesus, although as yet they were not an Order, nor had they a recognized rule or tradition. In order to survive as an entity, it was resolved that they should seek permission to form a new Order. There was much discussion, long scrutiny, and bitter opposition, but finally papal approval was given, and in the Spring of 1541 the Society of Jesus became a fact. A new and powerful force had entered the Church, and elected to head it, without surprise but with considerable and sincere reluctance on his part, was Ignatius, who in Rome had assumed the name by which posterity knows him.

The spectacular progress and success of the Society from its beginning is a familiar chapter in history. Equally well known is the persecution and opposition it has had to endure through the centuries. Sovereigns and governments have exiled and banned it. A Pope suppressed the Order, but another Pope revived it, and the miracle of St. Ignatius went on, and still continues. It is significant that, depending on the source of the comment, the very term "Jesuit" can be understood as a compliment or as a defamation.

Ignatius lived to see his followers penetrate the corners of the known world. They carried their work into palaces and hovels, marching along strange roads and invading foreign shores. Iron man though he was, he wept when Xavier died on an island off the China coast. After the foundation of the Society he never left Rome. His administrative genius was given tremendous scope, and a thousand projects occupied his agile mind. The Constitution of the Order was given form and the plans made to assure its permanence. The standards of discipline that had been set for the Society were never slackened for himself or anybody else. Always he set the example. Before his death he declared that, a single sign from the Pope, and he would willingly go off to the nearest galley, even though it be without sail or oars or food. "But where would be the prudence of this?" asked a noble friend. "Prudence, my lord, is the virtue of those who command, not those who obey," was the stern reply.

He was stricken with a fever in the hot summer of 1556, and the sickness proved fatal. He died as he lived, without ceremony, without ostentation. During the long hours of his last night he had been heard to murmur, "O God! O God! O God!" He was sixty-five years old. Catholic Europe mourned his passing. Princes and prelates jostled with the mob to touch his bier. Already he was venerated as a saint. No change came to the Society when his body had been carried to the tomb. This was his genius. The work went on.

The Society of Jesus was born when the fortunes of the Church were at a low ebb. Today an even graver crisis threatens not only Christendom but all peoples. As calamity looms, the sons of St. Ignatius make ready to take their share, and more, in attack and defense. Like combat-hardened troops, well-blooded in battle, they move to the enemy with efficiency and determination. Cast in the mould of their founder, they adhere to the life he patterned: teaching, preaching, converting men to God, upholding the natural law, fighting the evils of secularism, defending the Holy See—avoiding the purple, always bound to the lesson of the *Exercises*. The words of Christ, "Go teach all nations," are a command that is given strict obedience. They are everywhere and on all levels of society. Their number is only thirty thousand, but seldom have trained men been so strategically dispersed. They are in the jungles and on remote islands. They are in the great cities and distant villages. A Jesuit Hall is at Oxford, and in Washington they explain to aspiring diplomatists the intricacies of their trade. The famed Gregorian University of Rome is theirs, so too is the Pontifical Bible Institute, the Collegio Pio Latino Americano, the Brazilian College, the Maronite College and the Russian College. And so too are scores of kindergartens in dusty Hindu villages. Empty horizons of the Southern Seas are pierced by the thrust of a solitary schooner's masts, a Jesuit at the helm, bringing spiritual and material succor to lonely charges. Another of his comrades tramps the frozen wastes of the Arctic bearing comfort to the distant igloos. Chosen men work in laboratories and observatories and libraries. They control a hundred institutions of higher learning around the world, and they are the proprietors of lesser academies, seminaries, missions and asylums of all kinds.

Ignatian ideals, Ignatian obedience, Ignatian energy, continue to breed the type of martyrdom that is so gloriously manifested throughout the Society's heroic story. While Jesuits die in the Godless countries, others calmly prepare to cross the same forbidden frontiers. Few men are strong enough to thrust their will beyond the grave. Ignatius had this strength. The miracle that began at Loyola, the grace that was given at Manresa, did more than make one man into a saint. It made one man into many men, all with

185

the same goal of service and sanctity, all part of the never-ending Crusade, all fiercely devoted to imitating the Ideal, all dedicated to finding and following the Divine will.

When the Mexican martyr, Father Pro, faced the leveled rifles of the firing squad, arms outstretched, eyes upraised, he gave voice to that cry which is a continual echo in the hearts of his brethren of the Society. His farewell to this world and his greeting to the next was the brave salute, "Hail, Christ the King!"

KATE O'BRIEN

*

St. Francis Xavier

When I was a schoolgirl certain classfellows had leather-bound books, called "Confession Albums," in which they constrained one to set down in writing one's favourite colour, flower, historical character, fictional character, pet abomination, favourite quality in a man, favourite quality in a woman—in fact, to make two whole pagefuls of extremely difficult and arbitrary statements. I did not take to those "Confession Albums," but when, seeking to please, I filled in their questionnaires, I usually ran into trouble with my peers, bent inquisitively over my shoulder. I suppose their single virtue, those silly albums, was in that they made silly schoolgirls argue about ideas of excellency. But as to "Your Favourite Quality In a Man"—when, invariably, I wrote the word "Generosity," and opposite the next question: ". . . In a Woman," wrote "Ditto," I was, invariably, pounced upon. "What about justice?" some prig would say. "What about honesty?" another. "What about courage, what about modesty? What about intellectual curiosity?" And usually some ass would bleat that she did not see how a woman could be generous, anyway.

187

Well, we would toss all the noble qualities about, failing totally to understand each other or ourselves. And when I argued that I chose generosity because I did not see what it was unless it was compounded of justice, honesty, courage and modesty, I believe that I did not know very clearly what I meant. But I have learnt why it is the most complicated of the great virtues—and a rich source for discovery of its many-sidedness is the life, the personality of Francis Xavier.

Inherent in the character of the Society of Jesus is the total subjection of its members to its whole. The history of the order is an unbroken demonstration of that first principle which the *Spiritual Exercises* were designed to establish, i.e., the surrender, final and unquestioning, of personality to a fore-ordained plan imposed from without, infallible and immutable. The Jesuit is asked at the outset of his career for nothing less than this, and he gives nothing less. All that he is, all that he brings to his vocation will be used by the Society, but under a strictly impersonal discipline, and with only such remote and utilitarian reference to his individuality as will advance the organisation and the purpose to which he offers himself. And throughout four hundred amazingly filled and fighting years—*ad majorem Dei gloriam*—the sons of Ignatius have undoubtedly held to that hard, central exaction —have taken it, imposed it and handed it on as an ever-increasing strength in their far-flung and multiplying generations. The Society's absolute fidelity to this cold principle of abnegation has given it its unique history and its extraordinary success; and paradoxically, out of its proud and heroic refusal to its separate, human members of their rights over their personalities, it has created, recognisably to all the world, the personality of the Jesuit.

Qualities and virtues of a high order are needed to fit a man for the kind of self-subjection we are now discussing, and the Society has always picked its aspirants with great care; and in the exceptionally long and hard training which, as novices and as scholastics, these young men must undergo before they are admitted to the priesthood, an especial kind of intelligence, at once clear and generous, will be needed, an intelligence which will be able to see steadily beyond the particular to the general, able to forgive, or rather, welcome all that must be undergone of humiliation, of pettifogging, of suppression, monotony and frigidity throughout the long years wherein the young ego learns to die, giving place to the mature, the perfectly pruned Jesuit.

The system is clear cut and fundamentally changeless. It is all based in the *Spiritual Exercises,* and it works as Ignatius prayed and knew it would; and, as has been said, it attracts for the most part only men of especial intelligence, who can see the wood as well as the immediate prickly trees. Such men are usually of higher than average intellectual endowment—and their brains and talents are cultivated with infinite skill and liberality. If it is necessary to train them out of relation to the individual who is their source, and into the vast, unchanging, collective design of the Society, that is a part of what the Jesuit accepts, and gives to his vocation. Once he is of the Society he understands that his intellectual gifts are no more his than are his shoes or his soutane. They are, all these things, the property of the Order, under Christ, and he will use them or not as his superiors may direct. The surrender is unqualified and very generous, and it creates, as we have said, the paradox of Jesuit personality.

One consequence of this is that the amazing and stormy history of the Society of Jesus presents itself as the unified, solid story of an institution rather than as that of a long line of remarkable men. Its annals are heavy indeed with names distinguished in sanctity, in learning, in statesmanship, in apostolic gift, in all and any of the high qualifications necessary to its establishment, survival and increase. Yet that which is truly renowned is the Society—not this or that talent, triumph or glory won for it by this or that

189

individual life or gift, but simply the Society, behind the tranquil façade of which the centuries have assembled hosts and treasuries of effort in a sustained anonymity of service. Yet, if this is so it is so—another paradox?—because two of the most remarkably individualistic Spaniards of the sixteenth century, two men who in their beginnings at least could be described as almost wilfully self-expressive, were, together and apart, and in a span of years that were not many, to lay the plans and set once and for all the foundations of a citadel which was to withstand every conceivable shock and assault from without, and wherein the garrison would forever and in all circumstances do its duty, without comment and without reward.

Ignatius Loyola and Francis Xavier, both aristocrats of northern Spain, were superficially dissimilar in temperament, and we know that for more than the first year of their acquaintance in Paris the young man, Xavier, actively disliked and was puzzled by the grave, mature ex-soldier who, under God, was to be the inspiration and ideal of the rest of his short and brilliantly zealous life, and of whom he was to write—in the first of his letters which remain to us, from Paris in 1535—"he is, in fact, most thoroughly acquainted with my heart."

Francis Xavier was the slowest, the most reluctant, of the famous six young "elected" in Paris to accept Loyola's dream and plan of the Society, and he was the last of the six to submit himself to the test of the *Spiritual Exercises*. Loyola had indeed to devote years of tactful and gentle friendship to the winning of this apostle; and it must be conceded that he knew what he was doing. He was capturing for the Jesuits at once their greatest missionary and most attractive saint.

Like Ignatius, Francis Xavier was a Basque. He was born in 1506 in the kingdom of Navarre, on the northern border of Aragon. His father, Don Juan de Jassu, a grave and learned man, a Doctor of Laws of Bologna, was chancellor of Navarre, and married to Doña Maria de Azpilcueta y Xavier, a wealthy lady,

190

descended from two proud Basque families, and said to have been very beautiful. Francis, the youngest of their six children, was born late of this marriage, and when his brothers and sisters were already grown-up. For this reason he seems to have been particularly loved, and to have enjoyed a happy, sunny childhood in the old fortified castle of Xavier which stood on the slope of a fertile, wooded mountain and overlooking the Aragon river. In those years his father was much occupied by court affairs at Pampeluna, his two brothers had already departed to military careers, one sister was a nun and the other two married, so that he lived as an only child, and was very much the darling of his mother and of a saintly, indulgent aunt, "Tia Violanta." The tradition is that he was a child of singular grace, charm and intellectual promise, and that it pleased his father that his bent was, like his own, towards learning rather than for the soldier-life of his two brothers.

But in 1515, when Francis was nine, the fortunes of the family deteriorated, never to recover their old ease. In that year Don Juan de Jassu died, and in that year also Ferdinand of Aragon invaded the kingdom of Navarre, beginning a war which was to bring loss and poverty to the Castle of Xavier, as to many other Basque estates. For ten years Doña Maria's two elder sons were engaged in fierce fighting all over Navarre, from the Pyrenees to the Aragon border; meantime Francis grew up in the increasingly dilapidated and impoverished castle, but pursuing his studies there and in Pampeluna with gaiety and zest, until 1525 when, as he desired to enter the Church, it was decided that he must go to the University of Paris, celebrated above all European schools for its faculty of theology in the Collège de la Sorbonne.

Paris in the heyday of Francis I must have been a stimulating town, and to an educated, aristocratic but country-bred boy from the Basque country a strange and promising *mise-en-scène*. The imperialistic rivalry between the King of France and Charles V

191

of Austria, now also most inconveniently King of Spain, was in full tide. France was on a mounting wave, with the enlivening airs of the Renaissance blowing into her spread sails, and captained by a prince young, cultivated, courageous and of absolutist spirit. Against her pride rode well-matched menaces—the cautious, dangerous Emperor, the wilful King of England, the Turk, the Venetians, the eternal, cunning Papacy. Italy was the great prize, never in fact to be won; and Protestantism and the new learning were gathering up on the horizons of a reign and of a century that were to bring immeasurable troubles, glories and developments to Europe, but to leave France at its close much weakened, much the worse for wear. Still, in 1525 her king, Francis I, sat easily to his destiny and felt himself to be its happy and sole master.

Paris was expanding, by his will. North of the Town and east of the Cité he breached her walls and had begun to build the Palace of the Louvre; the new architectural style was a delight, and in such new suburbs as the Faubourg St. Germain the nobility was encouraged to express its high spirits in lordly modern *hôtels*. The University, long since great and crowded, and having provided the model for such places of learning as Oxford and Cambridge, was now withdrawn from Notre Dame and La Cité and had crammed its forty colleges on to the Left Bank of the river, about Sainte Géneviève and Saint Germain des Prés. In its four chief faculties, theology, canon law, medicine and arts, it was justly renowned; but greatest of all was its school of theology, and the fount and centre of this was the Collège de la Sorbonne. The *"thèse sorbonnique"* had come to be regarded, in the 13th and 14th centuries, as a supreme scholastic test, and the fame of the doctors and teachers of the Sorbonne was consistently so high that it grew above its many sister colleges to be the focal and chief school of the university. (This accidental distinction was such that when in 1808 and after the Revolution the University of France was reconstituted the Sorbonne was made its seat.)

192

To this crowded, brilliant city then, centre of all that was most cultivated, promising and *avant-garde,* came Francis Xavier in 1525, a student-pilgrim aged nineteen, a Spaniard and poor. (His brothers and his mother had only with difficulty been able to arrange for him to study in Paris; and all through his student days he was troubled about money.)

The students of the University were classified loosely under a heading of "nations," and although Xavier was registered as a student of France, this "nation" included Spaniards and Portuguese, who were chiefly housed in the Colleges of Sainte Barbe and Navarre. He was enrolled in Sainte Barbe, where his room-mate was a young Savoyard called Peter Faber.

Although he was poor, Xavier appears to have had control of his small patrimony, and to have lived in college as a "camerist," that is, paying his tutors, and also for his food and room, as well as employing a "burser" student to act as his servant in some measure.

He studied impetuously and with unaltering success. Before he was twenty-four he was a Master of Arts and took his licentiate in philosophy. Appointed then as lecturer in Aristotelian logic, metaphysics and physics in the Collège de Beauvais of the University, he was able to turn his attention to that which he had come seeking—theology in the Collège de la Sorbonne.

In the critical, jealous world of the Left Bank he was regarded as very able; an intellectual to watch. And he was being watched.

In the spring term of 1528 another Spaniard had made a pilgrimage, from Salamanca to Paris. This man was not of student age; he was thirty-seven; he was shabby and fragile, with a bad limp, and his earthly possessions were easily borne for him on a donkey's back. It is said that on the evening when he reached the end of his journey and was seeking lodging in the Rue St. Jacques he was observed by two Spanish students of the Collège de

Navarre, and one, Lainez, said to the other, Salmerón: "That, I think, might be the man they turned out of the University of Alcala." He was that man, who had more recently been ordered by his professors to remove himself from Salamanca, and who, before suffering either of these dismissals and having painfully made a pilgrimage to Jerusalem had been ordered off that territory also, by the Franciscan fathers, who considered themselves the owners then of the Holy Places. He was, in fact, this tired man with the donkey, Ignatius Loyola; and he entered himself as a student of grammar in the Collège Montaigu, on the roll of which institution there was also at that time, as it happened, the name of a nineteen-year-old student called Calvin. But for his philosophic studies Loyola was registered in the Collège de Sainte Barbe. And the tutors there directed one of their most gifted graduates, Peter Faber, to help the elderly neophyte catch up on his texts. Faber recommended that his pupil attend some lectures then being given by a fellow-countryman of his, Francis Xavier, in the Collège de Saint Rémy. So it was that the three first members of the Society of Jesus came together, with two of their immediate colleagues commenting, as it were, on the sidewalk of the Rue St. Jacques.

But Xavier was not easily to be interested in Peter Faber's elderly *protégé*. He was very busy, and was tasting success and *réclame*. Since he was passionately attached to his work it is probable that he liked well the rigours of university life. Bells ringing at four, candles lighted and lecture-rooms crowded at five. Mass at six, and then some rolls of hot bread to eat. Thereafter the real work, the important lectures, and at eleven o'clock dinner in college. Rest, for the lecturers at least, after dinner, until three, but then, until five o'clock, more classes, followed by tutorial work. Supper, night prayers in college, and curfew at nine. But candles might be lighted and study pursued until midnight. Feast days and days of religious obligation broke this routine, and there

194

were long vacations, and the quiet freedom of Sunday, and of appointed days of recreation. Francis, who was aware of his powers now and very ambitious, clearly had his work cut out, if he was to hold his reputation as a lecturer in philosophy and also pursue eminence in the school of theology, the most exacting faculty in Paris. He had no time to give to an ascetic who had come to the schools too late to be whipped into scholastic training. Moreover, he did not like his fellow-countryman, and it is recorded that he mocked at the humility and asceticism of Ignatius, which he may have considered an embarrassing affectation. This contempt of Francis for the self-denying manner of life of another is difficult to understand, and may indeed be no more than a legend born of his actual resistance to the assault which Loyola made on his ambition and his intellectual pride; because whereas it does seem to be true that Francis was impatient at first against Ignatius, and even repelled by him, it also seems to be established that his own life in Paris was entirely that of a scholar, and by reason of his natural disposition always ascetic and celibate. It may be that being born to live cerebrally, if not through the spirit, he was unable in his singularly blessed, cold self-assurance, to understand what Ignatius Loyola was making for. On all the evidence, Xavier was not a man like other men; he did not have to meet their troubles. As a boy he lived innocently, happily, by some great favour of God or nature; as a young man in Paris, he lived cerebrally and afterwards, quite simply he lived on, by and through his love of God—and because of God, on his amazing, tender love of God's children. Cynics, reading of his charm, his good looks, his easy success wherever he bent his mind, may doubt this sustained, happy indifference to those disturbances of the senses which have made such a plague of life for the common run of us. But I refer them to the evidence: the proof is in his letters.

I believe that Xavier, inexperienced in life and indifferent to all of it which did not come under logical or philosophic definition on his rostrum, found Loyola a somewhat eccentric character, whom he was glad to leave to the benevolent direction of young Peter Faber. His own intention was, eschewing all excess, to become a learned man, a doctor of the Sorbonne, to take Orders, and from a chair to direct the thought and doctrine of churchmen. Indeed had anyone told him then, in his proud and busy Sorbonne days, that soon, much sooner than he could dream, his greatest delight would be to hear little dark-skinned children singing the "Hail Mary" in an Asiatic dialect which he—accurate scholar of Greek and Latin— had feverishly skimmed and scamped on their behalf—had any prophet brought him that news, could he, one wonders, *would* he have believed it?

His life was to be short—its whole span forty-six years. Nineteen of those he spent in the random happiness of childhood and boy-hood at home; eleven were passed, proudly, successfully, in the University of Paris. That left only sixteen for his life-work. And we dawdle in reaching it. But so did he. He was, at first, a reluctant Jesuit.

However, since theology was his subject and since the Roman *curia* often submitted the knottier questions of the hour to the doctors of the Sorbonne, he was not unaware of the winds that were blowing through the Church. "Reform! Reform!" was every-where in Christianity the cry that dominated, and must be answered. Whether it rang from Wittenberg or Zürich or came in a more deprecatory form from the gentle Erasmus, it was the necessary word of the time, the irrepressible word, and it was as much the word of Loyola as of any other priest then at work. The student Calvin heard it in the Collège de Montaigu, and so did the young doctor Xavier, lecturing in the Collège de Saint Rémy.

Xavier's room-mate, Peter Faber, was from his first meeting with Loyola his unquestioning disciple. This Savoyard, Xavier's age, and distinguished like him in the University for his brilliance

196

in philosophical studies, seems to have possessed, for all his intellectual gifts, a curiously innocent sweetness very different in its outward expression from the proud Spanish charm of Francis. A born student, he has left it on record that when he was eighteen he foresaw no difficulty in secretly vowing himself to chastity in the service of God, as he cared only for learning. But as he grew into manhood in Paris, he was tortured by assaults on the virtue he had chosen to be especially his, tortured by scruples and—very touchingly—made unhappy and humiliated by his love of good food. However, he was so fortunate as to win the friendship, profound and never to alter, of his experienced, middle-aged pupil, Ignatius Loyola. Indomitable under all the rebuffs his high intention had suffered through the years since, dedicated to it, he had left the Cave of Manresa; indomitable, and with his *Spiritual Exercises* worked out and awaiting trial, Loyola was in Paris to look for men who should be as nearly perfect for his purpose as might on earth be hoped for. He must have been encouraged by his so speedy discovery of Peter Faber. He worked for him with all possible strength of will, intellect and spirit, and Peter Faber accepted delightedly all he brought to him. But it was only after four years of testing friendship and discussion that Loyola allowed his disciple to attempt to submit himself to the *Exercises*. Finally these were undergone during an extremely cold winter in Paris in 1533, and the physical mortifications of the ordeal, increased by the weather, are said to have corrected forever Peter Faber's weakness for good food. In the summer of 1534, Ignatius, not yet in Holy Orders himself, allowed Faber to seek ordination—thereby making him the first consecrated priest of his still hypothetical Society of Jesus. He must indeed, that severe perfectionist, have thought well of Peter Faber. For he was to spend a whole further year himself before accepting the powers and responsibilities of priesthood. And when on the Feast of the Assumption, 15th August, 1534, the Jesuit Order was, informally,

197

inaugurated, at Mass in the Church of Our Lady of Montmartre—when on that morning Ignatius Loyola and his six friends from the University of Paris, receiving Holy Communion, took their final vows of poverty and chastity and pledged themselves to the way of life outlined by the *Spiritual Exercises,* the celebrant of that historic Mass was Peter Faber, and he was on that date the only one of the seven who was a priest. But six of the seven had by then undergone the discipline of the *Exercises.* Six men famous in Church history: Loyola, Peter Faber, Lainez, Salmerón, Rodriguez, Bobadilla. Only one of them, taking his vows as gladly as them all, eager and holy, and already very precious and dear to Ignatius, and almost certainly marked down by him for great achievements—only this one, Francis Xavier, was still on that 15th August separated from his brothers; he had not yet been allowed the exacting discipline. His spirit was willing, and there is every evidence that he was all his life in contemptuous command of his flesh. But may we suspect, from Ignatius's extreme caution with him, that Xavier's menace in those Paris days was intellectual, and that his future General desired to force nothing, but to give the potentially great priest every possible freedom to turn right or left?

Within a very brief essay it is not possible to discuss the *Spiritual Exercises.* But our readers will know something of the book, will have read it, perhaps—even if in increasing despair, as they advanced through it. For it is, I think, for the layman very hard and alarming. That it is a key work, and one of Europe's most influential texts is well known; furthermore, it was written by a great and relentless mystic. But this latter fact is, I submit with all reverence, an accident. Ignatius Loyola was a mystic, but in relation to his time and his sense of duty he was primarily a man of action, an apostle and a friend of his fellow men—in fact he was very much more, on the evidence, a man with a conscience than a man with a dream. So it is true—though hard to catch in words—that his very difficult mystic's handbook is also a soldier's handbook. It is founded, rooted deep in the ineffable, in passionate acceptance of God, the Lord and Redeemer of us all; but it is, nevertheless, a kind of field manual—the most remarkable and ruthless ever conceived. Merely to read, it is a very exacting and amazing work. As an instructional text, under which to go into training for life-service, there can surely be no half measures about it. A man must either believe completely in what the *Exercises* exact, or speed away for ever out of reach of their relentless question.

Francis Xavier was intellectually equipped to confront the *Exercises* and decide for or against all that they meant. He submitted himself to their ordeal when Ignatius allowed him to do so; and thereafter, with all his wits and talents about him, with all his heart, with all his soul, he was Loyola's man, he was a Jesuit.

Since we must in this brief essay skip a great deal, we shall skip Francis's departure from Paris, his pilgrimage through Venice and Bologna to Rome, and his journey back across Spain to Lisbon. We shall skip also all the negotiations which at Rome and at the Pope's pleasure changed Ignatius and his gifted young men from being a few formidable soldiers of the church into that Society of Jesus which was to direct the Council of Trent, make history and trouble everywhere, and take the dangerous gospel of Jesus Christ to Travancore and Japan, to Paraguay and Peru.

Accidentally Francis Xavier took the Gospel to the East. John III of Portugal, troubled (and with reason) about the advancement of the life of the spirit in his rich Indian territories (discovered and annexed for his family in 1497 by Vasco da Gama) had been importuning the Pope for missions to Asia. The newly founded order of the Society of Jesus, including in its small membership one Portuguese aristocrat, Simon Rodriguez, interested the monarch, and he asked Paul III to command six Jesuits to proceed to Lisbon in time to set sail with the new Viceroy of Goa in 1541.

199

Ignatius, having only ten men in his order then, could not spare six, but told the Pope he would allow two, Rodriguez and Boba-dilla, to the Goa expedition. At the last minute Bobadilla was sick of a severe fever, and Ignatius—uneasily, reluctantly, one gathers —asked Francis Xavier if he would take his place.

The ships sailed for the East, round the Cape of Good Hope, only once a year. If a man could not go on a given convoy, then a vast period of time must be wasted. And Ignatius was an im-patient man and a great apostle. Nevertheless, one gathers from the documents that he was exasperated at having to offer the gifted intellectual, Xavier, in place of Bobadilla. Nor can the instruction to proceed to Lisbon and thence, under escort of the Portuguese governor, to Goa, have greatly pleased Xavier. However, so it was that the great saint came to India—and to that fame and vocation which were to seem to dismiss all that he had trained himself to be—but which were to seek and find in him the springs of perfect generosity.

The voyage from Lisbon to Goa normally, in the sixteenth century, took six months, but Xavier set sail, in the galleon of the Governor of Portuguese India, in April 1541 and did not reach his destination until May 1542. Five of these thirteen months were indeed spent in sheltering from bad weather on the island of Mozambique; but it must have been for the eager servant of God an extremely tedious and lonely expedition, and not alleviated by his discovery that he was a very bad sailor. However, he was to get used to seasickness, and to all the discomforts of sixteenth century sea-going, in the Bay of Bengal and the China Sea. But on this first long journey he began to exercise, of set purpose as it were, that personal charm and social grace which were to be his great missionary weapon. By the device of what he gaily called "apostolical conversation" he quite simply won the trust of every creature—all nine hundred of them—on the crowded and un-comfortable galleon. He learnt as he travelled towards Goa how,

200

in wisdom and goodness, to be all things to all men; he began to see what must be *his* way of manipulating human nature towards God's purposes. To charm, to relax, to gain access to men's secret hearts—and *then*, God willing, to win them to his faith. In the conditions of that ship, and in a situation where he was much more than literally at sea and at a disadvantage, it cannot have been easy for him to take such constant trouble to woo and please so many disconcerting specimens of the human race. It is not difficult to imagine the kind of person who would normally be sailing from Lisbon to Goa in 1541—and assuredly in any shipload of such there could only be one Francis Xavier. And he—granted the exaggerated generosity of his pilgrim life in Venice and Bologna and Rome, had nevertheless been companioned hitherto either by his own gentle, aristocratic relations, by University scholars, or by Ignatius and his hand-picked men. Now, save for two not very brilliant missionary assistants, Father Paul of Camerino and the Portuguese deacon, Mancias, he found himself associated only with the adventurous and licentious riff-raff of the world; high or low, grand or miserable, they were all uneasy and illiterate chance-takers on the make, and entirely given over to "taking care of Number One." Indeed, reading the letters and records of the time, one gets the impression that Xavier's fellow-travellers in 1541-42 were representative of what is to be found in large ships anywhere, first, tourist or steerage class, in any century. Yet, half-regretfully—and forgetting of course his great purpose—one has to record that this graceful, goodlooking and highly cultivated Spanish priest was the life of that long-drawn-out party, that terrible "pleasure cruise" which lasted thirteen months.

Indeed, throughout his short life his social gift, which he turned into a weapon in God's service, was to be questioned. Pious people, having heard of the great missionary, were disedified sometimes at first encounter, because they might meet him playing cards with half-drunk fishermen on a quayside of Travancore, or maybe

dining in luxury between some Mussulman prince and his favourite concubine, or sitting to talk with a prostitute on her doorstep
in a back street of Goa. But, like his great Exemplar, who had
frequented publicans and sinners, and who advised us all, so
vainly, against throwing the first stone, Francis desired to know
his fellow-creatures, their motives, their needs and their hopes.
Moreover, he was travelling into what was for him a very dark
continent, its spirit, history and idioms as dark to him as the
varying skins of its people. To be of any practical use he must
adapt himself to new habits of life, and as rapidly as possible
must get on working terms with some of the languages of the
Indian peninsula. Fortunately he was not merely a good gram-
marian-linguist, but that much more useful and quick kind of
person, an instinctive, irrepressible picker-up of new idioms. This
was a talent which Ignatius could not have foreseen in him, but
which was to be priceless. Xavier appears to have had that gift—
which I have seen, with envy, in certain of my own friends—for
getting a working grip on a new language in an amazingly short
period. In the various depositions for his canonisation many claims
were made for his having been granted by the Holy Spirit the
gift of tongues, and for his being able to speak, miraculously, in
languages of India which he could not have studied.

Now, in this brief essay I refuse outright to face the question
of Francis Xavier's miracles. That it is tedious to say "there are
more things in Heaven and earth," etc. is not Shakespeare's fault,
but ours, that we find it so necessary to repeat him. Still, I am in
no position to discuss events and actions which while appearing
incredible to me have yet been weighed, considered and accepted
as likely by Colleges of Cardinals. (I shall mention only one of
Xavier's deposed miracles—and that because it has the faultless,
delicious beauty of a fairy tale.) However, he did himself say
some very sensible things in his letters about how the legend of
miracle can grow in a simple community out of any fortunate set of

circumstances. But, leaving the question of the gift of miracles aside, we must remember that Francis Xavier was a man much in earnest when he set out from Lisbon, that he was exceptionally well educated, and had informed himself in his long months in Lisbon and Coimbra of where and into what conditions he was going. And apart from whatever searches and investigations he may have made whilst in Portugal, Francis had thirteen hard preparatory months on the sea, in association with sailors and adventurers, many of them natives of the South Indian coast, and most of them familiar with it. It is certain therefore that before he saw Goa, this very intelligent man had acquainted his mind with the forms of life and thought he must look for there, and had at least got a working familiarity with one or two of its chief languages. And thence I believe any real linguist would tell us that the power to handle various dialects in the expression of simple ideas need not be explained by visitation of the Paraclete. Anyway, Francis himself always resented talk of his miracles, and always worked hard and fast for that rudimentary control of Indian dialects which was essential to his work.

So—he landed in the harbour of Goa in May 1542.

He found a beautiful stretch of coast, shelving up, pearly and gentle, under the blue shadows of the Ghat mountains. He found tropical richness, stillness and mist, and a graceful, mannerly, dark-skinned race—sailors, fishermen, hawker-women, children, on the foreshore. But in Goa itself, the King of Portugal's town, he found wealth, gaiety, European architecture, churches, palaces, banks, convents, strolling monks and prelates, angelus bells, dance music, and money—fortunes of money. He found in fact European corruption, loose and proud. He saw that he could not yet, not without vast preparatory, and reparatory, work preach the God of these shameless and greedy colonists to the innocent people whom they were everywhere exploiting, up and down the conquered coast.

It is improbable that Francis Xavier ever met or saw Luis de Camoens in the year he spent in Lisbon before he left Europe forever. The poet would only have been eighteen then, and an obscure student in Coimbra. Yet it is conceivable that the two who of all Europeans were most lavishly to serve southern India and the Indian islands did brush and elbow against each other in the hilly streets of Lisbon in 1541. And it may be that when de Camoens came to Goa in 1553 he was in time for the exuberant home-bringing and obsequies of the greatly loved Father Francis. Certainly he would have come fresh to the legend of the missionary, and been shown his newly sealed sepulchre in the chapel of the college of Santa Fé, around which miracles were being recorded every day of that autumn and winter. But it may be as well for literature that de Camoens having rounded the Cape of Good Hope with his epic theme already a long time set and sounding in his breast, already since youth determined on poetic celebration of *Os Lusiadas* (The Portuguese), did not meet the formidable Spanish Jesuit who gave his burning life to salvage what Vasco da Gama's men had outraged. We cannot guess what Francis would have said to the poet, or how much he would have affected him. But it is worth noting that within a very close-clipped time Goa and the Indian seas created for Europe two of her glories, the *Lusiads* and the apostolic work of Francis Xavier.

The tangle of faiths and myths which Francis found all along the conquered Portuguese Indian coast, and in Ceylon and Bengal and the Moluccas is not to be unravelled here. Hindus, Mohammedans and simple back-of-the-hills heathens had had, confusedly mixed in through all their faiths and legends and for nearly fifteen hundred years, some remote suggestions and echoes of Christian teaching, left amongst them, it was thought, by St. Thomas the Apostle, Thomas "of little faith," who, tradition says, reached India with the gospel of Galilee and Calvary.

Marco Polo had found Nestorian Christians in Malabar, and

204

when Vasco da Gama conquered the coast in 1498, the sect was loosely reckoned at about two hundred thousand souls. But its practices were ruthlessly stamped out and anathematised by the Portuguese authority, which imperiously and pitilessly imposed upon all the queer flotsam of metaphysical conceptions abounding in their new territory the fixed and sweeping dogmatism, the formal, take-it-or-leave-it theology, and the impressive, attractive ritualism of the Roman Church in all its fifteenth-century and *fin de siècle* glory.

The confusion can only have been measureless. At least, this reader of the local history and memoirs of the time stares aghast at the spectacle of ethical, moral and mystical chaos into which Francis Xavier walked when he landed at Goa.

He was tired and lonely at the end of the long journey; and in a very few days he was, as nearly as he could ever be, disheartened. He had gladly obeyed Father Ignatius and accepted instead of the scholar's life the simple one of the apostle. He had prepared himself for that, rigorously—and long before he saw his dark-skinned, waiting flocks he loved them. He would bring them the simple rules of the Catechism, and the chief injunctions of the Sermon on the Mount. On the long sea voyage, playing cards with sailors of Goa and of the Travancore coast, he studied their dialects, and in his cabin slaved to get the rudiments of what he had to say to St. Thomas's children into words that would be theirs.

In Goa, he found between him and this pure mission a whole great city of voluptuousness, snobbery, intrigue and graft. He found Europeans at their worst, rapacious, imperialistic, and morally and physically defeated by the climate. He found jacks-in-office and jobbery, and churches and monasteries and chiming bells and wealthy priests—the façade, representing only pomp and circumstance, of imperialism. Nowhere did these conquerors seem to have troubled to meet, study or understand the people they were ruling, and savagely exploiting.

205

He was one young Spaniard, a very poor priest, with only two inexperienced lieutenants. True, he had the valedictions of the pious king, John III of Portugal, and throughout their long voyage he had made fast the friendship of the King's Viceroy in Goa, de Sousa. Nevertheless, he came with his truth, passion and loving kindness into a society where he saw at once that all of these, unless disguised—for there was plenty of religious hypocrisy —would be blocked at every turn. He might have decided to play in awhile with the *socialites* and find his way; he might have decided to lead through what the world calls "strength." He looked round him, and decided, one must suppose, that the only way to deal, to his purpose, with the shocking worldliness of the ruling Catholics, was to ignore them and to present Christ's idea—in their despite. So he began as he was to go on for the too-short, packed ten years of his earthly work—he lodged himself as an assistant nurse in the chief hospital, and when he was not helping or washing or amusing the sick, he walked in the streets and acquainted himself with the speech of the people of Goa, with the mingling of faiths and races in the region, and with the relation to the local life of the self-indulgent, greedy habits of his fellow-Europeans. And very quickly he saw that there was no way through the thickets of metaphysical and moral confusion in which he found the city save that of simple action. So he took a bell, and he went through the streets ringing it; and children and idlers and old men went after him and when he had enough of them round him he would pause, and in his rehearsed few words of their language he would say, and repeat, whatever he judged to be nearest to their understanding of God's law.

He was always very shabby-looking, they tell us. His soutane was a dusty, rusty garment, and his wide pilgrim's hat was battered. But he was a very handsome, slight man, and he was so aristocratic in manner and in thought that it was impossible for his advisers to prove to him that more respectability of appearance would be helpful; because wherever he went, ringing his incontinent bell, he got the young ones and the children following him. And then he would stop, and stammeringly, in their dialect— during his apostolate he made himself apprentice of more than twenty Indian languages—he would tell them of Bethlehem, Nazareth and Calvary, and of the Ten Commandments, and of the general idea of God's love of man. He set the words of the "Our Father" and "Hail Mary" to simple local tunes, and taught the children to sing them, and also to sing a very simple Catechism he had composed, in Malabar dialect.

On this direct method he founded his work. He invented, and indeed in his own example and success, he can be said to have perfected the Jesuit apostolic system, which is, first that the missionary get to know those to whom he comes as a stranger, next that he seek and win their friendship, and thereafter with the understanding so far won, he adapt the news he brings not only to their idiom but as far as possible to their whole field of tradition —rather than seek to startle or surprise them with stories and admonitions which they cannot relate to that which they already know and are.

This obviously intelligent and gentle way of going to work has been traditionally criticised and sneered at by enemies of the Society of Jesus, but it succeeded in its first few weeks of trial in the slums of Goa, it has succeeded since then throughout the world; and, whether they notice the flattery they offer or not, it *is* the method which has been sedulously aped by all kinds of Protestant missionary bodies, including some within which the word "Jesuit" still sounds with the effect of a blasphemy or an obscenity.

Another basic rule of Francis's mission was: take it *first,* always, to the children. The sung "Hail Marys," the little, brief Catechism, the short stories of Bethlehem and Cana and Bethany and Cavalry. Do not trouble the proud and the busy with it at first, seemed his idea. Ignore them, in this essential; tell the news to the very young, and with them, if they will gather round too—and the bell and the attractive foreign voice drew them into the street-corner groups— to the very poor, the down-and-out, the over-worked, and to the sick, and the people in the prisons. Get *their* attention and confidence first, and while doing so live amongst them, and truly in their way, whilst also as nearly as possible in the way of Him Whose story they are hearing for the first time.

That was the basic missionary principle of Francis Xavier, and he insisted on it—wrote it, preached it, begged it, commanded it of all his lieutenants all over the Indian seas and islands for all the ten years of his stormy, exhausting and incomparably successful apostolate.

And whilst he was establishing this simple but physically exacting form of itinerant preaching, he had, as may be supposed, a huge burden upon him of administrative, diplomatic and investigatory work. He had been sent to this confused and confusing great territory as the appointed Envoy of the Holy See and of King John III of Portugal; also he came as the first representative outside Europe of the newly constituted and already renowned Society of Jesus. He could not therefore ignore the rulers of Church or State, of Mosque or Pagoda, and simply go about in his shabby hat, ringing his bell and singing with the children. He had, as well, to establish his high office, spiritual and temporal; he had to examine conditions, religious, political, social and economic in Portuguese India; he must range over all its territories, reporting, revising, planning, preaching.

He had undertaken no sinecure. It is difficult to guess when he slept, especially in his first months in Goa. During that time perforce he must frequent the Viceroy, consult with the Bishop, become acquainted with all religious and educational institutions in the city, dine with the rich colonists and with the leaders of Mussulman and Hindu groups, while never failing to visit the lepers, the madhouses, the dancing houses, the market places, or to walk and talk and sing with his little ragged neophytes of the slums. He had indeed to be all things to all men, and to be utterly self-forgetting.

Goa, dizzily wealthy and corrupt, as has been said, and in all its crammed and overflowing life and beauty a truly shocking testimony of man's inhumanity to man, did indeed appal him. But it was its colonisers, its "civilisers," whom he had to contemplate in astonished horror. And although at first he felt and wrote that he could do little or nothing for Christianity in India unless he could Christianise the Portuguese, I believe it is just to say that he was wrong in this, for his work was given almost entirely to the native peoples, and there is little evidence that Portuguese Goan society was perceptibly influenced by the great saint's presence or example, or that it ever came to be regarded as honourable among colonial societies.

Francis grew to realise this as he worked among the oppressed and exploited races, and again and again in his letters spoke with forthright wrath and bitterness against the evil things he witnessed. ". . . There is here a power, which I may call irresistible, to thrust men headlong into the abyss . . . Robbery is so public and common that it hurts no one's character and is hardly counted a fault; people scarcely hesitate to think that what is done with impunity it cannot be bad to do . . . I never cease wondering at the number of new inflexions which, in addition to all the usual forms, have been added, in this new lingo of avarice, to the conjugation of that ill-omened verb 'to rob'. . . ."

Constantly in his letters he rages and mocks at the European standard of morality as presented to the helpless East. But if he saw it as a power which he called "irresistible to thrust men headlong into the abyss," there was moving through it, past it, and wherever it went, this evil thing, another kind of power, his own, and it too was irresistible; if it could not sweep away the

209

first—and how could it?—it could with assurance stand against it, act, live and speak against it, and let men judge between two ways of life. And for millions who witnessed it this second way of life *was* irresistible. Imperturbably Francis "went about doing good." On the one hand, oppressed and handicapped by the forces of wealth, graft, voluptuousness and demoralising climate, on the other, exposed almost wherever he went to several kinds of physical threat and danger, and living always in extreme privation, as the poorest among pilgrims and with no care at all for the morrow, he succeeded within ten years in taking Christianity all over Southern India, from Goa to Cape Comorin and Karthal, across the Manaar Strait of Ceylon, across the Sea of Bengal to the Moluccas, to Malacca, to the Spice Islands, and up through the China Sea to Japan. And in all these dangerous journeyings the Christianity which he preached, whether to proud Brahmin, heathen pearl fisher or cold, sophisticated Bonze, was identically, in word as in example the same which was manifested by the Lake of Galilee, at the roadside well of Samaria and in Jerusalem among the money-changers.

He became a legend wherever he passed, and the stories of his miracles, of healings, or raisings from the dead, linguistic miracles, miracles of prophecy and of bi-location, grew into a truly extraordinary saga. Yet he as he went on, always working harder and harder, changed only to become more himself, or perhaps more to resemble The Galilean whom he served.

His wonderful, lively, eager letters give him to us vividly through all the missionary years. And as we read him at first we are simply exhilarated by his warmth and goodness, by his fine impatience and his wonderful power to get things done, against crazy odds. *But,* as we go on through the letters, and relate them to authenticated biographical records, and the memoirs of reliable contemporaries, a more solemn feeling comes to us.

Those of us who were brought up as Catholics, those of us

210

especially who, or whose brothers, went to Jesuit schools, were always, as we thought, familiar with the great St. Francis Xavier. We heard wonderful stories of him, we knew his portrait in the Jesuit church, and we could have answered any reasonable question about him, from school chaplain or from bishop, with assurance. We may even have thought—and forgivably—that he was an unusually attractive-looking saint, and that perhaps after all it was a pity that he was so indubitably saintly. For the young can, averagely, only think the silly thoughts of youth—as Francis Xavier knew.

But if, grown-up, grown old, grown in general doubtful about missionaries and their merits, grown in any case entirely confused about saints and miracles, we come by chance to read, what we never did in our early, pious days, the letters of Francis Xavier and his life, then, as I have said, we may be visited by a solemn feeling, a solemn awareness of a great parallel.

So far as I know, the fast-thinking, desperately searching world, in its best and most civilised exemplars at least, has not been able —whatever it may have found to say against any of the forms of Christianity—to remove from His isolated place in history the modest, the lonely Son of Man. He is unimpeached, for all time. The crimes, atrocities, fatuities, follies and monstrosities that have flourished and will forever flourish under His name—ah, we all know some history, and each of us, according to our run of bigotry or ignorance, will take and thrash his favourite error. But Christ stands, in four short Gospels. In His sharp outline against the world He was to redeem, He must often seem—may He forgive me the word!—pathetic. Yet He stands; no matter what has gone wrong with all of us, He stands, and no civilised person can be unaware of what that awful permanence of one personality means.

Having read all the extant letters of Francis Xavier, and having read his chief biographers one moves, as I have said, from great admiration to a very solemn feeling—and a solemn conclusion.

I began in this essay by speaking of generosity as the greatest, because the most complicated and most tentacled of human attributes. And Francis Xavier's life, once he said goodbye to personal, intellectual ambition, was—and only the more so because of the hesitancy of that goodbye—a sustained expression of generosity. One cannot prove so vast a claim, in a few thousand words. All one can do is indicate it, and suggest that whoever cares to read of human excellence study the letters of Xavier. One could quote from them—but it is difficult to quote briefly from Xavier. He is neither epigrammatic nor lyrical in his letters; neither is he especially witty. What he is in them is in earnest, busy, informative, friendly, zealous, instructive; and, in his letters home—to Father Ignatius in Rome—desperately lonely, desperately hungry for news of his "beloved Father" and all the dear brethren, the dear Society. His loneliness must have been hardly bearable. He cries out against it constantly. Mail shipped at Genoa or Lisbon for Goa was officially supposed to reach its destination in six months, but almost certainly would make a year of the journey, and frequently was lost. "It is four years since we sailed from Portugal," writes Francis to Ignatius, "and during this interval I have received from you one letter and no more . . . I do not doubt that you write to me every year, as I do to you . . ."

To an impatient twentieth-century mind the idea of one letter in four years from the person who had directed one's destiny and was its master is hardly to be taken in, so bitterly lonely is it. Only Shaw's Methuselah group could live on such small help, we feel. But Francis Xavier died when he was forty-six. "The least and most lonely of your brothers," he signs a letter from Cochin in 1545. Always when he writes to Rome, to Ignatius, he begs like a child for news, for letters. Always he protests his loneliness. He is nothing if not human, tender and dependent upon his fellowmen, naturally and spontaneously so. And although he had to be severe and reprimanding at times to some serving under his wide-flung command, he was always considerate, in exhaustive detail, for the essentials of their welfare, and often playfully coaxing and paternal—as, for instance, in his messages to the young catechist Matthew in his letters to Father Mancias in Travancore. In the stories of his miracles too there rings an echo of the natural boyishness, sweetness he brought into human life.

For example, what of this "playful wonder," as it is called by his biographer, Father Henry Coleridge, S.J.? It is narrated that once when Francis and some companions were sailing to Baramua in the Malay Archipelago, they were caught in a great storm. The saint took a little crucifix ("one finger long") from his neck and, leaning over the boat's side, dipped it into the sea, which was instantly calmed. But greatly to Francis's grief, the little crucifix slipped from his hand in the water and was lost. However, the boat reached Baramua on the morrow of the storm, and Francis and his companions landed and began to walk along the shore toward the town of Tamalin. "And when they had walked half a mile, behold a sea-crab runs out of the sea on to the shore with the aforesaid crucifix, holding it in his claws on either side, and so ran to Xavier and stopped in his sight. And Xavier flung himself on his knees, and the crab waited until he had taken the crucifix from its claws, and then ran back again into the sea whence it had come."

It is indeed enough to say of this narration that it is a "playful wonder," and that he must have been a wonderful and strangely charming man of whom it could be written down some years after his death by one of the Filipino friends who had walked with him on the shore of Baramua.

Yet, though it makes us smile, that lovely story, it brings us back to our solemn conclusion. It is "a playful wonder," but Francis was, in matters not playful at all, a wonder-worker. So, when we have followed him through his ten unresting, lonely years of passionate service, when we have watched him in every word and

213

action of his life exemplify Loyola's great cry in the *Exercises*—
"Take Lord, and receive all my liberty, my memory, my understanding and my will, all that I have and possess—" and as we
wait with him on the Japanese island of Sancian for that ship
which will not indeed take him on to his last earthly desire, to
preach Christ's word in China, but instead will bear him in his
shroud to Travancore and Goa, as we see him close his eyes—
"*In Te, Domine, speravi*"—we recognise with awe that in this
man's life every major admonition of Jesus Christ was carried out,
in such pure and natural fidelity as almost to deceive us into believing that the perfect achievement had come easy to the saint.

That would indeed be self-deception; and we know that if a
man could live on earth in such a manner that Christ's expressed
human ideal was in all he said and did implicit and explicit, the
spectacle of such a life could only transcend mortal power of
admiration and comment. Yet such a man was Francis Xavier, on
all the evidence—one who lived *always*, sustainedly, at the highest
imaginable level of moral beauty. And this is what it means to be
the living embodiment of generosity, to be possessed, as it were,
by the most complicated of all human or heavenly excellences.

St. Pius V, Pope

Goddess, allow this agëd man his right
To be your bedesman now that was your knight.
   —George Peele to Queen Elizabeth, 1590

When the Furies finally caught up with Master Peele's goddess at Richmond Palace in the mid-March of 1603, the Flemish painter Marc Gheeraerts might well, if the Corsham Court portrait of the 1580-90's is rightly attributed to him, have been recommissioned to add one or two more symbolic figures to the pair he stationed behind the poor old woman's chair, obviously at her order.

It is a striking canvas. Leaning a haggard head on one hand and staring before her, the great Queen seems just to have caught what Death is grinning about over her left shoulder; just to have glanced round at the hour glass held aloft in skeleton fingers; just to have noticed the closed eyes of hoary Time drooping at her right elbow. Under the red wig, jewelled with what oddly recall the glass marbles of a money changer's abacus, the features are gaunt and

215

chalkwhite, the heavy-lidded eyes huge and hollow and bagged with weariness of life. Thus Gloriana certainly looked, if not a trifle more ghastly, as she sat day and night for nearly two weeks on the floor at Richmond, eyes fixed on the ground, muttering at intervals and sullenly stabbing her cushions, before her attendants finally prevailed and carried her off to bed. A Gheeraerts, not to mention a Hieronymus Bosch, could reasonably have ringed her now with phantom-shapes, Perjury, Mammon, and Murder looming well in the foreground. Perhaps also Bastardy, a lifelong incubus. Possibly, even, and despite all the fanfaronades of thirty years before, Excommunication, impassive and level-browed, armed like the angel of Eden.

To disturb the Whigs at their ungainly devotions with this last rude and plausible conjecture is such a pleasure that one is half tempted to embroider the theme in the manner of the nightmare-scene of *Richard the Third,* with the opening words of the Bull *Regnans in excelsis* tolling in that sick brain like the bourdon of Old St. Paul's. But one cannot linger overlong at Richmond. A holier martinet, Elizabeth Tudor's chief and chosen adversary, beckons from his tomb in Santa Maria Maggiore. In the enormous battle in which Michele Ghislieri, St. Peter's 227th successor under the title of Pius the Fifth, was engaged during the last half-dozen years of his life, the proscription of a persecuting Tudor apostate after eleven years of Roman patience and pleading and courtesy did not bulk so largely, perhaps, as it does in British history-books. England was but one lost (or temporarily lost) Northern outpost to set against the smashing of the Turk and the salvation of the West.

> *Llorad, naves del mar, que es destruida*
> *Vuestra vana soberbia y pensamiento...*

"Wail, ships of the sea, for your vain pride and imaginings are shattered!" Like the silver trumpets of St. Peter's the long exultant cry of Fernando de Herrera mingles with Chesterton's fanfare three centuries later to proclaim the world's lasting debt to the Pope of Lepanto.

Yet for any Catholic of British blood admiration must certainly begin on the Queen's threshold, since Pius' duty by this woman dedicated us to a couple of centuries of harrying on a pattern since familiar, and an outlawdom which ended, officially, in 1829; since when we enjoy, so far, the puzzled toleration extended to the Red Indian tribe we seem to our good-natured fellowcountrymen to be, as Mgr. Knox has pleasantly remarked. One of the many obstacles to being accepted as rational British citizens is undoubtedly an inability to join in the national cultus of Good Queen Bess. From the discovery that this great woman is essentially a bad woman—as John Richard Green, most amiable of Whigs, concedes in part, doffing a regretful top hat *en passant* to the most perfidious liar in Europe—a whole disconcerting and diverting sequence is apt to flow. The entire Elizabethan legend begins crumbling. Not a few of the heroes surrounding Gloriana lose their haloes, shrink to average stature, and begin remarkably to resemble their own portraits, in which the greedy cunning of the eyes is so often noticeable. The paladin Raleigh himself, viewed in strong daylight, tends to look like a man perpetually on the make, a ruthless go-getter little removed from the class of Hawkins of the Slave-Trade.

> Give me my scallop-shell of quiet,
> My staff of faith to walk upon . . .

The noble rhetoric, the superb poetry, the constant appeals to the Deity in which the Elizabethan master-clique indulged while founding the Big Business State thus acquire a certain piquancy. One is reminded somehow of those Italian cabinets of which they were so fond, those impressive Renaissance confections of ebony

217

and bronze and niello-work, with the secret nests of poison-drawers.

To St. Pius V such types as Gloriana's servants, not uncommon in Italy at the time, were apparently unfamiliar in a Protestant garb until the Bull *Regnans* (March, 1569) stung their mistress to final action. Pius was plainly unaware, when he added deposition to excommunication, of the Queen's hold over the still-Catholic English, whose rebels for the Faith had just been taught another bloody lesson. That mysterious, faster-than-sound international grapevine system centred at the Vatican, and part of the stock-in-trade of every No Popery lecturer, like buried Jesuit treasure and walled-up nuns, existed no more then than now. The chief result of *Regnans in excelsis* was to confront every militant English Catholic, for the first time in history, with a problem of loyalties as agonising, in its way, as his fate after arrest. And Gloriana, in whose worship her poets had long since been employing dithyrambs formerly reserved to the Mother of God, exacted full reprisals for her new title of Servant of Ignominies, *serva flagitiorum;* a phrase which, one gathers, no gentleman would apply to a lady. Echoes of that peacock voice seem still to haunt some of the rooms at Hampton Court. The Bull, I take leave to suggest very seriously, left a lasting, burning smart; perhaps something more, who can tell? Other eminent renegades than Voltaire and Talleyrand have dismayed their disciples at the eleventh hour. No wonder such surrenders are tactfully concealed from the polite, the noble, and the fair.

The Queen of England was only one of a numerous company to smart from the hand of Christ's Vicar. First to toe the line on his accession in 1566 were the *porporati*. Many of the cardinals resident in Rome, only dimly aware of the state of Europe, still kept up a pomp incompatible with existence in a citadel at siege. These Pius V immediately disillusioned, commending holy poverty to their disconcerted ears. The remainder of his subjects (since

218

reform, more than charity, begins at home) learned swiftly that a new discipline was in force. Like every cosmopolitan city, Rome, capital of the civilized world for centuries, had its usurers, its prostitutes, its shady innkeepers, its brotherhood of thugs. These were dealt with no less vigorously within twelve months than the brigands on the highroads of the Papal states and the wreckers and pirates of their seaboard. Another of Pius' domestic innovations, not yet adopted by the governments of Europe, was the abolition of imprisonment for debt. The poor, the sick, the unemployed, were his special care. Simultaneously the rest of Christendom received its orders. Simony, clerical and lay—this traffic was so rife in France, among other countries, that women and even Protestants drew revenue from benefices—absenteeism, and slack or scandalous behaviour among the clergy, high, low, regular or secular, degradation of the Mass and the Offices by frivolous composers, and a score more invitations to heresy were to cease forthwith. The Counter-Reformation had begun. Pius even achieved the feat of dulcifying the national sport of Spain to some extent by refusing Christian burial to bullfighters and *aficionados* alike, which should at least ensure him a purple grunt of approval from every British foxhunter. Himself he spared least of all men, living always as the Dominican friar he was, trained and stripped and girded for action by perpetual prayer and self-discipline and rigorous fasting.

Hardly a figure the world would idolise, then or now. Most of Pius' admirers, indeed, feel called upon (not I) to apologise for him. "I do not deny," says Newman, "that St. Pius was stern and severe, so far as a heart burning and melted with Divine love could be so. But . . . he was emphatically a soldier of Christ in a time of insurrection and rebellion, when, in a spiritual sense, martial law was proclaimed." Aubrey de Vere's remark on Newman's own austerity of expression—"that severity which enables a man to exact from others, and himself to render, whatever painful service or sacrifice justice may claim"—suggests a curious similarity. And in fact, except that Newman was a hypersensitive and St. Pius seems not to have had a single exposed nerve in his makeup, they have more than a little in common. The first demand of each was always on himself.

"Insurrection and rebellion" seem rather a meiosis when one contemplates the European bedlam at Pius' accession: the rival reformers, now a dozen or more, howling threats and abuse at Rome and at each other; the gallimaufry of excited dons prancing along the road to Millennium, bearing the flower-decked bones of pagan Greece and Rome before the human race like Constantine's labarum; the supporting literary horde, from Rabelais and, for a time, Ronsard down to the lousiest Gringoire of the slums, chanting a naive "darkness-into-light" refrain; the babbling oracles and illiterate Biblical experts; the looting and the wreckage and the bloodshed, the intoxications of the new nationalism, the well-organised ferocity in arms of the Church's enemies, and the pusillanimity and divided counsels of her defenders. As so often since Pentecost, the secular power was everywhere challenging the spiritual, and now with new intensity. Even in Spain what Pastor calls the "cesaropapalism" of Philip II was increasingly subjecting Papal decrees of every kind to the *placet* and usurpations of the civil authority, as was happening likewise in the Republic of Venice, in Milan, where the Spanish governor was at grips with St. Charles Borromeo, and elsewhere in Italy. In Germany the crypto-Lutheran Maxmilian II was plainly on the eve of granting everything the Lutherans cared to demand. In France, Catherine de Médicis—a worse headache for the Holy See than Elizabeth Tudor, since Catherine professed herself a Catholic—was giving way before the violence of the Calvinist offensive. In Poland, a perfect zoo of conflicting religions, Sigismund Augustus had been refused a divorce and seemed likely to throw the Catholic majority to the wolves in reprisal. The condition of Scotland

under Mary Stuart ("Knox and the horror of that hollow drum"...)
needs no comment. In Switzerland the four Protestant cantons
had an army of 32,000 and a highly efficient propaganda service
of printed slander. Only one ray of splendid light pierced the darkness; but even in America and the Indies, where the civilisation
of the Cross was steadily expanding, the Missions had constantly
to combat the greed and cruelty and arrogance of the conquista-
dors. And amid all the turmoil Suleiman the Magnificent was
known to be completing his plans to sweep Europe like a tidal
wave, as Attila had swept it centuries before.

Newman's military metaphor might be exchanged, perhaps, for
an equally apt one. Like some tall galleon of the period labouring
in angry Atlantic seas, the Bark of Peter was shipping it green,
as sailors say, lashed by squalls veering from every quarter,
under a sky more menacing every hour. But high on the poop,
driving steadfastly on his course, stood a captain evidently commissioned by God; spare, frail, aloof, autocratic, wasted by sickness, immovable, indomitable, patient, unpopular, assured. *Navis
Petri non quassatur*. Zucchero's portrait at Stonyhurst reveals more
of Pius' character than Pulzone's at Milan. The high, narrow forehead, the big imperious nose, the deepset challenging eyes, the
firm bearded lips are those of a man whose weakness, as some
assert, was his refusal to take advice; that is to say, human advice.
Long hours on his knees before the Blessed Sacrament recharged
Pius daily like a dynamo. St. Joan before him had needed no other
counsel on the eve of battle.

Nor, the world may be courteously reminded, were Pius' prayers
wasted. The Counter-Reformation gathered strength and advanced, the new religions fell back with great losses, the Turk
was defeated, despite the wrangling jealousies and apathies of
Catholic sovereigns and despite the business magnates of the
Venetian Republic, some of whom had more richly deserved to be
flayed by their Moslem friends and stuffed with straw than the

221

hero Bragadin. Lepanto was certainly a miracle. There is no doubt about the story of Pius' turning suddenly from his open study-window in the late afternoon of October 7, 1571, and announcing to those present that they could all praise God, for that Don John had just routed the Turk a thousand miles away by sea. The words were written down and dated as Pius passed to his oratory, signed by him later, read out to the Sacred College, and filed away until a fortnight later, towards midnight on October 21, the Doge Mocenigo's messenger, delayed by storms, arrived in Rome with the first news of a victory to the achievement of which Pius V had devoted so many months of exhausting toil and diplomacy and intensive prayer that the glory of Lepanto may justly be ascribed, under God, to him in chief. What was foreknowledge but one miracle more?

Pondering which deliverance in the presence of that masterful skull, enclosed since 1904 in its silver mask, no British pilgrim with a taste for comedy can help hearing the chuckle from Suleiman the Magnificent's Grand Vizier, assuring the Emperor's ambassador beforehand that the immediate first fruits of the rape of Europe would be the conversion—"at the lift of a finger"—of the English Court to Mahound. The Turk is traditionally credited with a sardonic humour. The Vizier's jape was probably not ill-founded. One good commercial treaty might have done it. For the Establishment she had created and forced on the English in 1559 Elizabeth Tudor had little veneration, judging by her attitude towards its chief ministers. Nevertheless, as she significantly cried when she drove her "hedge-priests" from her presence before accepting their ministrations, in default of any other, Elizabeth was no atheist. To her, as to many thoughtful persons since, the monotheist simplifications of Islam may at times have seemed the ideal religion for British business men in this world, over and above the black-eyed comforts promised to them in the next—and what a retort to Rome! Thus, but for Lepanto, the muezzins might be crying *Allah-ho-akbar* today from the minarets of the Great Mosque on Ludgate Hill, and the Chief Imam of Great Britain lamenting his lack of congregations in more nasal cadences. Of all the "ifs" of history this seems to me one of the most fascinating. Newman should have included it among those pearls of delicious satire known—to far too few connoisseurs—as *The Present Position of Catholics in England,* strewn before the citizens of Birmingham in 1851.

Compared with Lepanto such gifts to Christendom as the present Missal and Breviary, the purging of liturgical music under Palestrina, and the publication of the Trent Catechism may seem minor. They are all part of the unbroken rhythm of Pius' effort, like the increased and enriched devotion of the Rosary as we know it today, the mainspring of Don John's victory. This profound and inexhaustible synthesis of the Faith, profitable alike to intellectuals and illiterates, is so entwined with Lepanto that one should be unable to pick up the cheapest set of beads without a fleeting vision of the most glorious naval engagement in history, as Vincentino painted it for the Doge; the swaying, cracking forest of masts in clouds of smoke, the fiercely-interlocked galleys, the belching guns, the clamour of 150,000 men at death-grips, deciding the world's fate on a glassy, reddening sea; the final crisis, the heroic self-sacrifice of the Knights of Malta which won the battle. That European is little to be envied (one might say, adapting a famous passage of Dr. Johnson) whose patriotism and piety would not gain force and grow warmer while contemplating the shot-scarred Christ of Lepanto preserved in Barcelona Cathedral, or handling that rosary which was an additional weapon for every Christian combatant that day. Impossible not to be uplifted by such a vision in an age like ours, so swiftly rushing to resemble the age of St. Pius that the opening of the Office-hymn for his feast, May 5, might be written yesterday, or tomorrow. "Wars

223

and tumults fill the earth, men the fear of God despise; retribution, vengeance, wrath brood upon the angry skies . . ."

> *Quem nos in hoc discrimine*
> *Caelestium de sedibus*
> *Praesentiorem vindicem*
> *Quam te, Pie, vocabimus?*

And to which of the citizens of Heaven, indeed, can one call for spiritual aid, next to their Queen, more suitably and with more confidence? Since the time of Pius V the Ship of Peter has weathered more than one storm which, like that of his time, would infallibly have sunk any vessel built to human design. That wave of Renaissance revolt which looked for a moment as if it might become a second Noachic Deluge has dwindled into a maze of rivulets, many of them visibly drying in their beds. The French Revolution has thundered and flamed and died away in a dictator's Concordat. Bismarck and Combes, Calles and Hitler, Grand Orient Freemasonry and Atheist Liberalism and Communism have done between them all man can do to revive the onslaughts of the late Roman Emperors. Persecution, in fact, as somebody has remarked, is one of the ever-present marks of the Church, and there is hardly any part of Europe or America where it has not prevailed during the last hundred years. *Fluctuat nec mergitur*—more memorably than the galley on the shield of Paris, the Church survives everything. The tempest subsides, the sun temporarily comes out, the great shining hull emerges with a final heave from the waves. The rigging is mended, the torn sails replaced, the Ship sails on. Only yesterday, when another Pius, just beatified, rejected a hostile Third Republic's offer to supply all the material needs of the hard-pressed Church in France in exchange for total submission to the State, the enemy was making the usual buoyant predictions. World War II, as we know, was to have destroyed the Church finally and everywhere. H. G. Wells, shrillest and most unlucky of prophets,

224

himself wrote her obituary before leaving for (one trusts) a better and clearer-thinking world.

The storm now raging is certainly, in some ways, more menacing than the one through which Pius V steered us, in that Antichrist now has a greater number of allies, and, thanks to modern science, an immeasurably greater choice of weapons, from that continuous and deafening offensive over the air which is the daily torture of half Europe to the skilful employment of drugs which enslave the will and cripple the mind. It may well be that the Age of the Catacombs is upon us again, and the Mass due to be driven underground for a time, with the appropriate sanctions. If so, there can be no complaint of surprise or novelty. The Martyrology remains an excellent text-book for all concerned. Compared with what the Hurons did to Blessed Gabriel Lalemant of the Society of Jesus, the most interesting experiments carried out by Spanish Communists in the late Civil War seem amateurish. There is no reason to believe that ingenuity can improve on the Redskin technique. Yet, gloriously as the martyrs can teach us to endure, I think St. Pius V has especial aid to offer. He refused to compromise; for compromise, in this kind of war, is worse than death.

As a precept and a rule of life, compromise—defined by the Oxford English Dictionary as "adjustment of [between] conflicting opinions, courses, &c., by modification of each" is essentially a Renaissance benefaction, unless I err. Preceding ages had thought it odious and shameful, in matters of the Faith, at least. In St. Cyprian's time public penances were imposed on those of the Church's children who compromised with the persecutor, though an agreement under torture to make, say, a "token" sacrifice to the gods on alternate Fridays would seem reasonable enough to a liberal modern mind; nor can one begin to imagine St. Thomas More saving his life with a working formula enabling him to accept and reject the supremacy of the Holy See simultaneously. What Chesterton calls "the exalted excitement of consistency" is not merely lacking from nearly every aspect of what is nowadays called the British way of life. Its absence, as the most superficial observer can perceive, is a national virtue, loudly extolled as such by a myriad jovial voices.

Undoubtedly St. Pius V could have come to some arrangement with Elizabeth Tudor on these lines.* Many eminent Renaissance figures found no difficulty in facing both ways. The brilliant and spiteful Erasmus sat on the fence all his life, sneering impartially and leaning over to the Catholic side at the last moment. Rabelais' patron, Odet de Coligny, Cardinal de Châtillon, found Calvinism and marriage not incompatible with his Roman scarlet before he was duly excommunicated. Rabelais himself was plainly on both sides, though there is some evidence that his dying choice was that of Erasmus.

That all the turmoil and muddle and fever of the period gave birth to the Elizabethan Establishment, to elucidate the precise commitments of which men have wrangled ever since, is therefore not surprising; but Pius would have none of such things. Better, in his view, to lose England than keep it on any compromise: Our Lord had left the rule of His Church to Peter and his successors to the end of the world, and no arguments out of Germany or Switzerland could alter the fact. There was not, though Whigs have gladly suggested it, any financial motive involved in the Holy See's patience. Cardinal Pole had been empowered by Julius III in Mary's time to assure the nervous new-rich of England that they could keep all they had looted from the Church, and St. Pius—if there is any need to say it of such a man—was concerned with spirituals exclusively. Therefore, when Elizabeth Tudor finally rejected his spiritual authority, there was no more to be done. To inflexibility of this type in a matter of principle even our mushy modern thinkers occasionally pay lip-service, with the single reser-

* The oft-repeated story that Pius IV once offered to authorize the Book of Common Prayer is a fable.

vation that no Catholic candidate need apply; the case of James II, who gave up three kingdoms for his religion, being a perpetually fascinating example of this selectivity. Pius V is another.

> *. . . Que je pactise?*
> *Jamais, jamais!*

Cyrano's dying cry might well serve for a motto under the arms of Pius, so symbolically and severely simple with those three broad transverse bars of gules on a field of gold; standing, as one might say, for his three principal characteristics, goodness, fearlessness, and that impartial scorn for what is nowadays called "appeasement" which saved the Church from a disaster as great in its way as that averted at Lepanto. For appeasement was continuously in the air. The Council of Trent, long before its final session (December 1563) under Pius IV, had found it as formidable an obstacle to the launching of the Counter-Reformation as the new nationalism inspiring it. To appease the powerful leaders of the Reformation in Germany and France, or to nullify their efforts, all kinds of compromises were being put forward at the instance of the lay powers. Behind all demands for re-formulated doctrine, relaxed discipline, and revised liturgy lay an ominous objective: none other than the splitting of Catholic Christendom into national state-controlled churches and the destruction thereby of that unity on which Catholicity is divinely based. This major conspiracy the Council of Trent had defeated on the eve of Pius V's accession, but the poison was by no means expelled from Europe's system. The pride and folly of Catholic princes, their clashing politics and privileges, continued to thwart the Holy See's efforts to create a united spiritual front, and the agelong struggle between Church and State had broken out again in a form very pleasing to the Church's foes, who saw the God-State of Luther's ideal rising to challenge the Papacy as an equal in its own dominions.

Thus Pius V's holy obstinacy saved us once more. He made no concessions to policy or cowardice whatsoever. It would have been easy enough to grant one or two of the relaxations of discipline which "advanced" and timorous thinkers were urging. Several of the Eastern churches united to Rome retain from time immemorial a married clergy, a vernacular liturgy, and the administration of Holy Communion in both kinds. But the West was to continue as the West had developed, and would-be innovators could take it or leave it. In due course the great Suarez was to establish a formula defining the relations between the Universal Church and the noisy new world of competitive sovereign States, and to lay down the principles of modern international law. Had St. Pius V given in to the appeasers there might have been no foundations left for Suarez to build on, and no solid supranational rock of Christianity existing to block the Communist flood at this day. The increasing barrage of fury from Moscow and its jackals is, in a sense, a tribute to one strong Pope. The Comrades should know more about him.

For Pius' memory lives. I write these words on Rosary Sunday, a feast proclaimed in 1573 to celebrate Lepanto. All the world over, at a million altars, from St. Peter's in Rome to the soap-box to which some sick and ragged priest in some Central European or Chinese concentration camp has managed to drag himself to say his Mass, the Holy Sacrifice has been offered from dawn to noon this morning in thanksgiving to Almighty God and Our Lady of the Rosary for that victory which the Turk himself attributed to one man. If St. Pius is not mentioned in any collect of this Mass— he has his own feast in May, as already observed—his presence can be felt from the opening *Gaudeamus* to the *Ite missa est*. He kneels in the forefront of that great invisible company gathered round the altar at the Elevation; his frail white-clad figure can be imagined kneeling still, long hours after the church is emptied, as was his habit in life. It is particularly easy to feel Pius' presence in a British church. He loved and sorrowed for the nation he had

228

been forced to abandon, and his kindness to British exiles for the Faith was approached only by St. Charles Borromeo's. One day in his last sickness, a week before his death, as he gave up trying to struggle up the Santa Scala on his knees, a group of English waiting for his blessing moved him to tears and a loud cry "My God! You know that I would shed my blood for this nation!"

It was no merely emotional outburst. Had he been able, Pius would ardently have taken the place of any of that gallant procession of youth preparing at the English College six years hence for a life of peril and, quite probably, a hideous death, and each as aware of this as Regulus.

> *Atqui sciebat quae sibi barbarus*
> *Tortor pararet . . .*

Nor could the *Te Deum* at the College as the news of each fresh martyrdom came through have been sung in thanksgiving for a more heroic soul. Half Pius' life was, in fact, a kind of martyrdom. Increasingly violent pain from the stone which finally conquered him at the age of sixty-eight was an additional burden during all his Papal years. He bore it, like the soldier he was, without comment. Like him, one need not make an issue of it.

Heroic, an adjective freely lavished by the Press nowadays on firemen rescuing stray kittens up trees, is the final, banal, and inevitable adjective for this Pope, I find. It is amusing to reflect that but for being a saint, and on the wrong side, Pius V possesses every attribute of the Strong-Man-as-Hero postulated and proclaimed by Carlyle, and, except that he devoted it exclusively to God's service, all that Will-to-Power about which Nietzsche made such a hullabaloo. His chief reward therefore has been to be dismissed—not exclusively by enemies of his religion—as a bigot and a "typical Inquisitor." What sort of an Inquisitor Pius was before assuming the tiara, what kind of Inquisition he served, what the various Inquisitions were, why they were necessary, how they differ from

229

fancy pictures devised by Whigs to metagrabolise the vulgar—
such things are impossible to indicate within the limits of a pencil-
sketch like this, and I leave the dreary task to those equipped for
such labours.

No opposition of any kind, not even one known attempt to
poison him after accession, deflected Pius from his duty by a hair's-
breadth at any time during his life.

> . . . the general-in-chief,
> Thro' a whole campaign of the world's life and death,
> Doing the King's work all the dim day long,
> In his old coat and up to his knees in mud,
> Smoked like a herring, dining on a crust . . .

Browning's old Spanish officer in a shabby Dominican habit—
how can one describe or praise him better? Nerve us fumblers and
weaklings, Pius, when the storm breaks here.

KURT F. REINHARDT

*

St. John of the Cross

On July 27, 1926, the Prince of Mystics, the singer of the "dark night of the soul," the teacher of the "all and nothing" (*todo y nada*), was raised to the dignity of a "Doctor of the Church" by Pope Pius XI. The doctrine of the mystical life, as elucidated and lived by St. John of the Cross (1542-1591), was thereby given official sanction.

If one were to ask why this particular time was chosen for the papal declaration, several answers suggest themselves. A global war had been waged, but peace had only outwardly returned to an ailing world. Peace, "the tranquillity of order," was not residing in the hearts and minds of men. The Bolshevik revolution had passed through the early stages of its violent course, and at Fatima, an obscure Portuguese village, the Virgin Mary had spoken to three poor shepherd children and had asked them to convey to the world her request for a crusade of prayer.

But this had been only the first chapter in the contemporary epic of war, revolution, and attempted restoration; in the apocalyptic struggle of powers, of darkness and light; in the continuing efforts to destroy and the heroic endeavors to save the image of man and the meaning of human existence. The end was not yet. The battle grew more intense. There followed the internecine war in Spain, the extermination of ethnic and racial minorities, the horrors of the concentration camps, the second global war, the obliteration of cities, the unspeakable suffering of millions, the martyrdom of thousands.

Need the question be asked: why is St. John of the Cross the saint who speaks to this day and age directly, from heart to heart and from soul to soul—the contemporary of our deepest woes and our secret hopes, of our abandonment and our redemption? This generation is rapidly gaining experiential knowledge of one stage at least of St. John's way to the fulness of life. Many have learned to understand the meaning of the "dark night," the meaning of "nothingness," of forlornness, nakedness, and emptiness. To enter into this dreadful night their own experiences were pointing the way, and to make these experiences articulate the contemporary "existential" thinkers, such as Jaspers, Sartre, and Heidegger, were eager to extend a helping hand. But who was to aid in the attempt at finding an exit? Was there a trustworthy guide to lead men from the "nothing" (*nada*) to the "all" (*todo*)?

On the steep and narrow path from nothingness to the fulness of being, from the "naught" that man is without God or over against God to the "whole" that he is called to become in union with *Him Who Is,* St. John of the Cross is an authentic leader. Though he himself reached heights of the interior life and was granted a union of love with God to which only a few chosen souls have been admitted during their earthly pilgrimage, his life and his works hold consolation and encouragement also for those who are not privileged to follow him all the way on the ascent to the peak of the mountain. The saint himself has described this journey of the soul in a famous drawing. And we know from his testimony as from that of Christian mystics generally that the trials of the "dark nights" are necessary stages on the road from "things which, though seen, are not, to those things which, though not seen, are."

Those who have lost all their treasured earthly goods may learn from the Spanish saint how "to own nothing and possess everything." Those still in the possession of riches may learn from him the meaning of "detachment," so that, become spiritually poor, they will own their goods "as if they had them not." And those whose families have been disrupted, dispersed, and destroyed may find consolation in St. John's *cautelas* (warnings), wherein he speaks of and to souls who are willing to surrender everything, including their own selves, for love: "You must," he says, "detach yourselves in a way even from your relations, fearing that, through the natural love which always exists between members of the same family, flesh and blood may come to life again."

Is this a new doctrine? Certainly not. It merely restates and paraphrases Christ's saying, "If any man comes to me without hating his father and mother, his wife and his children, his brothers and sisters, and even his own life, he cannot be my disciple. A man cannot be my disciple unless he takes up his cross, and follows me" (Luke xiv, 26; 27). Is this severity incompatible with the tender love Jesus bore His own mother, or with the love His disciple, John of the Cross, bore his mother and his brother Francisco? By no means, if we have rightly understood the lesson of detachment: when we have offered up to God the precious gifts He has bestowed on us, they are then restored to us, so that we may truly own them with the freedom of children of God. Thus Isaac was given back to Abraham, "the Knight of Faith," and all his former possessions were doubly restored to Job, "the Knight of Infinite Resignation" (Kierkegaard). For to lose all is then to gain all, and he who possesses nothing is so much less possessed.

My own acquaintance with St. John of the Cross dates back about thirty years. I was a student at the University of Freiburg in Germany, engaged in writing my doctoral dissertation. It was

233

to deal with the mystical elements in the German literature of the seventeenth and eighteenth centuries. To place the writers whose works I analyzed in the proper historical perspective I had to delve into the mystical movements of the Middle Ages and of the Baroque period. It was then that I discovered St. John of the Cross.

Only a few years earlier I, who had grown up in the climate of modern paganism, had discovered and embraced Christianity. I had found Christ in His Mystical Body, the Church. The years 1918 and 1919 had turned out to be the decisive years of my life, years of physical and spiritual crisis. In the sanatorium for consumptives in the Swiss Alps I had lived in the vicinity of death. These years—following the war that Germany had lost, and the privations of the "hunger-blockade"—had begun for me with fear and trembling, but they ended in joy and peace of mind. I remember them as the happiest years of my life.

The message of St. John of the Cross was a strange one, hard to understand, harder to accept, and hardest to translate into terms of actual and personal life. Two men were instrumental in deciphering the saint's language for me, who was a bungling neophyte in the ways of the interior life. The one was the professor of dogmatics at the local university; he had just published a work on mystical theology, and he was a great admirer of St. John of the Cross. A saintly and sensitive scholar, he was also the fatherly spiritual guide of many young souls in search of truth. Two decades later, he underwent the fearful trial of the "dark night" when a large part of his beloved city, including the ancient structure of his family residence, was destroyed in a matter of minutes, with thousands of the inhabitants buried under the rubble. A cloud of incurable melancholy descended upon his brilliant mind. He has now entered into the mansions of eternal peace.

The other was a young Benedictine scholar of the monastery of Beuron in the valley of the Danube, who was enamoured of the Spanish mystics and had published several studies on St. Teresa and St. John of the Cross. It was he who further stimulated my interest in the two great saints and mystics, and I began reading their works in a German translation. Not until many years later did I become acquainted with Fr. Bruno's standard biography of St. John of the Cross and with Allison Peers's English translation of his works. Finally, I learned to master the Spanish language sufficiently to be able to read the saint's works in his own tongue. And I followed the trail of his life as it was dramatically traced out by Fr. Silverio de Santa Teresa.*

Not long ago, a friend in Germany sent me Edith Stein's *Kreuzeswissenschaft* (The Science of the Cross),† a profound phenomenological study and interpretation of St. John's personality and mystical doctrine. The author, a German Jewess and a pupil of Edmund Husserl, the founder of "Phenomenology," became a convert to Catholicism and later on entered the Carmelite Order as Sister Teresia Benedicta a Cruce. A true daughter of Our Lady of Mount Carmel, she learned to know the meaning of the "dark night" by passing through it on her way to the light of glory. She had entered the Carmelite convent at Cologne in 1934. When the persecution of Jews in Germany was nearing its climax, the ecclesiastical authorities ordered her transfer to the Dutch Carmelite community at Echt. There, in 1942, she was found by the German Secret Police. She was first thrown into a Dutch concentration camp, then deported to the notorious camp at Auschwitz in Silesia, and finally gassed and burned. Thus Sister Teresia Benedicta practised the "science of the cross" which she had learned from her spiritual father, St. John of the Cross. Serene and humble in her self-immolation, she followed in the footsteps

---

* Cf. *Obras de San Juan de la Cruz.* Editadas y anotadas por el P. Silverio de Santa Teresa, O.C.D. (Burgos: "El Monte Carmelo," 1929), I, pp. 7-262.

† Cf. *Edith Stein's Werke.* Herausgegeben von Dr. L. Gelber und P. Fr. Romaeus Leuven, O.C.D. (Louvain und Freiburg: E. Nauwelaerts und Herder, 1950), I.

235

of Him who had foretold that His disciples would stand in the world as a sign of contradiction, that they would be hated and persecuted, and that they would have to lose their lives if they wanted to gain them.

The age in which St. John of the Cross lived bore in many respects a close resemblance to our own. It was a period of unrest and violent change, of the social and religious upheavals marking the death-throes of the Middle Ages and the birth-throes of the modern world. The epoch was, on the one hand, rife with skeptical doubt, moral libertinism, and an iconoclastic frenzy and, on the other, filled with an as yet inarticulate longing for new spiritual and moral guideposts that might aid in restoring order and balance to human existence.

In Spain a vigorous renascence of scholastic theology and philosophy and a new wave of mystical devotion coincided with the "Golden Age" of Spanish culture and literature. Thus the brilliance of style and artistic form that generally characterizes the great literary and artistic creations of the *siglo de oro* is reflected in the writings of the theologians, philosophers, and mystics. The Spanish reform of ecclesiastic and monastic life achieved its most splendid successes through the labors of St. Teresa of Jesus and St. John of the Cross. Both were members of the Order of Our Lady of Mount Carmel, which had been formally instituted about the middle of the twelfth century as an order of hermits on Mount Carmel in Palestine. In A.D. 1206, St. Albert, Patriarch of Jerusalem, gave the Carmelite Order its first monastic rule. When, in the course of the thirteenth century, the Carmelites made their first appearance in Europe, they tried to combine the austere life of the early hermits of the Eastern deserts with the apostolic missionary zeal of the medieval Mendicant Orders. They vied with Franciscans and Dominicans in their efforts to kindle in the hearts of the people a special devotion to the Blessed Virgin. In 1432, the

236

rule of St. Albert was mitigated by Pope Eugenius IV, and the Reform of the sixteenth century was a protest against this relaxation of Carmelite discipline and an attempt to restore the full rigor of the cloistered contemplative life. The final result of the Reform was the division of the Order into two separate branches: (1) The *Calced* (shod) Carmelites, who continued to live under the mitigated rule; and (2) the *Discalced* (unshod; barefooted) Carmelites, who reverted to the original rule of St. Albert.

In closest collaboration St. Teresa and St. John of the Cross carried the Reform to a successful conclusion. They did so in the face of the most violent opposition on the part of the advocates of the Mitigated Observance. Undergoing incredible hardships and overcoming almost insuperable obstacles, they introduced the rule of St. Albert into many of the established communities and founded numerous new ones. Their extraordinary understanding of human souls was the fruit of a rare combination of gifts: spiritual inwardness, sober practical sense, and a sustained force of will. Both saints lived the lives of Mary and Martha in unison, knowing how to sit in stillness at the feet of the Lord, listening to His voice, but knowing equally well how to be busy with Martha after having refreshed and strengthened themselves at the font of Eternal Wisdom and Love.

As to St. John of the Cross, his significance as a Christian thinker and saint far transcends the boundaries of his country and his age. He is today generally recognized as the greatest among the masters of Mystical Theology. No one has either more lucidly or more succinctly spoken of the interior life of the soul—the experiential knowledge of God—and the way of the rational creature toward God. Nor has any one equalled him in the lapidary and beautiful simplicity of his language. Groping for the enunciation of the unutterable and ineffable, he succeeded in impressing the severe beat and rhythm of his life upon the style of his works.

St. John is a great poet, aside from being a great saint, and his strangely "surrealistic" drawing of the crucified Christ shows an immediacy and spontaneity of expression that have evoked the admiration of art connoisseurs. It is a receptivity indicative of that integrity with which—on different levels—the child, the genuine artist, and the saint experience reality.

Juan de Yepes, who later on was to adopt the name Juan de la Cruz, was born at Fontiveros near Avila, in the southern part of old Castile. He was the youngest of three sons. His brother Luis died as an infant, while his brother Francisco lived to testify during the initial stages of his brother's process of beatification. The father, Gonzalo de Yepes, was a member of the lower nobility, but he had been cast off by his family when, following the call of his heart, he had married Catalina Alvarez, who was of humble parentage, beautiful and devout, but poor. While Gonzalo was alive, the family lived on his meagre earnings as a weaver. When the father died, John was only seven years of age, and Catalina found herself and her children without even the bare necessities of life.

In Medina del Campo, to which the family had moved, John was apprenticed in the workshops of some of the local artisans and craftsmen, then became an attendant at a small-pox hospital. In the spare moments which care of the contagiously sick left him, he began his studies for the priesthood. At the age of thirteen he was sent to the new Jesuit college in the town.

John was twenty-one years of age when, in 1563, he entered the novitiate of the Carmelite Order. In 1564, he was sent to the Carmelite College of St. Andrew at Salamanca to finish his studies in theology and philosophy. Salamanca was at that time the center of Thomistic thought and widely renowned as "the Athens of Christendom." There he acquired the thorough knowledge of the principles of scholastic theology and philosophy of which there is such ample evidence in all of his writings.

238

In 1567, John was appointed master of students and commissioned to lecture to the scholastics of the Carmelite College. Ordained a priest in the same year, he returned to Medina del Campo and shortly afterwards he met Mother Teresa who had come to Medina del Campo to found one of the convents of the Carmelite Reform. For both saints, and for the future course of the Reform as well, this first encounter had far-reaching consequences.

Despite the fact that after his profession John of St. Mathias upon his request had been given permission to live according to the primitive rule of the Carmel, it now appeared that even so the cloistered monastic life did not fully satisfy his longing for solitude, austerity, and heroic discipline. At any rate, he had intimated to his superiors that it was his intention to become a Carthusian and that he hoped to be received into the Carthusian settlement of Paular in Segovia. Mother Teresa, however, succeeded in persuading him to defer a final decision in this matter.

Mother Teresa had been offered a small farmhouse in the hamlet of Duruelo, in the vicinity of Medina del Campo. It was little more than a shack, but for John of the Cross it had all the attractions he could have wished for: the place was lonely and desolate, the climate severe; he could live there in absolute poverty and practise total detachment. Already at the College of St. Andrew he had lived in a tiny cell whose single small window opened toward the tabernacle of the college chapel, and he had slept (he never needed more than about three hours of sleep) on an old board covered with straw, with a piece of wood as a pillow.

The ramshackle farmhouse at Duruelo became the first monastery of the Teresian Reform. John arrived there in 1568 and immediately began to undertake the repairs which were necessary to make the place habitable for a group of contemplatives. His knowledge of the mason's and carpenter's trade now stood him in good stead. His bed was the naked floor, his mattress a bundle

239

of hay, his pillow—an extraordinary luxury—a piece of sackcloth filled with straw. Again the small windows of the cells offered a plain view of the altar and the Blessed Sacrament. Seven Friars in all, the vanguard of the Reform, were joined together in the Carmelite community at Duruelo.

A few months later, Mother Teresa passed through the village on her way to Toledo, where she was about to establish another convent for her nuns. "When I entered the chapel," she writes, "I was filled with admiration, seeing the spirit of devotion which the Lord had diffused here. And I was not the only one so impressed; two merchants, friends of mine, who had accompanied me on the way from Medina del Campo, could not help but shed tears at what they saw . . . I shall never forget a little wooden cross that was placed beside the holy water stoup; affixed to the latter was a paper picture of Christ which, it seemed to me, inspired more devotion than if it had been a great work of art." John was fond of carving crucifixes and of drawing sketches of Christ in His agony.

John and his companions, at Duruelo as at all times, joined action to contemplation, preaching and teaching in the neighboring villages. When, after a year and a half, the place proved definitely too small to house the growing community, the monks gratefully accepted the more spacious quarters which had been offered to them in the neighboring town of Mancera. John had been appointed master of novices at Duruelo and he continued in the same office at Mancera and, two years later, in the newly founded monastery at Pastrana. In 1571, he founded a Carmelite College at Alcalá de Henares and became its first Rector.

In 1572, Teresa was made Prioress of the Convent of the Incarnation at Ávila, one of the largest communities of Calced Carmelite nuns and one in which laxity and a spirit of worldliness were quite conspicuous. The saint therefore assumed her new responsibilities with grave apprehensions. Almost immediately she called on John of the Cross to aid her in the difficult task of leading the nuns back to a stricter Carmelite way of life. John, though twenty-seven years younger than Teresa, became her spiritual director. Moreover, he and one of his companions were the confessors of the 130 nuns at the Incarnation.

Meanwhile, storm clouds had been gathering. They were threatening with destruction the still tender and fragile tree of the Carmelite Reform. During the night of the third to the fourth of December, 1577, Carmelites of the Mitigated Observance entered the little hut at the southeastern corner of the Convent of the Incarnation which housed the two Father confessors; they seized John of the Cross and took him to Toledo as their prisoner. A General Chapter of the Carmelite Order, convoked at Piacenza in 1575, had virtually outlawed the Discalced as dangerous innovators and rebels who must be subdued by force, if necessary. Father Tostado, a learned and energetic Carmelite of the Mitigated Observance, had been given authority to deal with the recalcitrant members of the Order and to put an end to the Teresian Reform. All the Discalced were to be compelled to rejoin the communities of the Mitigated Observance.

In the Carmelite monastery at Toledo, John of the Cross found himself face to face with Father Tostado, who tried every means of persuasion to make the saint renounce the Reform. John's refusal was taken as a sign of malicious obstinacy and flagrant disobedience, and he was thereupon imprisoned in the monastery. His prison cell was about ten feet long and six feet wide and so low that "he could hardly stand erect, even though he was very short in stature," as Mother Teresa wrote later on. In this airless and windowless dungeon the prisoner was to spend almost nine months. There was only a tiny grated opening, big enough for a cat (*una gatera*), near the top of the wall.

At first every evening, later on three times a week, the prisoner was taken to the refectory to eat his only meal—bread and water

241

—seated on the floor. Then, on his knees, he received a scourging from every member of the community. All this he suffered "in patience and love," without ever uttering a word of complaint. After the saint had regained his freedom, he called his jailers "his great benefactors," adding that never before had he received "such a plenitude of supernatural light and consolation" as during the time of his imprisonment. But whenever he was asked to recant and to renounce the Reform, he showed himself "immovable as a rock."

St. John's abduction and incarceration had taken place under the veil of deepest secrecy. For nine months Mother Teresa was entirely in the dark as to the saint's whereabouts. She had learned of his arrest, and that was all she knew. Her urgent letters to King Philip II produced no results. St. John had disappeared. As a matter of fact, he was leading a "hidden existence" in more than one sense. He was hidden from his friends and hidden in the love of God which bore down on him heavily, demanding that total surrender of self which marks "the narrow road" that leads on to Life. The disciple of the Lord was given what he had so ardently desired, "sufferings to be borne for Thy sake, and that I may be despised and counted as nothing." The "Doctor of Nothingness" (*doctor de la nada*) had come into his own: "Only when the soul in deepest humiliation has truly been reduced to nothing, can it become spiritually united to God . . . This union . . . consists solely in being crucified alive, in the senses and in the spirit, outwardly and inwardly" (*The Ascent to Mount Carmel*).

Speaking of John's imprisonment, Teresa not only laments the inability of his friends to come to his assistance: she is amazed that hardly anyone seemed to remember the saint. Meanwhile, St. John was cut off from all human consolation and—to increase his suffering—also from the sacramental life of the Church. But while his tortured body was slowly wasting away, his spirit was drawn to the eternal source of light and love. In the darkness and abandonment of his prison his soul began to chant the immortal songs of the *Spiritual Canticle*:

> In this blissful night
> Secretly, no man seeing me,
> I seeing nothing,
> With no other light or guide
> But that which burned in my heart.
> And it led me
> Surer than the light of the noonday.

In the dark nights of Toledo the ancient theme of the bridal song of the human soul—the Song of Songs—was born anew in St. John's heart. The *sponsa Christi* experiences her betrothal to the Divine Bridegroom as the eternal paradigm of all human and finite bridal relationships. In his prison the saint composed the first thirty stanzas of the *Canticle*. Without this total denudation and cleansing of soul, without this passage through the night of sense and spirit his future works might never have been written.

The way to the heavenly light leads through the fearful "passive nights of the spirit." The way of the Cross is the way of Life. But beyond this, St. John learned at Toledo the lesson of "the darkest night": he knew already that no human power could ever separate him from his Creator and Redeemer. But who can measure or comprehend the suffering of the soul that feels itself abandoned by God Himself? Who can fathom the forsakenness that overcame even the dying God-Man in the darkest hour of His agony?

> Where then hast Thou hidden
> O my Beloved,
> Leaving me alone
> In the tears of my grief?

And yet, for those whose love fearlessly follows their Master into this darkest night, suffering turns into bliss, death into life, night into light:

243

O night, thou hast been my guide;
O night, more lovely than the rosy dawn!
O night, thou hast united
The Lover with his beloved;
Thou hast transformed
The beloved into the Lover.

The story of St. John's almost miraculous escape is well authenticated and makes exciting reading. The flight was carefully planned and executed without any human help and in the face of overwhelming odds. The little "Brother of Our Lady" was guided by the exalted Patroness of his Order, who had appeared to him on August 15th, the Feast of her Assumption. Out of strips torn from two old blankets and a tunic he fashioned a sort of rope and, after having somehow managed to unscrew the heavy locks of his prison and of the adjoining hall, he let himself down through a window high up in the gallery overlooking the river Tagus. From the heights of the ramparts of Toledo he jumped into the darkness and found himself unhurt in the patio outside the enclosure of the Franciscan Convent of the Conception.

With the death of Father Rubeo, the Superior General of the Calced Carmelites, in May, 1578, the storms of persecution subsided. The next immediate goal of St. Teresa and St. John of the Cross was to bring about the complete administrative separation of the two branches of the Carmelite Order. But all efforts in this direction remained unsuccessful, for the time being. Sega, the Papal Nuncio, issued a decree which placed the houses of the Reform under the jurisdiction of the Mitigated Observance. St. Teresa, in this prelate's opinion, was "a restless vagabond woman."

At the General Chapter meeting of the Discalced, held in October, 1578, John of the Cross was appointed Prior of the Calvario, a monastery located in the vicinity of Beas de Segura, where Mother Teresa had established one of her convents. It was at the

Calvario that St. John wrote the commentaries on his *Spiritual Canticle* and in all probability also his treatise on *The Dark Night of the Soul* as well as the first draft of *The Ascent to Mount Carmel*.

The saint was enchanted with the peaceful solitude of his new abode and the surrounding scenery. Never before had he thus seen divine beauty reflected in the splendor of nature. After matins he would look out from the window of his cell into the majestically austere landscape, rapt in his admiration of the divine artist. In the countryside of beautiful Andalusia St. John fully matured as a mystical writer and as a poet. The *Spiritual Canticle* received here its final form, and the added stanzas were radiant with new poetic lustre.

The spring of the year 1579, bursting forth with an abundance of blossoms and flowers, filled the saint's heart with unspeakable gladness. Walking in this garden of delight as in a heavenly dance, he addresses himself to all the creaturely loveliness that his eye beholds, to groves and thickets, meadows and flowers. Have they not seen his Beloved, Him who has adorned them with all their splendor? And the lowly creatures make response to the soul wounded by love: hurriedly, they say, He has passed through these meadows, diffusing His gifts in a thousand ways, and by His fleeting glance He has left us clothed with the vestments of His beauty.

During the priorate of St. John the Calvario monastery became a model school of the interior life. "Sometimes," relates Fr. Alonso of the Mother of God, "he would take the religious entrusted to his care . . . outside the monastery, so that they might spend the hours of prayer in those groves and thickets . . . He would then withdraw to the most hidden part of the mountain. And when the hour to retire had arrived and they went to seek him, they found him in rapture, his face brightly shining. . . ."

In 1579, St. John assumed the rectorship of the Carmelite College at Baeza. This cultural center of Andalusia was a city with a university renowned for its contributions to scriptural studies. In the two years he spent there the saint worked out in great detail the rules and principles that were to guide the future establishments of the Reform in Andalusia. He had many friends among the learned men of the city; they regarded him as their superior in knowledge and wisdom and frequently asked for his counsel in controversial questions of theology and philosophy.

The prayers of the Discalced were finally answered when Pope Gregory XIII by his *Breve* of June 22, 1580, made it possible for them to elect their own Provincial and thereby establish their independence. In the following year St. John was appointed Prior of the monastery of Los Mártires at Granada. This house had been founded as early as 1573 and derived its name from the fact that it was located at the site where formerly the Moorish Kings of Granada had held their Christian captives. It was in the picturesque setting of this Andalusian city with its impressive monuments of two cultures—Christian and Moslem—that St. John completed most of his works, and it was here that his apostolate in the spiritual direction of souls bore its richest fruits. In 1585 John of the Cross was named Provincial Vicar of Andalusia, and during the following years he founded new houses of the Reform at Córdoba, Seville, Madrid, Manchuela, and Caravaca. In 1588, Nicolás Doria was chosen as Vicar General, and with his election new difficulties began to threaten the further consolidation of the Reform, difficulties which this time arose from the conflicting views of the leaders of the Discalced themselves. For John of the Cross this meant a revival of persecution and suffering. The favors he had asked for the declining years of his life, he now received: "Not to die a prelate; to die in a place where he was not even known; and to die after having suffered much."

As against those who wanted the Discalced to devote themselves to missionary activities in foreign lands, and those who stood for the opposite extreme—complete seclusion and the full rigor of the contemplative life—St. John, the faithful disciple of Mother Teresa (who had died in 1582), advocated a sane middle course. In 1588, the saint was named Prior of the Carmelite community in Segovia. Here his contemplative life reached its greatest heights, notwithstanding the fact that already at Granada, according to his own testimony, he had experienced the "bliss of mystical union" or "spiritual marriage."

St. Teresa tells of these highest stages of mystical prayer in her work on *The Mansions of the Soul,* ascribing them to the sixth and seventh "mansions." St. John describes the same experience in *The Living Flame of Love,* written at Granada in the course of two weeks. At the pinnacle of the mystical life the human soul becomes, as it were, "God by participation." It does not see the Tri-Une God face to face, as it will in the *"Visio beata"* of the life beyond, but it meets Him in a perfect union of will or of love. The Living Flame of Love is the Holy Spirit "Whom the soul now feels within herself as a fire which consumes her and transforms her into blissful love . . . a fire which erupts in flames of love." The soul stands here on the threshold of Eternal Life, "and everything is transformed and transfigured in love and praise." With her newly gained visual power the soul has become fully aware of the fragility of this earthly life. It appears to her "thinner than a spider's web; for now she sees things as God sees them; they are nothing, as she herself is nothing; God alone is everything."

The Chapter of 1591 stripped John of the Cross of all his offices and forbade him any kind of activity in the Order. There was even talk of expelling him from the Carmelite community. But had he himself not foretold that he would be "thrown into a corner like a rag or a dish-cloth"? He neither expected nor desired anything else.

It was finally decided to send him into the solitude of Peñuela in the Sierra Morena. There he became seriously ill. When his condition made it necessary to move him to another place, he was given the choice between Baeza and Ubeda. At Baeza was the college which he had founded; he had been its first Rector. There he had friends who would understand him and care for him. Ubeda was a new foundation, headed by Fr. Francis Chrysostom, one of his fiercest opponents. It goes without saying that he chose Ubeda, thus giving living testimony to what he had taught in the first book of the *Ascent to Mount Carmel*:

"Take care that you always choose
   not the easiest but the hardest;
   not the most agreeable but the most disagreeable; . . .
   not what consoles but what deprives you of consolation; . . .
   not attachment to things but detachment from them.

Desire nothing but to enter for Christ into absolute nakedness,
   emptiness, and poverty . . .
   If you want to possess all, you must desire nothing.
   If you want to become all, you must desire to be nothing.
   If you want to know all, you must desire to know nothing.
   For if you desire to possess anything, you cannot possess God
   as your only treasure."

It was in this spirit of total denudation that, on September 22, 1591, St. John, seated on the little mule which a friend had put at his disposal, began his last earthly journey. For days he had been unable to take any food or drink. His swollen leg was covered with festering sores and open wounds. In silence the little Brother of Our Lady and his patient beast of burden travelled over the seven miles of mountainous road.

At Ubeda the dying man is given the poorest and smallest cell. The physician, in an attempt to locate the seat of the infection, resorts to surgery, laying bare the nerves and bones. But the infection spreads; new abscesses appear on thighs and shoulders. The saint, meanwhile, is serenely rapt in prayer. He knows that he will die on Saturday. On Thursday he receives the viaticum. On Friday

248

ST. JOHN OF THE CROSS

by Thomas Merton

the Prior, in tears of sorrow and contrition, kneels at the foot of the couch, reproaching himself for not having done more to ease the sufferings of his dying brother. "I am perfectly happy, Father Prior," St. John says in reply, "I have received much more than I deserve."

In the night from Friday, December 13th, to Saturday the 14th, 1591, the saint listens to the twelve strokes from the belfry, announcing the midnight hour. "Brother Diego," he says, "give the sign to ring the bell for matins." Hearing the familiar sound, St. John pronounces his last words: "Into Thy Hands, O Lord, I commend my spirit." He dies in the arms of Brother Diego. "He shone," this Brother reports, "like the sun and the moon; the lights on the altar and the two lighted candles in the cell appeared as if immersed in a cloud; they gave no light."

John of the Cross was beatified on January 25th, 1675, and canonised on December 26, 1726. His Feast is celebrated by the Church on the 24th of November.

If you have never seen El Greco's view of Toledo, you might take a look at it. It will tell you something about St. John of the Cross. I say it will tell you something—not very much. St. John of the Cross and El Greco were contemporaries, they lived in the same country, they were mystics, though by no means in the same degree. In other ways they were quite different. Father Bruno, in the best life of St. John of the Cross so far written, reminds his reader several times not to go imagining that St. John of the Cross looked like an El Greco painting. He was more like one of Zurbaran's Carthusians. Even that comparison is not altogether exact. The original and authentic portrait of the saint (which my own sketch does not even faintly resemble) shows him to have an innocent and rather expressionless face. He does not look in any way ascetic. In fact you would think you were looking at the portrait of a Madrid shop-keeper or of a cook.

El Greco's view of Toledo is very dramatic. It is full of spiritual implications. It looks like a portrait of the heavenly Jerusalem wearing an iron mask. Yet there is nothing inert about these buildings. The dark city built on its mountain seems to be entirely alive. It surges with life, coordinated by some mysterious, providential upheaval which drives all these masses of stone upward towards heaven, in the clouds of a blue disaster that foreshadows the end of the world.

Somewhere in the middle of the picture must be the building where St. John of the Cross was kept in prison. Soon after the beginning of St. Theresa's reform he was kidnapped by opponents of the reform, and disappeared. No one had any idea where he had gone and, as St. Theresa lamented, nobody seemed to care. He was locked up in a cell without light or air during the stifling heat of a Toledan summer to await trial and punishment for what his persecutors seriously believed to be a canonical crime. The complex canonical and political implications of the Carmelite reform had involved the saints of that reform in the kind of intrigue for which they alone, of all Spain, had no taste. And even St. Theresa, whose dovelike simplicity was supported by an altogether devastating prudence in these adventures, seems to have rather enjoyed them.

John of the Cross found little that was humanly speaking enjoyable in his Toledo jail. His only excursions from his cell came on the days when he was brought down to the refectory to be publicly scourged by his jailers, who were scandalized at his meek silence, believing it to be the sign of a reprobate conscience, hardened in rebellion. Why didn't the man do something to defend himself?

Here in Toledo, in what he called "the belly of the whale," the saint, wisely more silent than the prophet Jonas, dealt not with men but with God alone, waiting patiently for the divine answer that would end this dark night of his soul. No one knows when or how the answer came, but when St. John made his miraculous escape during the octave of the Assumption, in 1578, he carried in his pocket the manuscript of a poem which respectable critics have declared to be superior to any other in the Spanish language. These critics range from Menéndez y Pelayo, who may be deemed to be respectable in a rather stuffy sense, to more recent and more advanced writers. Even the London magazine *Horizon*, which has a certain rating among intellectuals, included two very competent articles on St. John of the Cross in a series of "studies of genius." As far as I know, John of the Cross was the only saint in the series.

El Greco was painting in Toledo when St. John of the Cross was in prison there. But the imprisonment of St. John of the Cross, and the *Spiritual Canticle* which bloomed miraculously in the closet where he was jailed, had little to do with the exiled Greek. The color scheme is quite different. The painter's view of the city must be a winter view, black, purple, green, blue and grey. And the movement is a blind upheaval in which earth and sky run off the top of the canvas like an ebb-tide in the arctic ocean. The color scheme of John's imprisonment is black and ochre and brown and red: the red is his own blood running down his back. The movement is centripetal. There is a tremendous stability, not merely in the soul immobilized, entombed in a burning stone wall, but in the depths of that soul, purified by a purgatory that those alone know who have felt it, emerging into the Center of all centers, the Love which moves the heavens and the stars, the Living God.

The last place in the world where one would imagine the *Spiritual Canticle* to have been written is a dungeon!

I will try to translate a little of it:

> My Beloved is like the mountains.
> Like the lonely valleys full of woods
> The strange islands
> The rivers with their sound
> The whisper of the lovely air!
>
> The night, appeased and hushed
> About the rising of the dawn

The music stilled
The sounding solitude
The supper that rebuilds my life
And brings me love.

Our bed of flowers
Surrounded by the lions' dens
Makes us a purple tent,
Is built of peace.
Our bed is crowned with a thousand shields of gold!

Fast-flying birds
Lions, harts and leaping does*
Mountains, banks and vales
Streams, breezes, heats of day
And terrors watching in the night:

By the sweet lyres and by the siren's song
I conjure you: let angers end!
And do not touch the wall
But let the bride be safe: let her sleep on!

Only the saint and God can tell what distant echoes of an utterly alien everyday common life penetrated the darkness of the jail cell and the infinitely deep sleep of the peace in which his soul lay hidden in God. *Touch not the wall* . . . but the religious police could not disturb the ecstasy of one who had been carried so far that he was no longer troubled at the thought of being rejected even by the holy!

No one can become a saint without solving the problem of suffering. No one who has ever written anything, outside the pages

* I lift this line bodily from the translation of Professor E. Allison Peers.

of Scripture, has given us such a solution to the problem as St. John of the Cross. I will not speculate upon his answers. I will merely mention the fact that they exist and pass on. For those who want to read it, there is the *Dark Night of the Soul*. But this much must be said: Sanctity can never abide a merely speculative solution to the problem of suffering. Sanctity solves the problem not by analyzing but by suffering. It is a living solution, burned in the flesh and spirit of the saint by fire. Scripture itself tells us as much. "As silver is tried by fire and gold in the furnace, so the Lord trieth hearts" (Prov. xvii, 3). "Son, when thou comest to the service of God, stand in justice and fear and prepare thy soul for temptation. Humble thy heart and endure: incline thy ear and receive the words of understanding and make not haste in the time of clouds. Wait on God with patience: join thyself to God and endure, that thy life may be increased in the latter end. Take all that shall be brought upon thee, and in thy sorrow endure and in thy humiliation keep patience. For gold and silver are tried in the fire and acceptable men in the furnace of humiliation" (Ecclus. ii, 1-5).

Sanctity does not consist in suffering. It is not even directly produced by suffering, for many have suffered and have become devils rather than saints. What is more, there are some who gloat over the sufferings of the saints and are hideously sentimental about sufferings of their own, and cap it all by a voracious appetite for inflicting suffering on other people, sometimes in the name of sanctity. Of such were those who persecuted St. John of the Cross in his last days, and helped him to enter heaven with greater pain and greater heroism. These were not the "calced" who caught him at the beginning of his career, but the champion ascetics of his own family, the men of the second generation, those who unconsciously did their best to ruin the work of the founders, and who quite consciously did everything they could to remove St. John of the Cross from a position in which he would be able to defend what he knew to be the Theresian ideal.

254

Sanctity itself is a living solution of the problem of suffering. For the saint, suffering continues to be suffering, but it ceases to be an obstacle to his mission, or to his happiness, both of which are found positively and concretely in the will of God. The will of God is found by the saint less in *manifestations* of the divine good-pleasure than in God Himself.

Suffering, on the natural level, is always opposed to natural joy. There is no opposition between natural suffering and supernatural joy. Joy, in the supernatural order, is simply an aspect of charity. It is inseparable from the love that is poured forth in our hearts by the Holy Ghost. But when sanctity is not yet mature, its joy is not always recognizable. It can too easily be buried under pain. But true charity, far from being diminished by suffering, uses suffering as it uses everything else: for the increase of its own immanent vitality. Charity is the expression of a divine life within us, and this life, if we allow it to have its way, will grow and thrive most in the very presence of all that seems to destroy life and to quench its flame. A life that blazes with a hundredfold brilliance in the face of death is therefore invincible. Its joy cannot fail. It conquers everything. It knows no suffering. Like the Risen Christ, Who is its Author and Principle, it knows no death.

The life of charity was perfect in the great Carmelite reformer, St. John of the Cross. It was so perfect that it can hardly be said to shine before men. His soul was too pure to attract any attention. Yet precisely because of his purity, he is one of the few saints who can gain a hearing in the most surprising recesses of an impure world. John of the Cross, who seems at first sight to be a saint for the most pure of the Christian élite, may very well prove to be the last hope of harlots and publicans. The wisdom of this extraordinary child "reaches from end to end mightily." Lost in the pure wisdom of God, like God, and in God, he attains to all things. This saint, so often caricatured as an extremist, is actually beyond all

255

extremes. Having annihilated all extremes in the center of his own humility, he remains colorless and neutral. His doctrine, which is considered inhumanly hard, is only hard because it is superhumanly simple. Its simplicity seems to present an obstacle to our nature, which has sought to hide itself from God in a labyrinth of mental complexities, like Adam and Eve amidst the leaves of Paradise.

The hardest thing to accept, in St. John of the Cross, is not the Cross, but the awful neutrality of his interior solitude. After all, as he so reasonably points out, when the soul is detached, by the Cross, from every sensible and spiritual obstacle, its journey to God becomes easy and joyful: "The Cross is the staff whereby one may reach Him, and whereby the road is greatly lightened and made easy. Wherefore Our Lord said through St. Matthew: My yoke is easy and my burden is light, which burden is the Cross. For if a man resolve to submit himself to carrying his cross—that is to say if he resolve to desire in truth to meet trials and to bear them in all things for God's sake, he will find in them great relief and sweetness wherewith he may travel on this road, detached from all things and desiring nothing."*

The two words "desiring nothing" contain all the difficulty and all the simplicity of St. John of the Cross. But no Christian has a right to complain of them. They are simply an echo of two words that sum up the teaching of Jesus Christ in the Gospel: *abneget semetipsum.* "If any man would come after me, let him *deny himself. . . .*"

This total self-denial, which St. John of the Cross pursues into the inmost depths of the human spirit, reduces our interior landscape to a wasteland without special features of any kind whatever. We do not even have the consolation of beholding a personal dis-

---

* *The Ascent of Mount Carmel*, ii, 7. *Complete Works of St. John of the Cross.* Translated and edited by E. Allison Peers (Westminster: Newman, 1945). Vol. I, p. 91.

aster. A cataclysm of the spirit, if terrible, is also interesting. But the soul of the contemplative is happy to be reduced to a state of complete loneliness and dereliction in which the most significant renouncement is that of self-complacency. Many men are attracted to a solitude in which they believe that they will have the leisure and the opportunity to contemplate themselves. Not so St. John of the Cross: "These times of aridity cause the soul to journey in all purity in the love of God, since it is no longer influenced in its actions by the pleasure and sweetness of the actions themselves, . . . but only by a desire to please God. It becomes neither presumptuous nor self-satisfied, as perchance it was wont to become in the time of its prosperity, but fearful and timid with regard to itself, finding in itself no satisfaction whatsoever; and herein consists that holy fear which preserves and increases the virtues . . . Save for the pleasure indeed which at certain times God infuses into it, it is a wonder if it find pleasure and consolation of sense, through its own diligence, in any spiritual exercise or action . . . There grows within souls that experience this arid night (of the senses) care for God and yearnings to serve Him, for in proportion as the breasts of sensuality, wherewith it sustained and nourished the desires that it pursued, are drying up, there remains nothing in that aridity and detachment save the yearning to serve God, which is a thing very pleasing to God."*

The joy of this emptiness, this weird neutrality of spirit which leaves the soul detached from the things of the earth and not yet in possession of those of heaven, suddenly blossoms out into a pure paradise of liberty, of which the saint sings in his *Spiritual Canticle*: it is a solitude full of wild birds and strange trees, rocks, rivers and desert islands, lions and leaping does. These creatures are images of the joys of the spirit, aspects of interior solitude, fires that flash in the abyss of the pure heart whose loneliness becomes alive with the deep lightnings of God.

* *The Dark Night of the Soul*, i, 13. Peers, *op. cit.*, Vol. I, p. 393.

If I say that St. John of the Cross seems to me to be the most accessible of the saints, that is only another way of saying that he is my favorite saint—together with three others who also seem to me most approachable: St. Benedict, St. Bernard and St. Francis of Assisi. After all, the people you make friends with are the ones who welcome you into their company. But besides this, it also seems to me that St. John of the Cross is absolutely and in himself a most accessible saint. This, to those who find him forbidding, will seem an outrageous paradox. Nevertheless it is true, if you consider that few saints, if any, have ever opened up to other men such remote depths in their own soul. St. John of the Cross admits you, in the *Living Flame,* to his soul's "deepest center," to the "deep caverns" in which the lamps of fire, the attributes of God, flash mysteriously in metaphysical shadows; who else has done as much? St. John reveals himself to us not in allegory, as does St. Teresa (in the Mansions) but in *symbol.* And symbol is a far more potent and effective medium than allegory. It is truer because it is more direct and more intimate. It does not need to be worked out and applied by the reason. The symbols that spring from the depths of the heart of St. John of the Cross awaken kindred symbols in the depths of the heart that loves him. Their effect, of course, is supported and intensified by grace which, we may believe, the saint himself has begged for the souls of those who have been called to love him in God. Here is a union and a friendship than which nothing could be more intimate, except the friendship of the soul with God Himself. Earth knows no such intimacies. Those who love St. Peter from the Gospels and react in vivid sympathy for his all too human experiences, do not come as close to Peter as the one who meets St. John of the Cross in the depths of prayer. We know St. Peter on a more exterior surface of life—the level of passion and emotion. But on that level there is less communion, and less effective communication, than in the depths of the spirit.

And thus St. John of the Cross not only makes himself accessible to us, but does much more: he makes us accessible to ourselves by opening our hearts to God within their own depths.

In the end, however, I may as well have the courtesy to admit one thing: St. John of the Cross is not everybody's food. Even in a contemplative monastery there will be some who will never get along with him—and others who, though they think they know what he is about, would do better to let him alone. He upsets everyone who thinks that his doctrine is supposed to lead one by a way that is exalted. On the contrary, his way is so humble that it ends up by being no way at all, for John of the Cross is unfriendly to systems and a bitter enemy of all exaltation. *Omnis qui se exaltat humiliabitur.* His glory is to do without glory for the love of Christ.

John of the Cross is the patron of those who have a vocation that is thought, by others, to be spectacular, but which, in reality, is lowly, difficult and obscure. He is the patron and the protector and Master of those whom God has led into the uninteresting wilderness of contemplative prayer. His domain is precisely defined. He is the patron of contemplatives in the strict sense, and of their spiritual directors, not of contemplatives in the juridical sense. He is the patron of those who pray in a certain way in which God wants them to pray, whether they happen to be in the cloister, the desert, or the city. Therefore his influence is not limited to one order or to one kind of order. His teaching is not merely a matter of "Carmelite spirituality," as some seem to think. In fact, I would venture to say that he is the Father of all those whose prayer is an undefined isolation outside the boundary of "spirituality." He deals chiefly with those who, in one way or another, have been brought face to face with God in a way that methods cannot account for and books do not explain. He is in Christ the model and the maker of contemplatives wherever they may be found.

When this much has been said, enough has been said. St. John of the Cross was not famous in his own lifetime and will not be famous in our own. There is no need that either he, or contemplation, should be famous. In this world in which all good things are talked about and practically none of them are practised, it would be unwise to make contemplative prayer a matter for publicity, though perhaps no harm has been done, thus far, by making its name known. God Himself knows well enough how to make the thing known to those who need it, in His designs for them.

Let it suffice to have said that this Spanish saint is one of the greatest and most hidden of the saints, that of all saints he is perhaps the greatest poet as well as the greatest contemplative, and that in his humility he was also most human, although I have not said much to prove it. I know that he will understand that this article about him was written as a veiled act of homage, as a gesture of love and gratitude, and as a disguised prayer. He knows what the prayer seeks. May he grant it to the writer and to the readers of these words.

GERALD HEARD

*

St. Francis de Sales

A young man is kneeling in his room. His hands are pressed against the panelling. He is dressed in clerical costume. His whole attitude shows that he is absorbed, maybe entranced. But he is not praying. His eyes are neither raised to heaven nor reverently closed. He is looking intently, peering, peering through the panelling. He is not contemplating. He is eavesdropping through a hole he has bored between his room and the next. The room next his is that of his host. But his clerical dress is not a spy's disguise. Nor does his ungentlemanly behaviour show him to be a cad violating the commonest rules of hospitality. This key-hole peerer is Camus Bishop of Belley. He is a young man of good family, intelligence and devotion. He has lately been promoted to his first step in the episcopate which should lead (as indeed it did) to offers which would be grateful to the best born and most ambitious. But he is not a careerist. He has wished to take his "high calling" seriously. And Belley is a good training ground. It is a small semi-Alpine diocese. The people are poor, strenuous, yes and inclined to be dour. Their wine is the wine of the upland

261

Chablis—always dry and easily soured. And as the wine so the mind. They can easily come to see something attractive in Calvinism. Young Camus was shrewd enough to see that he had been put in a challenging position, and with enough humbling self-knowledge to realise his own unpreparedness. But Belley had one immense advantage. The very next diocese was that of Geneva, and Annecy where the present Bishop resided was not many miles away. For the city of Geneva had thrown off the lordship of the Duke of Savoy and had within its fortifications established its own grim Calvinist theocracy. Hence that city's rejected Bishop lived in exile from his cathedral. Soon, however, his amazing character had won for him a spiritual diocese which made Geneva a very little thing. Young Camus learnt as soon as he came into residence in his own see that already all Savoy and much of France was questioning whether his neighbour-bishop was not a saint.

Enquiry showed that at the very least a case lay for investigation. And Camus was clearly not the kind of enquirer who delays. To his own immediate need for counsel was added a really Boswellian interest in character. But the reports were almost too good to be true. His very need made him cautious. And the fact that his own first visits, observations and insights only confirmed and deepened what he had been told, roused his curiosity the more. François de Sales had then attained to the height of his unique achievement. For he is obviously a unique saint. No doubt all are, in the sight of God. But many saints wished (and He seems to have granted their wish) to be in the pattern of their Orders. He intended something different from His servant and friend, François. When young, François himself had felt drawn to what may be called the conventional pattern of heroic souls. Later he often smiles at these adolescent heroics. But they served to present him with his first true trial. Few men have been more gently affectionate. He was a boy of brilliant promise. In a world that was beginning to rate almost supremely, elegance, address, style, he had these supremely—to the pitch and point of that exquisite balance and restraint that made others' efforts seem laboured and his effects unstudied, inevitable. He was to refine and frame French prose—that unpretentious ease of expression which with apparent casualness continually commands *le mot juste*. And the style was the man. It was the precipitation of his spirit's perfect sincerity, its dread of sham, display or any extravagance.

He was the first-born of parents cultured and influential. His father naturally longed for his son's success and the son to give his father this seemingly intended fulfilment. The conflict gave precisely that unspectacular sacrifice which François' true nature would choose—instead of one of those spectacular torture-deaths which the immature mind loves to imagine. And to this painful test of divided loyalties was now added another. He had, after his "pre-teen" education at Annecy (which was the family's provincial capital) gone for eight years to Paris to study at the Clermont (Jesuit) College. There his temperament fell in love with France. Hence he suffered through his life the modern man's misery—loyalty to a small nation in conflict with devotion to an embracing culture. And a third and most acute distress was to be added by the very way in which his desire for the religious life was to be granted. When at eleven he had received the tonsure he knew he had a third and all-embracing loyalty, to religion. When in 1592, after he had returned to Annecy equipped with the necessary Paduan law degrees, he still sought time to win his father's willing consent to his abandoning a civil career, by qualifying to be an advocate to the Senate. His friends, however, worked more efficiently for him. They succeeded without his knowledge in having him appointed as Provost of the Geneva Chapter. The father was satisfied with the preferment and the son was set on a religious career. But for him his actual task was far more painful than the ardours of the mission field. To a nature as sensitive as his, fell the duty of winning back the Calvinists through the countryside. His preaching and example, his tact, courage, skill and method won over the greater part. It was the obdurate remnant that presented the tormenting problem. He made a distinction between those who he said, "Follow their heresy rather as a party than a religion." And, finally, when he decided that they must go, he secured that they should be permitted to sell their property before leaving.

Against the fortress of Geneva itself he made little headway. But year by year the light of his mind and heart had radiated, like a beacon from his Alpine station touching and kindling kindred spirits throughout the vast arch-diocese God grants to each of His saints.

It was this man, arrived at such proficiency, that young Bishop Camus was testing. He saw, with the surprise of the man who has closely observed his fellows, that Bishop de Sales was not only incessantly busy and yet never hasty nor hurried, but, close scrutiny showed, he gave total attention to each visitor, however exhaustive, however diffuse. De Sales' answer to Camus' question, "*Why* do you give so much to such time-wasters?" "It is God's will for me at that moment"—this answer met the problem at the height of theology. But all the more it seemed to leave it unsolved at the level of humanity. Camus was passionately interested in human beings, and, not mistakenly, in himself, in what he might hope to get out of himself. Hence his odd hole-in-the-wall procedure. Here he applied his final test. All day long for days on end he watched his amazing new friend. And as they went the unremitting round of innumerable duties—administrative, secular, religious; liturgy, negotiation, conversation, complaints, abuse, flattery—one thing was always the same in the tumbling flood, the complete equanimity, the unwavering interest, the just affection of the man who was so surged upon. From the moment the Bishop rose like a mouse, not to disturb even his valet; on through that lovingly-cross valet's stream of complaints because the Bishop had dared dress himself; through the bullying rudeness of highland chiefs; the more unpleasant carneying of dishonest suitors and scandalmongers; the meals where visiting churchmen ostentatiously abstained, looking pointedly at the way "the holy Bishop" ate all that was put before him; the presiding in a free law-court (set up by the Bishop, to the chagrin of the lawyers, to save his silly, cantankerous, litigious farmers from ruining themselves with their quarrels); the arrival of that modern misery, a large and pressing mail; right to the end of each distended day, de Sales' spirit never flagged, wavered or jarred. Then he went to his room. And then? That, Camus felt, and quite rightly as a psychologist, that was the moment, there was the final scene about which he must be informed, certain. Surely then the bow of steel must unbend. Human nature must relax. So, feeling that all's fair in such an issue of life and death, Camus bored his hole. He had bored well. His eye commanded his unconscious senior. "And he saw and believed." There sat his beloved, superhumanly kind, unwaveringly considerate hero. Yes, he was praying—apparently he always did. But now, alone, will he not unbend—not collapse but at least deliver himself? Camus shrewdly knew what the day had cost. François de Sales felt everything. There was no apathy in him. But there he sat alone in his room as quietly as on the bench, or caught on the steps of the church, or abused by valet or by peer, or patronised by a fellow Bishop proud of his own obvious austerities. Then Camus' generous soul could at last give itself completely, and the great master at whose feet he laid his devotion raised his younger brother to the amazing privilege of intimacy. They were brothers. François would take time off to let Camus row him out on the lake. They went Alpine walks, picking those small bunches of flowers, those "nosegays" which gave François one of his most beautiful and apt illustrations to us about prayer and how to carry its fragrance into the life of action. François teased Camus when Camus in hero-worship tried to change his

own tumbling oratory and to use the quiet method of his master
and joked him out of a too serious concern over secondary things
—e.g., whether troops in his diocese were keeping Lent as strictly
as they should. But it was through asides and silent example that
the disciple learnt what abysmal foundations of humility were
needed to rear this delicate, skyhigh shaft of sanctity, what sufferings were required to burn out the last alloy of pride from this
intensely gifted mind and give that ultimate resilience of temper
to the soul. St. François had no illusions about himself. His immediate predecessor in non-monastic sanctity "the Apostle of
Rome," Philip Neri, exclaimed once, "Lord, do not trust Philip,
he will betray Thee!" St. François, asked to berate into docility
an evil young scape-grace (whom the mother who had spoilt him,
had cast out and cursed), remarked in the same spirit as Neri's
humility, "It would not heal him and I might well lose in twenty
minutes what it has taken me twenty years to win!" What lowli-
ness to confess that his most wonderful characteristic was not
his at all; his most precious possession, his peace that made him
of constant service to the bewildered and passion-swept, and kept
him constantly open to the Peace of God, was never his own,
always an instantly renewed free Grace from the Eternal. So, too,
he could recognise, equally with his own utter dependence on
God, God's fullness in others, a fullness as utterly independent of
their worthiness as his own greatness was dependent on God's
momentary replenishment. When one of the outstanding "grand
prostitutes" of the day, summoning a desperate courage came to
him, made her confession and having made it collapsed in horror
at the exposure of her true self, St. François rose from his seat of
judgement and absolution. He raised the woman to her feet, himself knelt before her and, to fasten her grasp on God's granted
grace, told her that he so knelt because he was now in the presence
of a sinless soul.

His name, however, is of course connected for ever with another woman whose conversion was even more important than his long care for Camus. Round the triple theme of St. François, St. Jeanne de Chantal and the Order of the Visitation a whole library of spirituality now exists. Not only was a large portion of his incomparable letters written to St. Jeanne and members of their Order, but with his genius for humility, he learnt from them. His first great literary triumph, the *Introduction to a Devout Life,* had swept the secular world with a new hope. So God was not a hater of human happiness and fun! He really loved mankind. With perfect honesty the Bishop told lay-folk what were God's merciful terms. You must observe them and by His Grace you could. You could never be happy otherwise. It was disgraceful, it was the behaviour not only of a fool but of a cad, if you did not. "He could and would never reject you unless you first rejected Him." Further, as never before, the Bishop gave layfolk lucid instructions how they might day by day have God as their Companion in the world. Likewise when St. François came to planning for the specific vocation of the Religious he again is a modern and, at least in his mode, a moderate. The "Visitation" is one of those new inventions in which the modern Catholic Church has been so fertile. But in one way St. François is more modern than St. Ignatius with his encylopaedic, globe-circling Jesuits, or Neri with his Oratory-club centers for priests and their devout lay guests. He worked out a new religious pattern for women who were not sufficiently robust to stand the ancient Orders' traditional Rule. In all his planning we see a mind of lucid aptness. One of his epigrams illustrates this—"I will not have the home in the cloister or the cloister in the home," the latter being a too common confusion of vocations made by Puritanism. But when the Visitation was established (after protracted delicate negotiations in which the patience, tact and intelligence which he had in such high measure were all required) then this new variety of holiness showed its vitality by growing more vigorously, more originally than its founders in their fondest hopes had

267

expected. There was no greater fruit of that experiment than the second spiritual classic which the Order inspired St. François to write. It was the experience of St. Jeanne de Chantal and her daughters that gave him, the master exponent of the life of sane, adequate lay devotion, the opportunity to become, in the *Treatise on the Love of God*, an equally masterly exponent of devotion's highest range. He who had stooped to school beginners, now rose and reached to be the companion and recorder of those who, setting no limit to their generosity, wholly dissatisfied with a fulfilment of the Law's letter, asked to be permitted to offer everything. To write of that experience requires the rarest combination —a valid experience of the Ineffable and a mastery of expression. Perhaps no author-saint ever combined such height of divine devotion with such width of appeal. An essayist of genius, yet his incomparable lightness of touch accompanied the profoundest penetration of spirit. As Abbot Chapman says of St. François, in his own charmingly human *Spiritual Letters*, St. François under a tact that feels easy and even caressing, has a grip of steel. The very delicacy of his penetration (like the sharpness of a superfine hypodermic needle) prevents the patient from feeling how deeply he has been pierced. How did St. François achieve this spiritual tact—what *au fond* is its nature? It is certainly this feature of his holiness that made him the great modern, more than St. Ignatius or even St. Philip Neri. True, Neri is his pioneer in this endearing peculiarity. The Apostle of Rome realised that what stood most between Renaissance man and his God was Pretention. Somehow that terribly competent creature of intellect must be shocked out of his deadly self-complacency, which found the whole universe curious and none of it awe-inspiring. The only thing he really feared was laughter. If you could make him laugh at himself he might be saved. So Neri, as a true teacher, would make himself ridiculous, in order to exorcise by humour the demon of pride. St. François carried the lesson to a finer point, as the good taste of seventeenth-century France was a subtler disguise of Lucifer than the more ostentatious arrogance of sixteenth-century Rome. Neri had warned penitents that prolonged expression of remorse for a venial sin was often worse than the sin itself. St. François penetrates further the intricacies in which lurks spiritual pride. He is then probably the first great doctor of the spirit and director of the soul to bring to light the connection between holiness and humour. For he saw that self-humour, the gentle mockery of the ego, is the one way with modern self-conscious man, to bring him to a humility that is neither the blind alley of an inverted pride nor the precipice of despair. His last famous scene with St. Jeanne illustrates poignantly this delicate surgery of detachment. On what was to prove his last visit to France she had come to meet him. There were plenty of acute problems of the Order and of her own directorate and life to be discussed. He was her guide, director and inspirer. It was impossible that she should not be wrought up at such a crisis, expecting a culmination of insights, advices, illuminations to last her for a lifetime. The interview could not be lengthy; her longing was intense. Her orderly mind was ready to avail itself of every second. St. François was as instant as ever. When she would speak he asked her to listen. But not to him . . . to his footman Charles waiting outside and entertaining himself by whistling a casual tune. When St. Jeanne would have interrupted, he would beg a moment's more silence to appreciate the unselfconscious grace of the boy's ditty. It was like a scene between a Zen master and his pupils—the master listening to a bird and then telling the anxious class, "The sermon has been preached, did you not hear it?" And St. Jeanne when she and her dear master had parted for good realised, and told her daughters, how he had given her a message, the essence of his own detachment, richer than any amply answered questionnaire, however copious and itemised. For years he had instructed, advised, counter-checked with her.

Indeed from that day when she had first asked an interview, after the Lenten sermon he had preached at Dijon, had asked whether she was bound by a promise of absolute obedience exacted by an ignorant director, and he, after praying all night, had released her, he had been her guide in private and public affairs till they were known as the joint founders of the Visitation. Now the moment had come for final guidance. He was to commit her directly into the hands of God, for he himself was about to enter before the unveiled face of God. Henceforward, as he would see face to face, she must stand, though still veiled, without intermediary in that Presence, deprived of images, advanced beyond consolations (as she years after told one of her discouraged daughters). For the time of his departure was at hand. Though still in middle life he had already expended the energy of several lives of more than average usefulness. And maybe too his spiritual detachment was complete. He had long ago given as his motto, To ask for nothing and to refuse nothing. That achieved, what could detain him? He had also said with perfect truth, "I want little now: if I returned I would want nothing." His physical strength went from him at Lyons in his beloved France, attending a state function. His fame was as great as that of any of the great ones present. Even his death room was invaded by those who would gaze on a still breathing saint. Father Olier, then a youth, who was to attain high holiness, counted that sight as a signal grace. The doctors, however, felt that the bishop should and could be roused. So they put red-hot irons to his feet. Those standing by noticed how almost without a shudder he endured this inept attempt at stimulant. Then he was ready to go. He himself had given a number of convincing reasons why every devout soul should look forward to Purgatory. And the Church has considered him so sound a teacher as to raise him to the rank of one of her acknowledged Doctors. Above all, he tells us, look forward because after death the soul that dies in grace is ever after incapable of sin, and the cause of its intense suffering is due to God being beheld by a still imperfect spirit—a pain that rapidly purifies those of intense generosity.

For years the wise had felt that God was shaping this man for sanctity. On one of his few protracted visits (on a diplomatic mission) to Paris, the remarkable Madame Acarie and her circle had put themselves under his guidance, though they were clearly advanced people of great power of prayer, and St. Vincent de Paul kept close to him through those months, drawing on his spirit. Yet when the Church swiftly proclaimed him Venerable, then Beatus, and finally Sanctus, at every step in that heavenly elevation exclamations of surprise were heard among the applause. The Bishop was charming, of course; so affable, so accessible that we could all judge him to be a gentleman; so agreeable because so like ourselves. But surely holiness should be more emphatic, more awe-inspiring, yes forbidding! But God, who provides in His charity for each age its models of goodness, with St. François had made a style for the modern age. Generation after generation has therefore recognised that in the exiled Bishop of Geneva the modern gentleman of self-effacing humour was given his patron saint in the man who showed how with neither heroics nor spectacular self-humblings, the perfect anonymity of holiness could be attained.

Jean-Marie Vianney was born on May 8, 1786 at Dardilly, in the province of the Rhone and about eight miles from Lyons. His parents were small farmers. They had six children, of whom Jean-Marie was the third.

Three years later the French Revolution broke out. By the time that Jean-Marie was four years old the churches in France were served only by apostate priests who swore allegiance to the new State Church. Priests who refused to accept the Civil Constitution of the Clergy were deported or put to death. Among the only three bishops who conformed was the astute scallywag Talleyrand.

The Vianneys, who were good Catholics, went to distant farms to hear mass, celebrated clandestinely by loyal priests, who risked their lives to bring the sacraments to their flocks. From the very beginning, then, the practice of religion was, in the boy's mind, associated with heroism. Even Jean-Marie's instruction for his first communion had to be carried out in secret by two laicised nuns. The ceremony itself took place in 1799 in a private house at Ecully. While mass was being celebrated the windows of the

272

drawing-room were shuttered so that the light of the candles should not be seen.

The boy was naturally pious. His chief pleasure was prayer and his favourite recreation "playing at churches," when he instructed his companions in the rudiments of religion. Some of us, remembering the boyhood of A. J. Cronin's bishop in *The Keys of the Kingdom*, might be tempted to call him a milksop. But there were two differences between Jean-Marie and the future bishop: the young Marie really meant what he said and he spoke the truth at a time when it was dangerous to speak it, even in play. And hasn't contemporary history shown that playing at soldiers is not as sensible as the down-to-earth believe? Anyway, the boy said brave and important things in those early sermons. For example, he pointed out that it was a sin to beat beasts in anger. This is a truth which is still not said enough from more formal pulpits, and not only from those in Latin countries.

In 1802 a Concordat between Napoleon and the Pope re-established the Catholic religion in France. Jean-Marie was then sixteen and helped his father on the farm, watching the sheep and tilling the soil. A year later he became conscious of his vocation, but it was not until he was nineteen that his father allowed him to leave the farm and be tutored in Latin by M. Balley, the Curé of Ecully.

Most of M. Balley's pupils were boys of between eleven and twelve, who learned easily. Jean-Marie, who, owing to the recent lack of elementary school teachers, had had only a crude and interrupted education in French, was easily the dunce of the class. He found it almost impossible to memorise declensions and conjugations, let alone understand the differences between *se* and *ipse* and the gerund and the gerundive. In spite of his desire to be a priest he would have given up the struggle if M. Balley had not had the patience to encourage him to persevere.

But the young man had other difficulties to overcome before he became a priest. In 1809 he was called up for military service

273

with Napoleon's armies in Spain. The calling up was a mistake, as, in the archdiocese of Lyons, even theological students studying privately were exempt from conscription; but Jean-Marie had to obey. Through a series of mischances the young man became a deserter instead of a soldier, and it was not until January 1811, when Napoleon granted an amnesty, that he was able to begin his studies again. By this time he was nearly twenty-five years old.

For eighteen months the not so young Vianney crammed Latin with M. Balley in his presbytery at Ecully. Boning up on irregular verbs, however, was not enough. Although in those days only one year of philosophy and two of theology were required of candidates for the priesthood, for Jean-Marie's poor head these were more than enough. In the autumn of 1812 he went to the preparatory seminary of Verrières, near Montbrison, where, although the oldest student and not much younger than the professor, he came out bottom of a class of two hundred. This was largely due to his ignorance of Latin, but even when he was examined in French, he was still bottom. Although he bore cheerfully with the mockery of his fellow students he had, as he said years later in a smiling understatement, "to suffer a little" at Verrières.

He did so badly in theology at the Seminary of St. Irénée in Lyons that after five months he was asked to leave. M. Balley, however, undertook to coach him privately, and Jean-Marie was allowed to sit the May examinations. Again he lost his head as soon as he was questioned in Latin and failed to pass. The examiners' concession that they would not prevent him seeking admission to another diocese scarcely consoled him.

But M. Balley came again to his rescue. The Curé of Ecully persuaded the superior of the seminary to examine Vianney privately and in French. This time the young man answered correctly and the Vicar-General decided that the candidate's manifest piety must be considered to compensate for his equally evident lack of Latin. Accordingly Jean-Marie-Baptiste* Vianney was ordained sub-deacon on July 2, 1814, by Mgr. Simon, Bishop of Grenoble. He completed his last year of studies privately with M. Balley. He was ordained deacon on June 23, 1815, and priest on August 13th of the same year. For this last ordination he walked one hundred kilometres from Ecully to Grenoble through territory infested by Austrian invaders. Because he was the only ordinand and from a strange diocese, the clergy apologised to Mgr. Simon. "It's not any trouble to ordain a good priest," the Bishop answered.

The abbé Vianney's first appointment was as curate at Ecully to his benefactor and tutor, M. Balley; but, because of his incompetence in moral theology, his faculties as a confessor were not granted him till several months later. Although, according to his sister, the young priest was not very eloquent, the church was always crowded when he preached. And later, when his faculties were accorded, his confessional was besieged.

M. Balley was a saintly man who had remained in France during the penal days, exercising his ministry at the risk of his life. He wore a hair-shirt and scarcely ate at meals. Such an example impressed his curate, who also procured a hair-shirt and ate the same mildewy potatoes as M. Balley. Each reported the other to the Vicar-General for excessive mortification. Between rector and curate it was a race towards holiness.

The abbé Vianney remained for three years at Ecully, carrying out the heavier of the parochial duties and completing his studies. He became so popular that, when M. Balley died in December 1817, the parishioners petitioned the Vicar-General to appoint the curate rector. But the Vicar-General had other plans for the parish and for M. Vianney. At the beginning of February 1818 he summoned the young priest. "Thirty miles from here, my dear

---

* Jean-Marie Vianney took the additional name of Baptiste when he was confirmed.

friend," he said, "in the district of Trévoux in the Dombes, the village Ars is without a Curé. The church there is a chapel-of-ease, serving about two hundred souls. There's not much love of God in this village. Your job will be to instil it."

The last two sentences contained the operative words. If Saxon and Celtic Catholics are often embarrassed when they meet Latin Catholics, one of the reasons is because French villages are not, and have not been since 1789 at least, like Irish villages. Ars did not resemble Ballymacsnod. Although, to judge by the parochial records, the village was moderately pious in the eighteenth century, by 1818 only a few Christian families remained; the rest had either forgotten their religion or, having grown up during the officially godless days of the revolution, had never known it.

The abbé Vianney, in the words of his biographer, Mgr. Trochu, had almost "a physical impression of this" as he approached Ars on the evening of February 9th, 1818. He came on foot, his meagre luggage following him in a cart. Because of the mist he lost his way and had to ask a young shepherd to show him the road. When at last he caught sight of the lights of the village he fell on his knees and invoked his guardian angel. Then he made straight for the church.

The church consisted of a narrow nave and a tawdry altar. The sanctuary lamp was extinguished and the tabernacle empty. There were no side chapels. The revolutionaries had pulled down the steeple, and the bell now hung precariously between insecure iron supports. Next morning M. Vianney rang the Angelus himself on the groggy bell and said mass at an early hour; a few women attended, some out of piety, more out of curiosity.

Until Ars became a proper parish in 1821, M. Vianney was really only the *vicaire* or curate of Ars and under the authority of the Curé of the neighbouring village of Misérieux. The appointment was not well paid nor were there many perquisites: his salary was five hundred francs or a hundred dollars a year; the parish accounts might show a surplus of thirteen francs or a deficit of thirty-five francs. The presbytery, however, had five rooms, all of which had been comfortably furnished by the Châtelaine of Ars. Of this furniture the abbé kept only a bed, two old tables, a sideboard, a few chairs and a frying pan; the rest he returned to Mademoiselle d'Ars.

For the new Curé was convinced that there were only two ways of converting the village: by exhortation and by himself doing penance for his parishioners. He began with the latter. He gave his mattress to a beggar; he slept on the floor in a damp room downstairs or in the attic or on a board in his bed with a log for a pillow; he scourged himself with an iron chain; he ate scarcely anything, two or three mouldy potatoes in the middle of the day, and sometimes he went for two or three days without eating at all; he rose shortly after midnight and made his way to the church, where he remained kneeling without support until it was time for him to say his mass.

To a modern and predatory age, anxious to avoid discomfort at all costs, the abbé Vianney's mortifications will seem pointless, cruel, stupid and perhaps even perversely masochistic. But in his *The Perennial Philosophy* Mr. Aldous Huxley shows that it is only to the austere that a mystical knowledge of God is granted. He says that we do not know why this should be so; we know only that it is the rule. Catholic theologians, however, think that they know why it is the rule, and that is because all earthly suffering, supernaturally accepted, is a prolongation or completion of the Atonement. Sceptics will, of course, reject such an explanation. Mr. Somerset Maugham holds that suffering debases rather than ennobles the sufferer. Mr. Graham Greene, however, comes nearer the truth when he makes his whisky priest say in *The Power and the Glory*: "Saints talk about the beauty of suffering. Well, we are not saints, you and I. Suffering to us is just ugly. Stench and crowding and pain. . . . It needs a lot of learning to see things with a saint's eye. . . ."*

In other words, all depends upon the disposition of the sufferer. The argument of the theologians, however, that suffering, properly accepted, is rewarded even in this life is backed by results. The abbé Vianney was to have proof of this. Years later, when he had converted his parish and "Ars was no longer Ars," he said to a priest who was distressed by the tepidity of his own parishioners: "You've preached? You've prayed? Have you fasted? Have you scourged yourself? Have you slept on bare boards? As long as you haven't done that you've no right to complain."

The abbé discovered that there were three main evils in his parish: religious ignorance, pleasure-seeking and Sunday work. He set out to combat all three, and he condemned them forcibly from the pulpit. Benedictines will be glad to learn that, although he relied chiefly on penance and preaching, he did not neglect the liturgy. Although all through his life he wore his cassocks till they fell off him, he bought, with the aid of the Châtelaine, the finest vestments he could find in Lyons. "An old cassock goes well with a beautiful chasuble," he said, knowing that each was worn for a different purpose. He paid for a new high altar out of his own slender funds. Even the indifferent came out to see. And M. Vianney preached to them.

At first his sermons caused him a great deal of trouble: he wrote them out and memorised them. "If a pastor wishes to avoid damnation," he thundered at the congregation, "he must, if there is scandal in the parish, overcome motives of human respect and the fear of being despised or hated by his parishioners; and, were he certain of being killed when he got down from the pulpit, that must not stop him." The abbé Vianney preached as well as practised what he preached. "Away with you, reprobate fathers and mothers, down with you to hell, where the anger of God

* (Viking, 1946).

awaits you and the good deeds you have done in letting your children go gallivanting. Away with you. They won't be long in joining you." Contemporary Redemptorists could scarcely be more menacing.

It would be interesting to know what the Curé would have made of the boogie-woogie or the bebop. "Why," Mgr. Trochu asks, "this condemnation of an exercise which St. Francis of Sales calls 'an indifferent thing'?" The Curé's biographer gives the Bishop's own answer: because "according to the normal manner in which that exercise takes place, it's a steep and slithery slide down towards evil, and consequently dangerous and perilous." The Curé spoke with a vehemence which may make us smile: "The devil surrounds a dance as a wall surrounds a garden." But was the Curé so very far wrong? A glance at the photographs in a society weekly of illustrious degenerates attending hunt balls may lead us to suspect that he was not. Even if there is no direct connection between nuclear fission and the can-can, a generation which sends its bravest to die while wealthy imbeciles gamble and consume strawberries out of season at Deauville seems to deserve the destruction which threatens it.

Naturally the abbé Vianney did not win his battle quickly or without opposition; but within ten years public dancing, semi-public boozing and even clandestine Sunday work had ceased in Ars. And it was not only the "sights that dazzle" which had disappeared. The villagers no longer stole, swore, or gave false measure. When the Bishop came to visit the parish he found that the children of Ars were the best instructed in the diocese.

The abbé Vianney, however, didn't always threaten, and as he grew older he threatened less. He gradually gave up writing his sermons and finished by preaching extempore. Thus very few of his words remain to us, and such we owe to the good memories of his listeners.

"My children, as soon as one sees a small stain on one's soul, one must act like a person who takes good care of a crystal globe. If he sees that the globe has become a little dusty, he sponges it and the globe is again clear and shining. My children, it's just like a person with a slight illness: he doesn't need to go to the doctor: he can get well all alone. He's got a headache: he's only got to go to bed. But if it's a serious illness or a dangerous sore, he needs the doctor. And after the doctor, the medicines. When one falls into grave sin, one needs the doctor, who is the priest, and the medicine, which is confession."

You've heard it all before, of course, and probably dozed off in the middle? A simple metaphor and rather jejune? The Curé would probably have agreed. He knew that he was no great preacher. When Lacordaire preached at vespers in the Curé's church in 1845 the abbé Vianney, who himself had preached at high mass, said next day: "You know the saying: extremes meet. Well, that's what happened yesterday in the pulpit of Ars, when you saw extreme knowledge and extreme ignorance."

But nobody ever went to sleep during the Curé's sermons and nobody ever found them trite or platitudinous. His words moved as even the great Dominican's never did. To understand their power one would require to have heard the abbé Vianney say them. Perhaps the secret was that those simple words were said by a very holy man who meant every syllable of them. Strong men wept when they heard the Curé preach, and the haughty became humble.

The Curé himself wept when he preached, and he smiled when he spoke of things which made him happy. And he wept or smiled as he said mass, according to whether he was sad or glad. His demeanour at the altar was perfect: every word was properly pronounced, every gesture clear; there was no rushing back to the centre of the altar muttering the *"per omnia saecula saeculorum"* of the last postcommunion as he went. He went neither too quickly nor too slowly. Thirty minutes *ab amictu ad amictum*

280

ST. THÉRÈSE OF LISIEUX

by Thomas Merton

was the Curé's time, and his aspect during those thirty minutes often converted unbelievers.

In Ars the school was open only for three months in winter, and not at all in summer when the children worked in the fields. The teacher was a farm hand. The abbé Vianney undertook both the religious and secular instruction of the children and combined the two by teaching them to read the catechism. He held his catechism classes every day, at six o'clock in the morning, and punctuality was encouraged by rewarding the first child to arrive with a holy picture. None of the Curé's pupils would have been able to pass their *baccalauréat,* but the education which he gave them was sufficient for the rough life they had to lead. From a worldly as well as a religious point of view, the Curé was probably right: his own secular knowledge was too limited for him to produce scholarship in others, and it is the half-educated who work the most harm in the world; both the simple and the learned share the wisdom of humility. Indeed, the ineptitudes of the popular press would suggest that it is a mistake to teach the majority of people to read at all.

Because he disapproved of boys and girls being educated together, the Curé founded a girls' school, which was later known as "La Providence." In 1823 he chose two young girls of the parish, Catherine Lassagne and Benoîte Lardet, and sent them to the nuns of St. Joseph at Fareins, to learn to be teachers. Next year he bought, with money inherited from his father and with donations received for that purpose, a house near the church, and opened his school.

As no fees were charged the Curé soon had plenty of pupils. Girls came from neighbouring villages as well. At first the parents provided the bedding and the food; but in 1827 the success of the school was so great that the abbé Vianney decided to establish an orphanage under the same roof. After that only orphans were taken in as boarders and children of well-off parents were accepted

only as day pupils. Generally the orphans came at the age of eight
and left when they had made their first communion, but often
girls of nineteen or twenty years were sheltered until work was
found for them. All the money the Curé had inherited from his
father went into the school and for the rest the Curé relied on
subscriptions. The Curé ran this school until 1847, when it was
transferred to the nuns of St. Joseph.

It was at "La Providence" that the Curé's famous "catechisms"
took place. At eleven o'clock every day the abbé Vianney visited
the school to instruct the children in religion. When the pilgrimages
began adults came to hear him and soon there were crowds in
the street. In 1845 these instructions were transferred to the
church, where every morning the Curé mounted a low pulpit and
preached a short sermon.

Even in a cynical country like France it was natural that such
zeal should impress the Curé's parishioners. There was none of the
"Do as I say, but don't do as I do" about M. Vianney. Although
the application of military metaphor and simile to religion has
been overworked by the hymnologists, one cannot but compare
the Curé with a good modern general who is always in the front
line with his troops. And the Curé's front line was his church.
Except when called away on duty he was never out of it. He went
there in the middle of the night. He recited there his office on his
knees. He practised all the heroisms. He scarcely ate. He mortified
himself. He was stern in the pulpit, gentle in conversation. He
gave to the poor.

If European Christians hadn't been such tightwads, the philosophy of communism and its bogus benevolence would never have
been invented. The inadequacy of our past charity is the cause
of our present troubles. M. Vianney's charity was never inadequate. To be able to help others according to the fulness of
their needs he practised an apostolic poverty. Until he took his
scrappy mid-day meal at "La Providence" he generally did his

own cooking. As long as he had the time he mended his own clothes. He never polished his boots, because he wished to humble his feet. He gave to the poor not of his surplus but what he himself required. At Ecully when he was presented with a new pair of breeches he gave them to a beggar and wore instead the beggar's. He gave his mattress and his cloak to tramps. He wore the same cassock the whole year round.

Soon the report of the Curé's holiness began to spread. People from the surrounding countryside came to hear him and he was asked to preach in neighbouring villages. He preached missions in Villefranche-sur-Saône, Trévoux, Montmerle, Saint Trivier, Saint Bernard, Savigneux, Misérieux. At the forty hours' adoration at Limas he was embarrassed to find prelates and ecclesiastics assembled to hear him.

To the end of his life the poor Curé could never understand the reason for his own fame. And to begin with, many of his colleagues couldn't understand it either. An abbé Borjon wrote to him: "Monsieur le Curé, a man with as little theology as yourself ought never to enter a confessional." The Curé of Ars replied: "My very dear and respected colleague, how right I am to love you. You alone really know me. As you are good and charitable enough to deign to take an interest in my poor soul, help me to obtain the favour for which I have been asking for so long, so that I may be moved from a post I am unworthy to fill because of my ignorance and retire into obscurity to atone for my wretched life." This long and awkward sentence was written without irony, but with humility, and its recipient was touched. Fortunately, M. Vianney had his bishop behind him. One day when a priest said to Mgr. Devie: 'The Curé of Ars is looked upon as being rather uneducated," the Bishop answered: "I don't know whether he is educated or not, but what I do know is that the Holy Ghost makes a point of enlightening him."

The boozers in the cabarets also attacked him. Furious at the

283

interruption of their pleasures, they spread rumours that the Curé's pallor was not due to asceticism but to the practice of vice. They sang lewd songs under his window at night. They spattered his door with filth. They said that he was the father of a prostitute's child. These tales reached the Bishop, who felt obliged to send the Curé of Trévoux to conduct an enquiry. Although the slanders, were all disproved, the Curé suffered greatly.

To these troubles were added the nightly visitations of the devil, whose operations are now so evident that his existence has been discredited. For thirty-four years, from 1824 to 1858, the Curé's scanty sleep was disturbed by manifestations similar to those now ascribed to poltergeists. The chairs in his room were moved about, the furniture rocked, curtains were ripped, bears growled, dogs howled and the Curé's bed was pulled across the floor. In the end the abbé Vianney came to bear these visitations with a smile. They were always the prelude to the conversion of a notorious sinner, he said.

In 1827 what was later known as the pilgrimage began. At first the visitors numbered about twenty a day and came from the surrounding district. Most of them came to make their confessions to the Curé and to receive holy communion from his hand, but some came out of curiosity, to crane their necks at a saint as they would have craned them at the bearded woman at the fair or a pair of Siamese twins. Their number increased gradually, as did also the distance which they travelled. From 1830 to 1859 four hundred strangers arrived daily in Ars and the majority came from pious motives, to confess to the Curé. Special coaches had to be arranged to transport such numbers. As a pilgrim had to wait several days before his turn came to enter the Curé's confessional, the Paris-Lyons-Méditerranée Railway issued cheap weekly return tickets from Lyons to Ars. By 1855 there was a daily service of two horse buses between Lyons and Ars, and two other buses met the Paris train at Villefranche. Other pilgrims came in private carriages, others in boats along the Saône and others on foot. Among them was Mgr. Ullathorne, Bishop of Birmingham, England. It was a sort of holy free-for-all: prelates, priests, monks, nuns, aristocrats, commoners, society women, intellectuals and peasants came to seek counsel of the man who still called himself "the least important priest in the diocese of Belley."

All day the church was crowded, and from the small hours of the morning. People queued for the sacraments as they were later, when progress had got going properly, to queue for soap, nylons and bread. People knelt in the side chapels,* behind the high altar, in the sanctuary or stood on the steps of the church. Penitents had to pay substitutes to keep their place for them while they went to lunch. Bishops waited their turn like anybody else. Only the sick and the disabled were allowed the privilege of jumping the queue, and their presence the abbé Vianney seemed to discern by intuition, opening the door of his confessional and calling them out of the crowd. New hotels had to be opened to accommodate the pilgrims at night, although in summer many of them slept in the fields.

The Curé devoted the greater part of the day to the pilgrims. He began hearing confessions at one o'clock in the morning and sometimes at midnight. He went on hearing them until six or seven o'clock, when he said his mass. As soon as he had finished his thanksgiving he entered (until 1834 without breaking his fast) his confessional again and remained there till half-past ten, when he recited prime, terce, sext and none on his knees in front of the high altar. At eleven o'clock he preached a catechetical instruction, after which he heard more confessions. At noon he lunched, standing up, at "La Providence" on a bowl of soup or milk and a few grammes of dry bread. After visiting the sick he went back to the church, recited vespers and compline and heard confessions until seven or eight o'clock, when he said the rosary in the pulpit.

* These were added by M. Vianney when he enlarged the church.

Five hours later he was back in the church, beginning another day's work. And this went on, day in, day out, for more than thirty years.

It is not astonishing that such a routine should tire even a saint. Physically and morally, sitting in a confessional is the most wearying part of a priest's duties. Henry Morton Robinson's Father Fermoyle was so flat out after his first four hours' spell in the church of St. Margaret's, Malden, that he had to take aspirin. The abbé Vianney never took aspirin, and not only because aspirin had not yet been invented; and he sat in his confessional, not for four hours once a week, but for from sixteen to eighteen hours a day. In winter the church was like ice and in summer it was baking hot. But in freezing cold or in sweltering heat, M. Vianney sat in his little box listening to the unvaried tale of man's ignominy.

This existence was all the harder for the Curé because he was a natural solitary and had always desired to lead a life of contemplation. *"Il y aura toujours de la solitude pour ceux qui en seront dignes,"* says Villiers de L'Isle-Adam. For the Curé of Ars there was not. Worn out and ill, he tried to escape three times. In 1840, after writing to the Bishop, he set out by night for the Trappist monastery of Saint Lieu at Septfons, but changed his mind on the way and returned to his church in time to hear the next day's confessions. In 1843, after double pneumonia, the Bishop granted him a transfer to Notre Dame de Beaumont, but when, on his way there, the Curé reached his native village of Dardilly he found that the pilgrims had followed him: he had to ask the Archbishop of Lyons for faculties and shut himself up in the confessional of his old parish church. He went on to Notre Dame de Beaumont, said mass there, and returned to Ars. Ten years later he again tried to steal away by night to join a contemplative order but was stopped on the road by a crowd of parishioners and pilgrims who had learned of his intentions.

What was the secret of the Curé's power? To the unreflecting he may suggest the modern hot gospeller. Such a parallel cannot validly be drawn because, unlike Elmer Gantry, the Curé of Ars had got his doctrine right and was sober and well-mannered. What he said to his penitents was simple and untheatrical. To a priest who had committed a venial sin he said: "What a pity!" and to a religious: "Love God." Once again, what mattered was not what the Curé said but the way he said it. With recidivists, however, he was energetic. "My son, you are damned," he would say to such. But the Curé had a gift which is given to few confessors: he could reveal to penitents sins which they themselves had forgotten, or wished to conceal. "Ah, there you are," he greeted a woman through the grille. "You're the one who refused to go and fetch your husband back from hospital."

This intuition extended sometimes to a knowledge of the future. To a girl, whose brother had run away from home, he said: "Tell your mother that her son is quite well. He's working underground with decent people, far from her and from his home. But don't worry, either of you. He'll come back to you on a feast day." Five or six years later, on the evening of the Assumption, the young man returned and told his mother that he had been working down a mine in Montceau-les-Mines. To future religious the Curé foretold their vocation and to others the approaching deaths of their relatives.

Unlike many other saints, the abbé Vianney accomplished miracles during his lifetime. The first two took place at "La Providence." In 1829 the wheat, which was then stored in the attic of the presbytery, ran out. The Curé couldn't hope for any help from his parishioners, because the harvest had been bad. He placed under the few grains of wheat which remained a relic of St. Francis Regis, to whom he had already had recourse when unable to learn Latin, and prayed. "Go and tidy up the remainder of the wheat in the attic," he said to the school cook. When the cook went to the attic she found it full of wheat, piled up in the

287

shape of a cone. A little later, when there was enough flour in the house to bake only three loaves, the Curé told the cook to put it in the mixing bowl; when water was added there was enough dough to bake ten big twenty-pound loaves.

When such miracles became known the Curé's modesty was disturbed. Convinced that he was an unworthy priest, he could not bring himself to believe that miracles could be operated through his intercession, and he was unwilling that others should attribute them to a merit which he was certain he didn't possess. He himself ascribed them to the intercession of St. Philomena, an early child martyr, recently canonised, who, he was sure, had been responsible for his own recovery from double pneumonia in 1843. "Go and pray before St. Philomena's altar," he told the sick, to make sure that their recovery would be ascribed to what he honestly considered the proper source.

A woman, who had suffered from tubercular laryngitis for eight years, came to Ars: because of her illness she couldn't speak and had to use signs or write on a slate instead. It was by the latter means that she informed the Curé of her illness. "Go and lay your slate on St. Philomena's altar," the abbé Vianney told her. She did so and was cured. A mother carried her paralysed son of eight into the sacristy for M. Vianney to bless. "That boy's too heavy for you to carry," the Curé said. "Put him down and go and pray to St. Philomena." Clutching his mother's hand, the boy staggered to the saint's altar and knelt there. Three quarters of an hour later he was completely cured.

So many similar miracles took place that in the end the abbé Vianney had to ask the saint to work them in the sick person's own parish, so that his own person might not become too notorious. For the hand of the child martyr was not always visible. One day a semi-paralysed woman on crutches approached the Curé as he was leaving the church for "La Providence." "Well, walk," the Curé said. The woman hesitated. "Do as you're told," the

abbé Vianney's curate said. The woman let go her crutches and
walked. "And take your crutches with you," the Curé called
after her in an attempt to hide the miracle from the crowd. On
February 1, 1850, a woman, deaf and blind as a result of brain
fever, was brought before M. Vianney. He blessed her and at
once she both saw and heard. "Your eyes are healed but you'll
become deaf again for another twelve years; such is God's will,"
the Curé told her. The woman's ears closed at once. On January
18, 1862, two years and five months after the Curé's death,
she recovered her hearing.

However, it was not only because of his humility that the
Curé wanted to hide his miracles; it was also because he himself
considered that people's souls were more important than their
bodies and that the afflictions of the latter were often a means
of acquiring merit. This doctrine will offend an age in which
progress seems to be measured in terms of the number of comforts one can cram into a transatlantic airplane. Of course, the
fact that one philosophy is obviously false does not prove that its
counterpart must be right. Even the normally worldly must be
tempted to approve anchorites when they listen to crooners or
watch fat women waddling into beauty parlours. It is the Curé's
own life that is the best answer to those who would question his
wisdom; and the conversions that he made, no less than his
miracles of healing, are a testimony to the favours which are
granted to the integrally unworldly.

Even so humble a man as the Curé d'Ars must have known that
it was himself that so many pilgrims came from so far to see. But
he was never proud in word or thought. There was in him none of
the vanity which one of the characters in Mr. Somerset Maugham's
Ashenden says "leers even cynically in the humility of the saint."
M. Vianney was so humble that he was unaware of his own
humility. "It's a terrible thing to have to appear before God
as a parish priest," he used to say, and almost gave way to despair

at the thought that no parish priest had ever been canonised. I don't suppose that he had heard of the contention of St. Odo of Cluny that the floor of hell is paved with the bald pates of clergymen. Nor had any need to know of this warning, any more than he required to have read St. Thomas' *Summa*. The Curé knew his theology intuitively and his virtues were as natural as his knowledge. If pilgrims came to Ars, he argued, and if conversions and miracles took place through the unworthy agency of so unimportant a priest as himself, it was only in order that the power of God might be more clearly shown.

Worldly honours came to the Curé although he tried to avoid them. In 1852 the new Bishop made an unexpected visit. The Curé hurried out of his confessional to offer incense and holy water to his ordinary and made a short speech of welcome. But when the Bishop tried to invest him with a Canon's cape he protested. "Give it to my curate," he said. "It will suit him better than me." The new Canon had to be invested by force, and as soon as the Bishop had gone he sold the cape for fifty francs, which he gave to the poor. His cross of the Legion of Honour was seen by the public for the first time when it was placed on his coffin.

His humility was constantly put to proof. During the last twenty years at least of his life he must have known that he was considered a saint. The indiscreet deportment of many of the pilgrims could have left him in no doubt. Vulgar collectors of relics snipped pieces off his cassock as he passed through the throng and stole his breviary or his catechism from the pulpit when he preached. When he went to the barber he had to pick up the locks of his hair which had been cut off and burn them in his fireplace. Although he never allowed himself to be photographed, his portrait was on sale throughout the village. The Curé tolerated this only because it was a means for the shopkeepers to earn their livelihood. "They've made a new picture of me," he said

290

one day to Catherine Lassagne. "It's me all right this time. I look stupid, as stupid as a goose."

Until the pilgrimages began to swell in 1830 the Curé's duties were not heavy, but after that they became overwhelming. For thirteen years, until his illness in 1843, he spent sixteen or eighteen hours a day in the confessional, preached, said his office and carried out his ordinary work as a parish priest without a curate. And when the Bishop did send him a curate, he sent him a bumptious oaf, an abbé Raymond, who had recently been Curé of Savigneux and now thought that he had been appointed Curé of Ars. He signed as such in the baptismal register. He even contradicted the abbé Vianney publicly from the pulpit. How did the Curé take it? "I regret only one thing," he said later about the abbé Raymond, "and that is that I didn't learn more from his example; I count, however, on the tender and fatherly affection which he bore me."

The wickedness of the world hurt the Curé because he saw it as a deliberate laceration of the goodness of God. As he sat in his confessional he wept that men could be so mean. And as he suffered in his soul so he suffered in his body. On his left arm he wore an iron band with four spikes on the inside. For fifteen years he was tortured from acute neuralgia contracted through deliberately sleeping in a damp room in the presbytery. Lack of exercise brought on fainting fits which made it necessary for him to be bled once a year. He had such violent toothache that he had to ask the schoolteacher to pull out several of his teeth with pliers. In the confessional his headaches were so severe that he often had to sit with a poultice on his forehead. And still he wore his hair-shirt and scourged himself in his room.

Towards the end of his life his sufferings became more and more terrible. He kept fainting in the confessional, and in the pulpit his voice was so feeble that the congregation could scarcely hear what he was saying. They could, however, see him weeping and smiling as he preached, and occasionally they were rewarded with an audible and slightly acidulous witticism. "The Emperor has done fine things, but he's forgotten something. He ought to have made doors larger so that crinolines could get through."

Such a rebuke may recall the Hibernian fulminations of the 1920's against the scantiness rather than the volume of apparel. And indeed the Curé of Ars ruled his parish à l'irlandaise and was almost certainly the only priest in France who could do so. He was conscious, too, of his own power. "Listen, we're not in England," he said to a female busybody who was trying to show him how to run the parish. "In England it is Queen Victoria who gives orders; here it is I."

For during the last years of his life the Curé encountered none of the opposition by which he had been faced when he first came to Ars. Quite apart from the fact that the worldly tolerate sanctity more readily in the old than in the young, the heroism of his life had made even the most recalcitrant love him. And among the new righteous there were perhaps some who kept the commandments more to please their Curé than to please God. In 1818 there were few men in the parish who made their Easter duties; in 1859 there were fewer who failed to make them.

During the thirty years in which the Curé sat day and night in his confessional philosophies were being hatched which were to rock the world even more than the French Revolution of 1789. Darwin was preparing *The Origin of Species* and Ernest Renan left the Church. In his high house in Passy, Honoré de Balzac was writing his *La Comédie Humaine,* and the first railways were built. Two more revolutions took place in France. Slowly but surely science, scepticism, disillusionment, speed and greed were setting the stage for the tragedies of 1914 and 1939.

As he went to and fro between his church and his presbytery the Curé must have heard some echo of the rumblings in the outside world. Some even say that he foretold the war of 1914, but

292

whether this is true or false he must have known that men were marching towards disaster. His remedy was simple, and he preached it with his lips and with his life: the practice of integral Christianity. He was a parish priest and his pulpit was in Ars, but to the people of Ars he told the truth with such simple sincerity that people from all over the world came to listen to him.

In the last seven months of his life a hundred thousand pilgrims came to Ars. His "catechisms," Mgr. Trochu says, were a long string of exclamations and tears. He could speak only with difficulty and his feeble words were cut short by coughing fits. He was too ill to scourge himself any more. In his bed he lay sleepless, but he still rose at midnight and went across to the church to hear confessions. On the feast of Corpus Christi he was too weak to carry the Blessed Sacrament in procession, but could only hold the monstrance in his hands to bless the people. And still he wept as he wondered: "I do not know if I have carried out properly the functions of my ministry."

He foretold that his death would take place at the beginning of August, 1859. On July 29th, although very ill, he rose at one o'clock and went down to the church. During the day the heat was so intense that he fainted several times in the confessional and had to be taken out of the church to get air. At eleven o'clock, before preaching his "catechism," he asked for a little wine and drank it from the hollow of his hand. When he climbed up into his little pulpit his voice was so frail that nobody could hear what he was saying; but the congregation knew that he was talking about the Eucharist, because he kept looking at the tabernacle.

At one o'clock the next morning he knocked on the floor of his room. Catherine Lassagne came running. "It's my poor end," he said. "Go and fetch the Curé of Jassans."

He was so ill that he did not protest when they slid a proper mattress on top of his pallet of straw. He swallowed all the medicines they gave him. The only complaint he made was when a nun flapped away the flies from his forehead. "Leave me alone with my poor flies," he said. "Sin's the only thing that worries me."

He made his confession humbly and coherently to the Curé of Jassans. At three o'clock in the afternoon he received Viaticum. A procession of twenty priests carrying lighted tapers preceded the Blessed Sacrament. When they knelt round the bed the heat was so great that they had to extinguish the candles. The abbé Vianney wept. "It is sad to receive communion for the last time," he said.

But even on his deathbed he was not allowed the solitude which he desired so greatly. People came with rosaries and medals to be blessed, and to be blessed themselves. Unable to speak, the Curé raised his hand and made a feeble sign of the cross.

On August 3 he was still alive. At seven o'clock that evening the Bishop of Belley came. The Curé was too ill to speak and could only smile. The Bishop kissed him and went down into the church to pray for him. At two o'clock next morning Jean-Marie-Baptiste Vianney, Curé of Ars for more than forty-one years, died; he was seventy-three years old.

Miracles continued to be wrought through the intercession of the Curé of Ars after his death. He was beatified on January 8, 1905 and canonised on May 31, 1925, a fortnight after St. Thérèse of Lisieux. Although this juxtaposition may have been accidental, the lesson seems clear. In an age whose selfishness and rationalism led inevitably to the tragedies of today, both Jean-Marie-Baptiste Vianney and St. Thérèse of Lisieux lived by sacrifice and faith. To those who contend that their example has been without effect Maxence van der Meersch cites the resignation, the courage and the fortitude which millions have acquired through praying at their tombs. It is true that if we all lived as they wanted us to live there might be no radios, refrigerators or air-conditioned movie houses; but there might also be no bomber airplanes and no angry poor to train their cannon on civilisation.

St. Thérèse of Lisieux

For

Miguel Prados y Such

On November 20th, 1888 Friedrich Nietzsche wrote in a
letter to the Danish historian of literature, Georg Brandes: "I
have now revealed myself, and I have done it with a cynicism
which will have its effects on the course of history. The name
of the book is 'Ecce Homo,' and it represents a sort of assassina-
tion, without any mercy for the Crucified one; it ends with thunder and lightning against anything which is Christian or in any
way contaminated by Christianity. Now, at last, I have become the
first psychologist of Christianity. I am an old artillery man, and
I draw up heavy guns of whose existence no enemy of Christianity
would ever have dreamed. The whole thing is a prelude to 'The
Revaluation of All Values,' a work which I have already finished.
I tell you that within two years I'll have the whole earth in convulsions."

About the same day on which Nietzsche wrote this, an unknown
lady of the French provincial middle class, a Madame Guérin re-

ceived a letter (dated November 18th) from her niece, Thérèse Martin, a fifteen-year-old postulant in the Carmel at Lisieux. This is what Thérèse said in her letter: "This morning, at Communion, I prayed hard to Jesus to fill you to the full with His joys. . . . alas, joys are not what He has been sending us for some time, it is the Cross and only the Cross that He gives us to rest upon. . . . oh, my dearest Aunt, if it were only I that must suffer, I would not mind, but I know the great part you take in our trial. I should like to take every sorrow from you for your feast, to take all your burdens to myself. That is what a moment ago I was asking of Him whose heart was beating in unison with mine. I felt then that suffering was the very best gift He had to give us, that He gave it only to His chosen friends; this answer made clear to me that my prayer was not granted, for I saw that Jesus loved my dear Aunt too much to take away her Cross!"

The two letters quoted here, written nearly simultaneously, are remarkably dissimilar in content and in mood. They really are, as the saying goes, poles apart, and it is not difficult to see that everything which has occurred in the history of the world since that November 1888 has occurred in between these two poles.

To be sure, it is quite unfair to Nietzsche to quote him in such a manner. That letter was written shortly before the outbreak of his mental illness. Hence the extravagance of phrase, although the content reflects a good deal of the thought of the writer's creative years. Moreover, it reveals only one side of this remarkable thinker. He has, on other occasions, written on Christ and Christianity in a way which is nearly the opposite of our quotation. Moreover, there were virtuous sides to his life, and he was anything but the nihilist or immoralist which the uninitiated reader might surmise behind those lines. He was a truly modern man. He was not only complex but he allowed his complexity to get the better of him. He finally broke under the weight of a paradox. This is the reason why one cannot really quote him with

296

any fairness, and any quotation, no matter from which one of his works, would contradict another quotation. In a way, one always quotes him out of context.

Not so Thérèse Martin. Our quotation is a fair sample. It is quite impossible to be unfair to her by quoting her out of context because, in a sense, one is always in context. She said at one time that she began to accept the love of Christ and His Cross at the age of three. She died at the age of twenty-four under incredible suffering, with the words: "My God, I love you!"

In other words, the writer of the first letter is typical of all of us "modern" people by the many facets of his personality, the multiple roots of his thought and his glittering complexity. The writer of the second one showed, in contrast to this, a remarkable single-mindedness. This single-mindedness becomes more startling the more one gets acquainted with St. Thérèse.

To be sure, single-mindedness was not natural with her. If it were it would hardly constitute a heroic virtue. Precocious geniuses, in music or in mathematics, are also single-minded. In fact, they often make great material sacrifices in order to pursue their vocation. In a sense they live heroic lives. But I do not think that they ever have serious temptations, let us say on account of poverty, to give up music or painting and go in for banking. Not so St. Thérèse. From the meager hints she gives us it becomes obvious that she must have been tortured to the limit by the possibilities of many other lives she could have led—the life in the world, the life of natural peace and happiness as she had known it in the home of her childhood, the life of a housewife and a mother. Saints are the geniuses of religion, but not all geniuses of religion are saints. In fact, there are precocious mystics, very much as there are precocious musicians or precocious mathematicians. Guardini speaks of "religiously talented" people. It is highly probable that there is, on the natural plane, a gift for mysticism as there is a gift for playing chess. From this point of view the whole Martin family was not unlike one of those families of talented musicians. To use an American idiomatic expression, little Thérèse was a "natural." But—and this is the way in which saints differ essentially from other geniuses—her single-mindedness, her monolithic life, was most strenuously acquired and had to be re- conquered every day in a struggle for which there is only one word —mortal. We should not underestimate the sufferings of the geniuses or underrate their merits. But they are naturals and, in a way, always remain naturals. They are never tempted to be non-geniuses. Not so the saints. If they are naturals, as St. Thérèse obviously was, they cannot afford to remain so. They are tempted to be non-saints almost every second of their lives.

The fact that St. Thérèse's "simple" life was a most bitter and terrible conquest is not at all obvious from her writings. You can read a lot of her letters and a large part of her autobiography, and never guess the existence of potential negation. From that early age of three to her death at twenty-four she seems to have been flying in a straight line towards a goal, unwavering, like a homing bird whose instinct does not present him with alternatives. The deception is emphasized by her style of expression.

This brings us to another point. When we compare the two quotations given in the beginning we are struck by an obvious difference not only in content but also in expression. Although Nietzsche's letter is far from showing him at his best as a writer, there is something very personal and provocative in the way in which he expresses himself. The quotation from Thérèse Martin, on the other hand, sounds like a religious cliché. One has the feel- ing that letters like this must have been written by thousands of French girls to thousands of aunts at all times. Now this apparent lack of originality is a most important feature of her personality, of her life, and of the effect she has had on people. The word original is derived from origin, and the paradoxical fact exists that those who go straight towards the origin are, in temporal

298

terms, often quite unoriginal. After all, Christ Himself has summed up the Law and the Prophets in two sentences, and there is not much variety of expression possible. But there seems to be an infinite variety in the possibilities of being different. Nietzsche's attack on Christianity was highly original. He had an angle entirely his own. So had Voltaire, so had Lenin, and so has Bertrand Russell. Even people of much lesser intelligence, when they come out with platitudes along those lines, always seem to manage to sound smart. They have it all over a Carmelite nun, particularly if that Carmelite nun couches her statements in "poetic" language. The poetic taste of the middle-class of the French province (the flowers, the perfumes and the toys, and all the other sweet and little things of this world) is an obstacle for a great number of people. It was an obstacle for me. Moreover, it emphasizes the surface lack of originality. That such a searing flame should have hidden under the camouflage of *fin de siècle* ornaments is somehow a challenge to us modern people. It is not at all smart. It is a trial to our intellectual pride.

Her apparent lack of originality is so significant because it adds another element of anonymity. It is this hiddenness which is so important in the picture of St. Thérèse of the Infant Jesus and the Holy Face. Hiddenness, for some reason, seems to be an essential element in the economy of salvation. Abraham was a big herdsman but he was nothing compared with the powerful Chaldeans and the other nations of his time. He was told "In thee shall all the kindred of the earth be blessed" (Gen. xii, 3), and "Look up to heaven and number the stars, if thou canst . . . so shall thy seed be." The Jewish people were the smallest, most insignificant tribe in the Near East. They were altogether inconspicuous within the framework of the political history of their time. The Blessed Virgin was an unknown and hidden girl when she received the salutation from the angel. People often do not realize that Christ Himself, in terms of temporal fame and in terms of political history, was quite unknown. There is hardly any reference to him in Roman history books of the time. You may remember Anatole France's famous story "The Procurator of Judea." In it we meet Pontius Pilate as a retired civil servant who lives in a health resort and nurses his arthritis. A friend from the time of Pilate's procuratorship in Judea meets him and reminds him of several incidents of those bygone years. The friend brings up, quite incidentally, the case of Jesus. Pontius Pilate tries hard to remember. But finally the old civil servant, who has had so many legal cases to deal with, admits: "I do not recall him." The great skeptic Anatole France has here, with artistic intuition, given us an eternal truth. Compared with the matters of state of the Roman Empire, Jesus was nothing. He never made the headlines, to use the current expression. The procurator Pontius Pilate, in order to remember, would have had to look up the old files, provided there were any left. It is most important to realize that within the colossal Imperial machinery of Rome the story of the man with the blood-stained face, mocked by occupation troops, is not much more than a police incident.

Thus we see that a curious incongruity exists between the political and the spiritual history of mankind. It seems almost as if a thing to be world-shaking in spiritual terms had to be inconspicuous and unknown in temporal terms. Those who are familiar with St. Térèse's life remember the incident when she was on her sickbed and overheard the remarks of young novices outside her window. It is customary that after the death of a nun the superior should send a death notice with a biographical note to other communities. Referring to this, one of the novices said: "I really wonder sometimes what our Mother Prioress will find to say about Sister Thérèse when she dies. . . . she has certainly never done anything worth speaking of." (This remark, in the light of subsequent events, sounds somewhat like the punch-line in Anatole France's story.) Sister Thérèse was happy overhearing this. Com-

300

plete and utter anonymity was one of the essential features of her "way." It is one of the elements of "littleness," that concept of hers which often leads to so much misunderstanding. The idea was precious to her "that no one may think of me, that I may be forgotten and trodden under foot as a grain of salt." In speaking of the Carmel she speaks of "virgin forests" in which "there grow flowers of a fragrance and brilliance unknown to the world."*

This touches upon one of the essential points of the life of the Christian in the world, of the life of the contemplative, and particularly of the teaching of St. Thérèse. I never had any understanding for the contemplative life, or for the role of contemplation in our life until one day, many years ago, I came across a remark in a book of letters by Father Peter Lippert. This letter was written to an old priest stricken with a chronic infirmity. The priest had apparently complained that he was of no use to anybody any more. Father Lippert in his reply said something to the effect that in order to be of use one did not at all have to be useful in a practical sense. He went so far as to say that if he were alone in the desert, and with his body in a state of disintegration, his life might be most useful. This remark struck a chord in me. It was one of those simple truths which one seems to discover accidentally.

This fact, namely that nothing which is directed either towards or away from God can ever be lost, this inestimable preciousness in the economy of the universe of every hidden movement of every human soul, this Law of the Conservation of Charity—this is the central idea of the contemplative life. At the same time, it forms the centre of Christian teaching. Christianity stands and falls with it. This idea is a scandal and a contradiction in the face of all present-day philosophies of life. It scandalizes those who see "re-

* Shortly before her death she appears to have had a notion of her subsequent fame which belonged in the order of "prophetic gifts." If it did, it was one of the very scant supernatural manifestations during her life. It is accidental, and does not at all change the significance of hiddenness and anonymity in her "way."

301

ligion" as "useful in terms of interpersonal relationships," those who
think of the Communion of Saints as a General Brotherhood Week,
and those who want to apply the laws of advertising to the Church.
Compared with people in her and our century, Thérèse had a
peculiar sense of statistics. "Zero, by itself, has no value, but put
alongside *one* it becomes potent, always provided it is put on the
proper side, after, and not before . . ." With this goes an immediate, almost natural, awareness of the infinite value of each single
person, an idea which occurs over and over again, from her earliest
to her last recorded sayings. When speaking of what God has
done for her sister Céline, she remarks that "He is prouder of what
He has done in her soul, of her littleness and poverty, than of
having created millions of suns and the whole expanse of the
heavens . . ." It should be noted that on such occasions she speaks
no longer in clichés but in a daring and, in a sense, shocking
language. Think of such imagery in comparison with our current
concept of the human person and of the cosmos! Suddenly you
have something like an optical illusion—the "sweet" and "little"
French girl disappears, and before you stands an immense, awe-
inspiring timeless figure, a companion of the Prophets, the Apostles,
the Fathers of the Church and of the great mystics of the Middle
Ages.

But this lasts only for a moment. Back you are again in the
nineteenth century, in Alençon, France, in a comfortable bourgeois
family, with the atmosphere of velvet, embroidery, plaster statues,
knickknacks, little garden houses, fishing expeditions, flowers in the
meadows and games on the swing. The photographs look like all
children's photographs from our parents' generation, with the ex-
pensive Sunday dress and the stiff pose. There has never been
a milieu or a period more contrary to our common idea of greatness. There was nothing extraordinary in the fact that she wanted
to be a religious. Both her father and her mother had tried to
enter the religious life. All her sisters were nuns. The only un-

usual thing about her was that she was impatient. By persistency and a combination of circumstances she was able to enter the Carmel at the age of fifteen.

The Carmelites are a contemplative, enclosed order. Daily life begins in the summer at five, in the winter at six in the morning, and ends at ten-thirty in the evening. There is a rigid schedule of prayer, meditation and work, with little time for meals or recreation. Sister Thérèse was stationed at various times in various places, in the refectory, in the sacristy, in the linen room, as a doorkeeper, and as a porter.

Now first of all you must visualize a child who leaves the happy atmosphere of the bourgeois home, with the eager impatience of the lover unable to wait, and who finds herself, on arrival at the goal, for long stretches of time devoid of any glimmer of inner satisfaction. Then there is the story of the Mother Superior. A good deal of historical controversy has arisen as to whether that woman really was the tormenting psychopath she appears from some descriptions, or whether she was just an ordinary fault-finding chief who did not understand the people living under her rule. I am inclined to believe the first of these two possibilities; from clinical experience it is hard to see how the stories which have been told about her could have been invented. Actually, it does not make much difference. All that matters is the general setting. It was in this setting that the young girl conceived a plan and carried it out.

In order to present the basic idea of her plan to modern readers it is best to look first at our own setting. To begin with, every one of us has to make a choice between the demands of God and the demands of the world. Actually neither of them allows half-measures. God was the first totalitarian. He insists on having every one of us completely. We are to say Yes, Yes, or No, No. We are to be hot or cold. He will not hear of anything in between.

"The world" has also been totalitarian in its demands from the beginning. What we commonly call "the world" manifests itself socially more and more in such a manner that less and less half-measures are permitted to the individual human person. We have to surrender totally. To begin with, the advancement in the field of techniques, not only mechanical but also organizatory, brings with it danger of de-humanization, of a cooling-off of our planet, not physically as happened long ago but in terms of relationship of man to man. The frightening efficiency of the social systems of certain dictator countries is a particularly blatant example of this.

Secondly, with the mastering of the forces of nature there goes, paradoxically, a greater awareness of the fortuitousness, the hit-or-miss, in the existence of every individual. Curiously enough, present-day man is not reassured by the great decrease of the death rate. Everyone is afraid he might belong to the encouragingly small percentage of people who are going to die tomorrow. We become like actuaries who are able to work out, with ingenious formulas, to the third decimal, how many people in a given area will have bricks fall on their heads during the coming year; the fact, however, that nobody knows whether he himself will be the recipient of such a brick becomes disquieting in the measure in which our applied mathematics improve.

Thirdly, the potential power of one single individual has increased to an incredible degree. This is another of the possible draw-backs of technical progress. It has often seemed to me that the idea of a "push-button-war" is so fascinating to people because it is a stark symbol of how much one person might be able to accomplish today just by moving his little finger.

The three examples I have just outlined come down to something rather simple. They illustrate the way in which our present-day world, the social structure of the twentieth century, endangers our charity, our confidence and our humility.

Now in the face of these two conflicting totalitarian demands, that of Christ and that of the world in which we live, what are we to do? To be totalitarian is a great thing. Nietzsche's insane prediction that no enemy of Christianity would ever have dreamed of the existence of such heavy guns came true to an uncanny degree, even if it came true in a way in which he did not mean it at all. The earth *is* in convulsions. It is Big Stuff all right. Where in the world is the Big Stuff which *we* can use in the face of all this?

Now this is where we have to come back to Thérèse's plan. Point number one, she would say if she were here with us right now: Don't use any Big Stuff, use Little Stuff. An all-out surrender does not have to be spectacular in worldly terms. Not everybody can be a St. Paul or a St. Joan of Arc. Only a few people are meant to be stoned, suffer shipwreck, spend a night and a day in the depth of the sea, or don armor and ride at the head of a regiment. As a matter of fact, with the world becoming more and more totalitarian, a Christian should think twice before he goes in for the Big Stuff. There is in everybody's life, in every place and at every moment, a lot of Small Stuff around which would provide excellent material for sanctity if one only exploited it. Céline said about Thérèse that she revealed her strength "in a multitude of slight, almost microscopic acts." At first sight you are disappointed. It sounds like the Boy Scouts' rule (which, incidentally, most of us don't follow either, perhaps because it is so far below our "spiritual level"). To understand its real meaning you have to study her biographies. It would go far beyond the scope of this essay to relate those "microscopic acts" in detail. No single incident illustrates sufficiently what is meant by all this. There is the story of the Sister towards whom she felt an instinctive antipathy. There is the story of the old Sister whom she looked after and who found fault with her endlessly. There is the series of events during the influenza epidemic in the convent. And there are many more stories. With all this go the misinterpretations and rebuffs to which she was subjected every day, the coldness, both emotional and physical, of the atmosphere, and those endless nights without sleep, with physical and mental torture, with the torment of doubt and the withdrawal of all natural and supernatural consolation. "When my heart, weary of the enveloping darkness, tries to find some rest and strength in the thought of an everlasting life to come, my anguish only increases. It seems that the darkness itself, borrowing the voice of the unbeliever, cries mockingly: 'You dream of a land of light and fragrance, you believe that the Creator of these wonders will be forever yours, you think to escape one day from the mists in which you now languish. Hope on! Hope on! Look forward to death! It will give you not what you hope for, but a night darker still, the night of utter nothingness!'" This was the raw material out of which, miraculously, she made her "little, nameless, unremembered acts of kindness and of love." This is the same Thérèse of whom one of the Sisters said when she did not show up for recreation: "There will be no laughing today, Sœur Thérèse is not here."

Ivan Karamazov, that fictitious and very real contemporary of St. Thérèse, says: "I could never understand how one could love one's neighbour. It is precisely the neighbour (the one who is physically close to us) whom one cannot possibly love, in my opinion; at best one can love those who are far away . . . the love of Christ for human beings is, in my opinion, a miracle which cannot be realized on this earth. All right, he was God. But we are no Gods. Let us assume, for instance, that I suffer deeply, and that another one never realizes how much I suffer—well, he just is *another one* and not I; moreover, a human being will only rarely admit the suffering of another one—as if there were something like a rank involved. Why does he not admit it, what do you think? Well, perhaps because I have a bad smell, or a stupid face, or because I stepped on his toe. And with all this, there is a difference between suffering and suffering: ordinary suffering which humiliates me, let us say hunger, might still be acknowledged by my benefactor. But very rarely will he acknowledge in me a higher form of suffering, for example, suffering for an idea. The moment he sees me he'll find that my face does not at all resemble the face he had imagined a man who suffers for an idea ought to have. He'll withdraw all his good deeds, and, mind you, he won't do it out of a bad heart. . . . One can love one's neighbour in an abstract way, occasionally, perhaps, even from afar, but in close contact almost never." He stated the problem very neatly. The obstacles to a Christ-like life are trivial, almost ridiculous, often in the nature of psychological subtleties. Therefore, the method, too, has to be one of trivialities and psychological subtleties. Thérèse's so-called Little Way is the exact complement to Ivan's remarks. He had a clear notion of what seemed to him a hopeless position, and she evolved a strategy.

The fact that the fictitious Ivan and the historical Thérèse are contemporaries is perhaps not as accidental as it looks. Ivan says it is easy to love human beings in a far-away, abstract manner. There are, as everybody can see, great possibilities for self-deception. And the general cultural atmosphere of the nineteenth century as of the twentieth lends itself particularly to this kind of thing. If the Gospel appeals to you, it is easy to come out against general social injustice, against the exploitation of the poor, in favor of pacifism, ethical vegetarianism or other "isms." But it is a thousand times harder to tackle problems of hostility or coldness or injustice in the relationship with those with whom you are in everyday contact. It is also much less spectacular. Tolstoy is a case in point. As a husband and family man he was often torn by hatred and injustice. For many reasons he somehow never came around to parting with his possessions. And it seems almost that in the same measure in which these conflicts mounted he went into the big sweeping issues of the society of his day and became more radical in his demands. Soloviev was perhaps the first one to see the pitfall in this. He himself came out on such issues as capital punishment and antisemitism. He sacrificed even his professorship, the source of his livelihood, for his convictions. But he saw in a purely externalized morality such a grave danger that he branded Tolstoy's way as the way of the Anti-Christ. This is strong language. It is heresy, he said, to preach vegetarianism to the masses. But after his death it became known that he himself had lived a strictly ascetic life and a life of voluntary poverty. All this only goes to show how highly topical St. Thérèse is.

Now to point number two of her program. Be in your relationship to God like a little child. "Unless you be converted and become as little children, you shall not enter the Kingdom of Heaven." "Ah," you will say, "that little child! Has not modern psychology done away for good with that picture of the utterly loving, utterly confident and utterly humble child? A poetic myth!" It is true, children do hate, they do distrust and they are proud. The ambivalence, the two-pronged nature of our feelings, develops early. But we all have gone through an early phase of complete and utter dependence. We were helpless without our mother. We needed her in an all-out way. We could do nothing without her. We simply had to trust her, there was no alternative. We could not foresee future hazards and had to leave all those blindly to her foresight. That earliest Little Man, that Arche-Child of our ontogenetic story, is still alive in every one of us. To regress to it on the natural plane, in our relationship with people, is a most serious form of neurosis. To find our way back to it on the supernatural plane, in our relationship with God, is the highest degree of maturity. "As one whom the mother caresses, so will I comfort you," says God (Is. lxvi, 13). But for this to be possible there has to be a child on the receiving end.

One minor aspect of this spiritual childhood is often overlooked. This is a sort of intellectual simplification. One does not at all need to be anti-intellectual, but one must look out not to become top-heavy. Many of us read entire libraries of philosophy and theology from St. Augustine to Karl Adam. Before we know it we have attained a sort of mental obesity instead of spiritual growth. St. Thérèse first read quite a few spiritual treatises (not always the most sophisticated ones, it seems); later she read only the *Imitation* and the Gospel, then only the Gospel, and in her latest phase she did not read anything at all. She said at one time that not three consecutive minutes of her life passed without her thinking of God. But that does not mean that she speculated. These thoughts were movements of the heart. St. Seraphim, that greatest modern saint of the Eastern Church, who died forty years before she was born, and in whose life and teaching there are a few striking parallels, confined himself for years to a prayer consisting of one sentence. He repeated it thousands of times a day. It was the sentence uttered by the publican in the parable of the proud Pharisee.

Point number three of her "way" is often entirely neglected. That is her devotion to the Holy Face. It will be remembered that she adopted, in addition to "Child Jesus," the name of the "Holy Face." Apart from the quotations referring to the "child," one of her favorite Bible passages was the famous one from Isaiah: "There is no beauty in him nor comeliness: and we have seen him, and there was no sightliness . . . despised and the most abject of men, a man of sorrows and acquainted with infirmity: and his look was as it were hidden and despised. Whereupon we esteemed him not." At one time she said that all her piety had been based on these words. Her relationship to the supernatural attained such a degree of concreteness and immediacy that she was able to *see* in all forms of suffering the suffering of Our Lord. The closer to her the sufferer was, the more abject the forms of suffering were, the more real became this identity. There was a most extraordinary interpenetration of concrete situation and supernatural meaning. They are nearly fused into one image. This is the aspect of her life most difficult to understand for most of us. It comes out most clearly in the way she experienced her father's illness. It is easy to approach things of this sort with psychoanalytic concepts. But this means to miss the point entirely.

There is in our relationship to the saints a limitless possibility for fooling ourselves. We all admire St. Francis of Assisi. When we come to analyze what attracts us to him, we may find that he represents to us a phantasy of escape rather than a true hero. He may actually appeal to the Rousseauist who is still alive in every one of us. In the mind of many people he has become a kind of nature boy who lives as the friend of birds and squirrels and does not have to pay any income tax. The fact that he experienced the agony of Our Lord is a small-print footnote. Moreover, there is no need to do anything about it, because our station in life is such that we could not possibly all try to be St. Francises.

I have a particular personal devotion to a Pastor Schneider, a Lutheran minister who died in Buchenwald concentration camp. Father Steinwender, a priest from Austria and a fellow-prisoner of Pastor Schneider, tells us his story. During a solemn ceremony in the camp Pastor Schneider refused "to take his cap off to the swastika flag. He was dragged into the bunker, the ill-famed prison within the camp, which he was destined not to leave. For thirteen months he suffered the tortures of a sadistic form of separate treatment. Prisoners who temporarily shared his cell were overwhelmed by the spiritual greatness of this man. In spite of a diet which was scarcely enough to maintain life, he refused on Friday, the day of the death of Our Lord, all food. In front of the one-story bunker was the big gathering place on which prisoners had to appear twice daily, in the morning and in the evening, to be counted. . . . On the high feast days one would suddenly, during the quiet of counting, hear the powerful voice of Pastor Schneider through the grates of the bunker. Like a prophet he made a feast day sermon, that is to say he tried to begin it. On Easter Sunday morning, for example, we heard suddenly the powerful words:

'Thus speaks the Lord: I am the Resurrection and the Life!' There the prisoners were standing in long rows, stirred to the innermost by the courage and tremendous will power of a man. It was as if a voice from another world were calling them, as if they heard the voice of John the Baptist from the dungeons of Herod, the mighty voice of a Prophet calling in the desert. He could never say more than a few sentences. Then one heard the truncheons of the guards beating him, or the blow of a fist throw his tortured body into the corner of the bunker. . . . Since they could make no impression on a conviction which was of the hardness of granite, they declared him a madman who had to be silenced by beating. For over a year he bore the tortures of the bunker, until even his strength succumbed to brute force. There was nothing whole on his entire body when he was carried dead from the bunker."[*]

But even with Pastor Schneider I have a first-class excuse. I am not in a concentration camp and I am not called to witness. There is nothing here and now calling upon me to follow his example.

With Thérèse it is different. With her no excuse is possible. Pope Benedict XV says: "There is a call to the faithful of every nation, no matter what may be their age, sex, or state of life, to enter wholeheartedly into the Little Way which led Sister Theresa to the summit of heroic virtue." It sounds easy. Depend on God like a little child. Trust Him blindly no matter what happens. Use the inconspicuous events and situations of everyday life as material for sanctification. Do it in obscurity. And in view of all suffering think of that Face.

It is just about the most difficult thing to do. Littleness, as she understood it, and mediocrity as we live it—I could not conceive of two more contrary ways of life. It often occurred to me that poor tortured Nietzsche with his violent cry of "No, No!" was in

[*] *Christus im KZ*, by Leonhard Steinwender (Otto Müller Verlag, Salzburg, 1946).

the eyes of God closer to her "Yes, Yes!" than we are. But then there is that terrible word of their fruits by which you shall know them. I have known the boys who continued with the Revaluation of All Values. I have known them at high school and at the university. I have run into them in the most unlikely places. From all this arose such an army of lying and murder as the world has perhaps never seen before.

St. Thérèse, like Nietzsche the old artillery man, was fond of military metaphors. She spoke of an army she was going to raise and of conquests she was going to make. I have come to know her followers too. There too, I must say, it was in the most unlikely places and the most unexpected situations that I met them. I am tempted to write instead of this essay the stories of all the various persons I have met who are attached to her. But this would make a book all by itself. As a composite picture it would constitute a sort of "Life" of the saint, although beginning quite some time after her death.

Her death occurred, in complete obscurity, on September 30th, 1897. Two days later Tolstoy, in faraway Yasnaya Poliana, made the following entry in his diary: "I imagined vividly what a joyful, peaceful and completely free life this would be: to be able to dedicate oneself entirely to God, i.e. if one intended in all situations which life presents only to accept his will—during illness, when one has been insulted, in humiliation, in suffering, in all temptations, and in death. In that case death would be nothing but the taking on of a new task." There he was, that great and tragic genius of our time, struggling for a goal to which he had come so much closer than most of us, clearly beholding it, yet far removed. And Sister Thérèse had made it.